Translation, Sociolinguistic, and Consumer Issues in Interpreting

Studies in Interpretation

Melanie Metzger and Earl Fleetwood, General Editors

Translation, Sociolinguistic, and Consumer Issues in Interpreting

Melanie Metzger and Earl Fleetwood, Editors

GALLAUDET UNIVERSITY PRESS

Washington, D.C.

Studies in Interpretation

A Series Edited by Melanie Metzger and Earl Fleetwood

Gallaudet University Press
Washington, D.C. 20002
http://gupress.gallaudet.edu

ISBN 1-56368-360-1; 978-1-56368-360-2
ISSN 1545-7613

Interior design by Richard Hendel

∞ The paper used in this publication meets the minimum requirements of
American National Standard for Information Sciences–Permanence of Paper
for Printed Library Materials, ANSI Z39.48-1984.

Contents

Part I Translation Considerations

Handling and Incorporation of Idioms

in Interpretation

Roberto R. Santiago and Lisa Frey Barrick

The importance of idioms has been identified and discussed by language scholars from many different disciplines such as language acquisition (Lupson, 1984; Boatner & Gates, 1966; Ichikawa et al., 1964; Taylor & Gottschalk, 1960), translation studies (Larson 1984; Horodecka & Osadnik, 1992; Rosenthal, 1978; Vilar-Sánchez, 2002), and psychology (Gibbs, 2002; Keysar & Bly, 1999; Titone & Connine, 1999). All of these authors have noted that idioms are an essential component of language and that mastery of idioms is a determiner of linguistic competence. Therefore, it is surprising that so little empirical research has been conducted on what interpreters do when faced with source language idioms or how they incorporate idioms into their target texts. While there is plenty of discussion in the literature on what interpreters and translators *should* do (Larson, 1984; Horodecka & Osadnik, 1992; Hatim & Mason, 1997), very little empirical research focuses on what choices interpreters actually make.

This chapter discusses interpreters' actions when working between an idiom-rich language like English and American Sign Language, whose idiomatic tendencies have not yet been fully investigated. The data consist of several interpretations of a single source text by both hearing and Deaf interpreters. Analysis of the data shows how interpreters deal with idioms and how native ASL users differ from second language learners in their interpretations. Our focus is not on interpreter comprehension of source text idioms but rather on what interpreters do with idioms while interpreting. We examine emergent patterns in the interpretations and study the ramifications they have for our work as interpreters.

Larson (1984) states that "All languages have idioms, i.e., a string of words whose meaning is different than the meaning conveyed by the individual words" (p. 22). Indeed, several works focus on helping both second language users (Taylor & Gottschalk, 1960; Ichikawa et al., 1964; Lupson, 1984), and native speakers (Rawson, 1995) understand the wide variety of idioms that occur in language. Writing about figurative language in general, Rawson states, "They are embedded so deeply in our language that few of us, even those who pride themselves on being plain spoken, ever get through the day without using them" (ibid.). Additionally, Horodecka and Osadnik state that "Idioms are not separate parts of language that one either can choose to use or omit, but they form an essential part of the vocabulary of English" (1992, p. 37). These comments support Rawson's claim that idiomatic language is ingrained in language users. These authors identify idioms as a prevalent linguistic feature. Because interpreters encounter idioms in their work, these expressions are a topic worthy of further research.

LITERATURE REVIEW

The Functions of Idioms in Language

Several authors have discussed the functions of idioms in language in general and in English in particular. Lupson (1984) says, "Idioms can be a most rewarding aspect of language study, offering a fascinating glimpse into the forms of thought unique to a particular language community" (p. v). Rawson (1995) provides several examples of the ways in which euphemisms are used to discuss delicate topics such as bodily functions, socially awkward situations, and death. Tray (2005) also addresses these topics when discussing indirectness in American Sign Language. These observations lead to a related study of idioms since they are also a way of being indirect. Idioms may be used to discuss taboo topics, but they also spruce up more mundane topics like the weather. In their 1966 book, *A Dictionary of Idioms for the Deaf*, Boatner and Gates write, "Since idioms are the idiosyncrasies of our language, and they transgress either the laws of grammar or the laws of logic, writers on grammar and language down through the years have given idioms such descriptions as 'the spice of language' or the 'soul of language'" (p. vii).

Definition and Perception of Idioms in Discourse

Having established that idioms are important to language, we now define and explain how language users perceive them. For this we have adopted Rosenthal's definition: "1. Idioms consist of at least two or more words, which may or may not be contiguous, inflected or in a specific order. 2. Idioms are recurrent constructs. . . . (Some degree of recurrence is necessary to distinguish idioms from metaphors and other style figures)" (1978, p. 1).

Horodecka and Osadnik (1992, p. 27) cite Norrick (1985) when they claim that idioms are perceived as "independent textual units, i.e. discrete little texts." Wood (1986) claims that "An idiom is a complex expression which is wholly non-compositional and wholly non-productive in form" (p. 95). Rosenthal (1978) in turn quotes Chafe (1968), who appears to have influenced the previous writers and presents a view that combines the preceding two ideas. In discussing the way in which language users perceive idioms, Chafe writes, "First . . . the meaning of an idiom is comparable to the meaning of a single lexical item ('kick the bucket'). . . . Second, most if not all idioms exhibit certain transformational deficiencies ('kick the bucket cannot be passivized'). . . . Third, there are some idioms which are not syntactically well formed, which could not be generated by a base component designed to produce well-formed deep structures (by and large). . . . Fourth, an idiom which is well formed will have a literal counterpart, but the frequency of the latter is usually lower than that of the corresponding idiom ('kick the bucket' means 'die' more often than it means 'strike the pail with one's foot')" (p. 111).

There is, however, some debate as to whether idioms are processed as long words (noncompositional) or whether their literal meaning (kick the bucket = strike a pail with one's foot) is processed along with their idiomatic meaning. Giora and Fein (1999) claim that literal meanings are indeed processed when people are exposed to figurative language. Titone and Connine (1999) suggest a hybrid model in which "idiomatic expressions function simultaneously as semantically arbitrary word sequences and compositional phrases." This line of reasoning implies that idioms may have some compositional components that make sense. That is, the meaning can be found by looking at the individual lexical items along with the syntactic structure.

Gibbs (2002), Keysar and Bly (1999), and Virginie (2003) refute these ideas. Gibbs claims that "Most of the psycholinguistic research shows . . . that given sufficient context, people understand nonliteral meanings without first analyzing the complete literal meaning of an expression (i.e., the direct access view)" (2002, p. 1159). Virginie (2003) also mentions context as a substantial factor in understanding figurative language. Keysar and Bly state, "We claim that idioms cannot, in principle, be used to argue for the existence of such conceptual structures. To support this argument we demonstrate that people's intuitions about idiom transparency vary as a function of what they believe to be the meaning of the idiom" (1999, p. 159). Keysar and Bly go on to explain that some people, because of their personal invented etymology, have internalized opposite meanings of a particular idiom and therefore cannot see how it could mean anything other than what they believe. By examining these texts we can deduce that idioms are figurative language constructions that become static and therefore well-known, widely used, and commonly understood by members of a linguistic community. Also, as the preceding authors (as well as Gibbs, 2002) have pointed out, native language users can identify and understand idioms that are not a part of their personal idiolect if the idiom is presented in context.

GENERAL TRANSLATION AND INTERPRETATION THEORY

The debate over the merits of *literal* (form-based) versus *free* (meaning-based) translation has raged for centuries. Hatim and Mason (1997, p. 5) cite a critique of literal translation methods written by "fourteenth-century translator Salah al-Din al-Safadi" seven hundred years ago. Today the discussion continues, as evidenced by Vladimir Nabokov's (1955) defense of literal translation. Contemporary translation theorists propose that literal and free represent opposite ends of a continuum rather than polar extremes (Larson, 1984). Both Hatim and Mason (1997) and Gutt (1991) use the literal versus free debate to frame an exploration of the translatability of figurative language and poetic discourse.

Larson (1984) states that "A truly idiomatic translation does not sound like a translation. It sounds like it was written originally in the receptor language. Therefore a good translator will try to translate idiomatically" (p. 18). Hatim and Mason (1997) add, "A sentence or text is composed of the sum of the meanings of the individual lexical items, so that any attempt to translate at this level is bound to miss important elements of meaning" (p. 6). Horodecka and Osadnick (1992), citing Klemesiewicz (1955), place an even greater emphasis on free translation: "The task of the translator consists of neither reproducing nor transforming the elements and structures of the original, but grasping their function and introducing such elements and structures of his own language that could, as far as possible, be substitutes and equivalents of the same functional coherence and efficiency" (p. 93).

Current literature indicates that the free—or idiomatic—theory of translation has been accepted as the norm although the interpreter may sometimes choose to transmit some of the source text form, as well as the meaning. Hatim and Mason (1997) note that translating the form may at times result in an equivalent response from the target language audience. Larson (1984) addresses one such instance in which it may be appropriate to include the form: "For some purposes, it is desirable to reproduce the linguistic features of a source text, as for example, in a linguistic study of that language ... although ... they are of little help to speakers of the receptor language who are interested in the meaning of the source language text" (p. 17).

Seleskovitch (1978) links the fields of interpreting and translation by maintaining that "they are—or can be—based on the same theory" (p. 2). She goes on to show how interpreters also interpret meaning beyond the level of the individual lexical items in the source text. Since then interpreting theorists have accepted this idea as a given when examining the interpreting process. Cokely (2001) gives examples of phrases that have both a literal and a figurative meaning. He shows that a skilled interpreter uses contextual information drawn from the rest of the source text and the communicative situation in order to select the correct meaning before rendering an interpretation. Cokely also shows that savvy interpreters automatically recognize polysemous words and phrases, and instinctively seek more information about their meaning.

Idioms are a focal point in some texts in terms of the free versus literal question. Tytler (1907) points out that both interpreters and translators face this issue: "While the translator endeavors to give to his work all the ease of the original composition, the chief difficulty he has to encounter will be found in the translation of idioms, or those turns of expression which do not belong to the universal grammar, but of which every language has its own that are exclusively proper to it" (p. 135).

We have already shown that idioms are an integral part of language. Horodecka and Osadnik (1992) combined the problems of integrating general translation theory and the importance of idioms: "The way in which the words are put together is often odd, illogical, or even grammatically incorrect. These are the characteristics of some idioms and that is why one must adopt the idiom as a whole, why one cannot translate it word for word" (p. 27). Lupson (1984), in discussing the importance of not only understanding but also using idioms, writes that "Idioms tend to be used strategically; that is, they capture and express particular states of mind or particular observations of the speaker, at moments when maximum effect is desired with a minimum of language. An appreciation for their content and sensitivity to their use in the correct context are, therefore, a mark of competent language use" (p. v).

Cultural mediation also becomes a factor when interpreting idioms. Vilar-Sánchez (2002) supports the importance of idiomatic competence. In the same vein as Hatim and Mason (1990), Vilar-Sánchez (2002) writes that "It is well known that one does not translate words and structures but text or discourse. In order to do so, the translator/interpreter must understand the communicative intention of the original text or discourse and reproduce it in the target text. That means, not only does he/she need a solid idiomatic knowledge (knowledge of grammar, vocabulary, phonology, suprasegmental and extralinguistic elements in both languages) but also a good knowledge of the expressive aspect of all these linguistic resources (i.e., which resources are used to express which function in what kind of situation or text and with what effect)" (p. 109).

By considering the observations of Vilar-Sánchez and Lupson we can deduce that idiomatic language contains more information than either the literal or the figurative meaning provides. Indeed, figurative language includes information about the speaker's affect and discourse style. Idioms are used for effect, be it humor, obfuscation, or emphasis. It is important for interpreters to understand not only the meaning of the idiom but also its purpose in the discourse. Ideally, the interpreter will be able to get across all three of these levels of meaning. Effective interpretation of idioms will help uphold the six parameters of an equivalent interpretation as set forth by Isham (1986): content, style, contextual force, affect, function, and register. Significantly, five of Isham's six parameters relate to meaning that is outside of either the literal or the figurative interpretation of the text. That is, Isham acknowledges that the meaning of a text relies not only on *what* is said but also *how* it is said.

Horodecka and Osadnik (1992) add that idioms are often tied to the history, beliefs, religion, customs, cuisine, and culture of the people in a particular language community. Therefore, interpreters must not only find phrases that capture the meaning and the spirit of the original phrase, but they must also do so in a culturally appropriate way. Tytler (1907) sums up the interpreter's ultimate goal: "The translation is perfect when the translator finds in his own language an idiomatic phrase corresponding to that of the original" (p. 138). Even with this as the ideal, Horodecka and Osadnik (1992) note that, because idioms are tied to language and culture, idioms are replaced rather than translated, resulting in the replacement of the source language and culture by those of the target text. Larson (1984) emphasizes the use of idioms in translation: "Use them naturally to make the translation lively and keep the style of the source language" (p. 12).

Thus far, the literature reviewed has taken a prescriptive stance on what interpreters should do when faced with an idiom in the target text. However, few researchers have looked at what they actually do. This question is further complicated when examining interpreters who work between English, which has a rich assortment of idioms, and ASL, which is thought to have relatively few idioms. There is some ambiguity in defining and identifying idioms in American Sign Language as little is known of its use of idioms. Cokely and Baker-Shenk (1980) write that "it is interesting to note that ASL seems to have *very few* widely used idioms, according to the standard definition of 'idiom'" (p. 119). Indeed, some authors have stated that many signs that people often think are ASL idioms (e.g., OUT-OF-SIGHT, ON-THE-FENCE, FUNNY NONE) are in fact either sign compounds with transparent meaning (FUNNY NONE means "not funny") or single-sense lexical items that either cannot be translated into English by using a single lexical item or require an English idiom for translation.

According to Battison in Valli and Lucas (1998), "We can show that things that are often called sign 'idioms' are often just ordinary signs that are difficult to translate into English" (p. 225). When compared to the sign SUCCEED, which is made with two movements, the sign AT-LAST is one sharp movement and has historically been called an ASL idiom for the very reason of its nontranslatability. But Battison maintains that, because the "two signs are made differently, they have different meanings. . . . They are two separate signs" (ibid.). By "misusing" the term "idiom" as it applies to American Sign Language, the result is an "obscure" understanding of how "the language really works and it makes it seem as if the language is unstructured and simple. Of course, nothing could be further from the truth" (ibid.).

THEORETICAL FRAMEWORK

If Battison and Cokely and Baker-Shenk are correct, then interpreters working from English to ASL cannot satisfy the ideal set forth by

Tytler (1907) because the target language will often have no corresponding idioms. Horodecka and Osadnik (1992) claim that plain language replacement of a source text idiom achieves zero equivalence. Therefore, it stands to reason that ASL, without a large corpus of clearly defined idioms, has some other way of expressing and fulfilling the functions of idiomatic language. Because American Sign Language utilizes both space and movements and occurs in three-dimensional space, its constraints differ greatly from those of spoken languages, which must be conveyed linearly. Battison (1998) explains: "One way that ASL expands its vocabulary is through . . . changes in movement. (This is one more reason for paying attention to the fine details of how signs are formed)" (p. 225).

A second concern facing interpreters who work with ASL and English is culture. Unlike many interpreting situations, ASL-English interpreters work with consumers who are often from the same country and share some of the same cultural norms. This can be both a help and a hindrance for interpreters. Shared cultural histories can help bridge the language barrier. However, interpreters must remember that hearing consumers often have little or no knowledge of signed languages or Deafness. Moreover, Deaf consumers have varying degrees of bilingualism and exposure to those parts of mainstream American culture that are transmitted aurally: music, television, and film iconography, or English idioms and puns that are based on English phonology.

In this chapter we apply empirical data to the question of how interpreters handle idioms when interpreting from English to ASL. Two researchers contributed greatly to our theoretical framework: Ressler (1999) and Tray (2005). Ressler's study addresses the issue of interpreters working into their native language (L1), as it applies to signed language interpreting. Tray's study focuses on the ways in which interpreters convey innuendo, a form of language comparable to idioms in that both are figurative.

Ressler's (1999) examination of the differences between a direct and an intermediary interpretation posits that the end product of a relay team in which a hearing interpreter accesses the source text directly and feeds an intermediary interpretation to a Deaf team interpreter, who then reformulates the message into ASL, will be a more natural, cohesive, and coherent target text. This is based upon the Deaf interpreter's greater fluency in ASL. Ressler cites Baker-Shenk (1986) in saying that hearing interpreters are often "far from fluent in ASL" (Ressler, 1999, p. 72).

Ressler also states that, "for most interpreters whose second language is ASL, the form of the English utterance often takes precedence over the content. As a result, pieces of the English form often appear in these second language learners' ASL-rendered product" (ibid.). Ressler suggests that using a Deaf interpreter as part of a relay team can result in a "culturally appropriate, accurate interpretation from English to ASL" (ibid.).

The second source of our theoretical framework is Tray (2005), who examined the manner in which innuendo is handled in ASL. Like the authors noted earlier, Tray also acknowledges that, "For interpreters, figurative use of language presents a potential difficulty because they must determine the speaker's intent for those choosing the non-primary meaning" (p. 2). His stated purpose is to "uncover similarities and distinctions in the strategies employed to convey the English-based humor in ASL" (ibid., p. 25). To do so, Tray compares two interpretations of an English source text by two hearing interpreters with two translations of the same text by two Deaf native ASL users. In comparing the two groups, Tray notes that both of the hearing interpreters and one of the Deaf translators tried to include some of the form of the figurative language, along with its meaning. Though his study deals specifically with innuendo, the conclusions he draws can be applied to other forms of figurative language. We borrowed aspects of Ressler's (1999) and Tray's (2005) methodologies for our study.

METHODOLOGY

In her examination of intermediary interpretation, Ressler (1999) sought out an experienced relay team. She analyzed the interpretations of a single hearing interpreter who first worked as part of a relay team and then later worked alone. Following Ressler, we too looked for a hearing interpreter who had several years of experience as a member of a relay team. However, we asked the relay interpreter in our study to work with several Deaf interpreters. Also, in an effort to create a lab environment that simulated real-world interpreting situations as closely as possible, Ressler brought her participants into a lab setting and provided them with a spoken English stimulus text, as well as an introduction to the content of the text they would be interpreting. We too sought to create as real a situation as possible in a lab setting by providing the participants with introductions to the speaker, the Deaf audience member, and a written description of the context of the communication situation. Tray (2005) used both hearing interpreters and Deaf actors in his study of how innuendo in English is conveyed in ASL. He included the two groups (Deaf and hearing) in his study based on the hypothesis that "analysis would reveal differences between the two groups.... Moreover I anticipated the [Deaf] actresses' ASL utterance to reflect greater communicative competence through the use of different contextualization cues than those of the interpreters whose native language is English."

In order to determine whether Deaf interpreters and their hearing counterparts use different strategies when interpreting idioms from ASL to English, we drew upon Ressler's and Tray's assertions regarding the greater ASL fluency of native Deaf ASL users in our decision to include Deaf interpreters as part of a relay team in our participant group.

DATA

The source text (see appendix A) contained the following ten English idioms:

just fell off the turnip truck	"innocent or inexperienced"
my own back forty	"my land or property"
bitten by the gardening bug	"enthralled by gardening"
green thumb	"expert gardener"
bent out of shape	"upset"
blood, sweat, and tears	"extraordinary effort"
fruits of my labor	"results of my hard work"
under the weather	"sick"
down in the dumps	"depressed, sad, melancholy"
chase the blues away	"feel better, improve one's mood"

PARTICIPANTS

We collected data from a pool of nine interpreters. Of these, four were hearing and five were Deaf. These interpreters were screened for RID CI/CT, CSC, CDI, or RSC certification and/or at least five years' experience in the field (see table 1).

TABLE 1. *General Demographic Information on Interpreting Participants*

	D1	D2	D3	D4	D5	H1	H2	H3	H4
M/F	F	M	M	M	F	M	M	M	F
Certification	None	None	CDI	CDI	CDI	CI/CT NAD V	CI/CT	NAD V	CI/CT
Number of years certified			3	5	11 months	5	10+	6	3
Years working experience	4	10+	10+	10+	5.5	5	10+	10+	5
Age	25–34	35–43	35–43	35–43	25–34	35–43	44–53	35–43	25–34
First language	ASL	ASL	ASL	English	English	English	English + other	English	English
Started learning ASL	29 years ago	since birth	22 years ago	31 years ago	11 years ago	9 years ago	34 years ago	24 years ago	10 years ago

D = Deaf interpreter
H = hearing interpreter

DATA COLLECTION

The participants were each asked to interpret a brief text, and their interpretations were videotaped for subsequent analysis. The participants were told that the study was focusing on the translation of idiomatic language as a discourse process. This wording was used so that they would not focus on any particular language feature in an unnatural manner. We placed several English idioms in the final third of the text so that the interpreter would have some time to warm up before encountering the linguistic feature in question. The source text was read aloud on video by an actor hired to recite the text as though she were giving a presentation to a group at a community event. This context was explained to the interpreters prior to our asking them to interpret (see appendix B for the explanation of the context).

The interpreters were asked to imagine themselves interpreting to an educated Deaf audience who is familiar with English but prefers ASL to contact variety signing. The videotape opened with an introduction to the speaker and the Deaf consumer. These introductions were provided in order to further establish the context of this imagined communication event, as well as to give the interpreters an imagined audience. After they completed their interpretation, the interpreters were offered the chance to view their work and comment on what they found challenging, confusing, or interesting.

The interpreters were divided into two groups. The first consisted of four hearing interpreters, who were shown the videotaped source text that was developed for this study. The second group consisted of five Deaf interpreters, who accessed the same source text as part of a Deaf/hearing relay team. The hearing member of the relay team was consistent for all five Deaf interpreters. In this case the hearing relay interpreter was an RID-certified interpreter who had many years of experience both working with and researching Deaf/hearing relay teams. This person was a member of the research team and knew the research questions for the study. This was essential because we wanted to ensure that the source text the Deaf interpreters received remained consistent throughout the interpretations. The hearing relay interpreter worked with us to establish a way of transmitting the English idioms in a manner that was consistent with how Deaf/hearing relay teams work in the field. Also, prior to interpreting the source text, the two interpreters discussed how to work together, including how they preferred to receive information and what techniques they would use for clarification.

TRANSCRIPTION AND CODING

After this phase of the data collection was completed, we transcribed the portion of each interpretation that contained the most idiomatic language (see appendix C). This means that we did not examine the first two-thirds of the text since it contained no idioms and was included only to give the interpreters time to warm up (Ressler, 1999). We used a variation of the Vista College transcription conventions to transfer the signs into a written (or "glossed") format (see appendix C).

We then made three comparisons of the English idiom interpretations. The first compared the sign choices in each interpretation to those of other interpretations from the same group (hearing interpreters compared to other hearing interpreters, and Deaf interpreters compared to other Deaf interpreters). This was done in order to identify patterns of similarity and difference within each group. Next we compared one group's interpretations to those of the other group and paid specific attention to the trends within each group. Through this method we were able to find features that were representative of each group's handling of the source idioms. We also identified patterns that occurred across both groups and may be representative of how interpreters work regardless of hearing status or ASL/English competence.

ANALYSIS

In this section we describe the trends we found in each group's handling of the source text idioms. We also analyze these trends across groups and provide theories based on participant interviews, as well as our own observations, as to why each approach was employed.

After making our transcriptions we found that the interpretations of the English idioms fell into the following six general categories:

1. meaning only
"Meaning only" interpretations are those in which the meaning—but none of the form—of the English idiom was interpreted. For example, two interpreters chose to interpret the idiom "blood, sweat, and tears" as WORK with nonmanual intensifiers (see appendix C).

2. omissions
"Omissions" are instances in which the interpreter left out both the form *and* the meaning of the English idiom. In these cases, the idiom was not interpreted.

3. form only; meaning skewed
Interpretations in this category contain only the form—but not the meaning—of the English idiom. By form we mean that the English lexical item is represented in the interpretation by the commonly accepted ASL sign for its gloss. Through the interview process we were able to ascertain that these interpretations were due to the interpreter's misunderstanding of the English idiom.

4. form and meaning

The interpretations in this group contain both the meaning of the English idiom and some of the form. For example, an interpretation of the idiom "blood, sweat, and tears" contained the concept of hard or rigorous work, as well as one or more of the ASL signs glossed as BLOOD, SWEAT, or CRY. (See appendix C, "blood, sweat, and tears.")

5. form, meaning, and marker

These interpretations adhere to the same basic principles as those in the form and meaning category. However, some sort of indication to the audience that the next chunk of language is marked in some way precedes these interpretations. The most common marker was the sign glossed as QUOTE-shake. This sign is similar to the "air quotes" gesture used by native English speakers in the United States. There are several uses of QUOTE-shake in ASL. Semantically, QUOTE and QUOTE-shake are clearly delineated, and the latter appears frequently in the interpretations. Whereas QUOTE is produced in one large motion and alerts the audience that the next segment of the interpretation is either a direct quote of the source text or a title, QUOTE-shake is commonly used to mark a sarcastic or humorous remark. Both markers can alert the audience that the next utterance may contain a borrowed or otherwise marked phrase.

Other markers in the form, meaning, and marker group include nonmanual signals (NMS) such as head wobble or a combination of head tilt and eyebrow raise. For example, the source text sentence "Now, I've had mosquito bites . . . and I've had spider bites . . . but I never knew how sweet the itch could feel until I was *bitten by the gardening bug*" was interpreted as follows:

INFORM PRO.2 HAVE MOSQUITO BIT "hand" SLAP
SPIDER (1h BUG BITE BAD BITE WOW NOW)
(new space BITE #BY WHAT (pause NMS **head tilt + eyebrow raise**) fs-GARDEN
fs-BUG QUOTE FEEL HOOKED NOW
(see appendix C, "gardening bug")

In this example the signs and NMS that mark the idiom are in boldface text.

6. wrong path and save

This category includes those cases in which the interpreter began an interpretation that failed to match the meaning of the idiom, then realized the mistake, and fixed the interpretation (see appendix C, "fell off the turnip truck").

Analysis Phase One: Raw Data

The first step in our analysis was to examine and compare interpretations within each group. By doing so we found clear patterns in how both the hearing and the Deaf interpreter groups interpreted each individual idiom and the idioms overall. The raw numbers for each group show similar approaches by the Deaf and the hearing interpreters, though the numbers are slightly different. When comparing the raw data, we found one point that merited further discussion. First, the Deaf interpreters included some of the form of the English idiom (form and meaning, form only, and form, meaning, and marker) in 30.0% of their interpretations, while the hearing interpreters included the form in only 17.5% of their interpretations.

Interviews with the Deaf interpreters revealed that they often did not process the idiom as a marked phrase until after they had begun their interpretations because the feed they had been receiving up until the introduction of the idiom was in ASL. This in effect caught them unawares and led them to reproduce the form of the idiom rather than provide an interpretation of its meaning. The interviews also showed that in the case of form-only interpretations among the Deaf interpreters, the idiom was not processed but rather taken directly from the intermediary interpreter and placed into the interpretation. The Deaf interpreters then gave either the form but not the meaning (14.0%), the form and meaning (14.0%), or the form, meaning, and marker (2.0%).

Additionally, the few times in which the hearing interpreters from the first group gave the form of the idiom, they gave either the form only, without the meaning (7.5%), or the form, meaning, and marker (10%) but never gave the form and meaning without the marker, which implies that for the Deaf interpreters, the inclusion of the form (unmarked) is, at least in part, induced by the manner in which the idioms were presented by the relay interpreter. This implication is supported by the fact that the discrepancy between instances of meaning-only interpretations between the hearing (60.0%) and Deaf interpreters (42%), a difference of 18.0%, is almost entirely accounted for by the difference in form-and-meaning interpretations (hearing [0.0%] vs. Deaf [14.0%]; see appendix D).

Analysis Phase Two: Adjusted Data

In the next step of our data analysis, we adjusted the numbers to represent only idioms that were omitted or whose meaning was evident in the interpretation. When an idiom was not readily understandable and an interpretation was rendered that varied from its actual meaning, we removed the item from the final data analysis. We excluded instances in which the form but not the meaning of the idiom was interpreted because interpretation of the form without acknowledgment that the phrase is marked in any way generally indicates the interpreter's noncomprehension. This assumption was supported by both groups of interpreters during the interviews.

The rationale behind this decision also relates to one of the delimitations of the study. Namely, we are interested in how interpreters deal with idioms when they are understood. It is an accepted idea that interpreters often miss information due to a lack of comprehension or an overload of their capacity to process information (Gile, 1995). We wanted our numbers to reflect the interpreters' decisions about how to interpret the idioms, not their comprehension of any specific idiom. As noted earlier, interpretations that fell into the form-only category were based on lack of comprehension rather than conscious decision making. Though omissions may result from lack of comprehension, we could not always be certain. Omissions are often due to cognitive overload or interpreters' decisions about what information is most important or relevant, and we found clear patterns as to which idioms were omitted and why. During the final interviews, we discussed the possibilities for breakdowns in comprehension or other factors contributing to omission. These are discussed in more depth later. Precedent for the decision to eliminate data that may be misleading appears in Winston's (1989) examination of transliteration.

Once we had eliminated these data points, we calculated our adjusted numbers (see appendix E). These adjusted numbers reflect the way that interpreters handle idioms when comprehension is not an issue. Finally, we combined the numbers in order to get an idea of what interpreters do, regardless of how they access the source text (see figure 1).

MEANING ONLY, ADHERENCE TO DOCTRINE
The overwhelming majority of the time (56.3%) the interpreters in this study relayed the meaning of the English idiom without any reference to its form or the fact that the language choice was marked in any

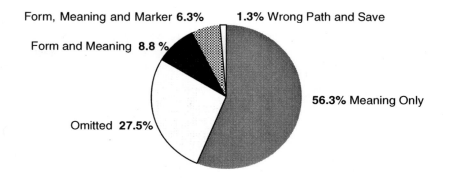

Form, Meaning and Marker **6.3%**   **1.3%** Wrong Path and Save

Form and Meaning **8.8 %**

56.3% Meaning Only

Omitted **27.5%**

FIGURE I. *How interpreters handle idioms.*

way. This may have happened for several reasons. First is adherence to the current theories that form should be stripped away and only meaning should be interpreted. Many of the hearing interpreters indicated in their interviews that they did not notice that an idiom had been used. This is consistent with Rawson's (1995) suggestion that idioms are so embedded in our language that they often go unnoticed. This also indicates that the interpreters carry out an "immediate and deliberate discarding of the wording" and interpret only what they understand the meaning to be (Seleskovitch, 1978, p. 8). With regard to the Deaf interpreters, there are three possibilities: Either the form of the English idiom was not transmitted, they chose to omit the form and interpret only the meaning, or depending on their English fluency, they also missed the fact that an idiom was used. Though possible, this last option is unlikely since a native ASL user would almost immediately mark a phrase bearing English grammar placed in the middle of an ASL text.

The second factor that may contribute to an interpreter's discarding the form of an English idiom is processing time. Depending on their lag time and personal perception of textual density (Palma, 1995), interpreters may decide that giving the form or otherwise indicating that an idiom has been used (i.e., with a marker) is not efficient or at times even possible. Finally, an interpreter may decide that the fact that the speaker has used an idiom is not relevant to the text.

OMISSIONS

In this study we found that 27.5% of idiomatic phrases were omitted altogether. Two of the idioms most frequently omitted were "back forty" and "under the weather." In both instances, six of nine interpreters gave neither form nor meaning. Our interviews did not fully clarify the reasoning behind these two omissions; however, we have come to several possible conclusions, none of which can be proven empirically, but they may nevertheless provide some insight. Consider, for instance, the following passage: "I've always lived in apartments in the middle of a big city. So when I moved here, it was a great chance to start planting things in *my own back forty*" (see source text, appendix A). The interpreters all utilized different signing spaces to depict the transition from city life to a life conducive to gardening. Also, the interpreters seemed to consider it more important to communicate what was being done (i.e., MOVE, PLANT) rather than to talk explicitly about the pride of ownership, which is represented by the phrase "back forty." They also did not show the pride of ownership in their affect (see figure 2).

In the following portion of the source text, the idiom "under the weather" was also omitted six times: "So if I'm feeling *under the weather* or *down in the dumps,* it's there to *chase my blues away*" (see source text, appendix A). Because it contains three idioms, this sentence is particularly dense. When contemplating possible reasons for the majority

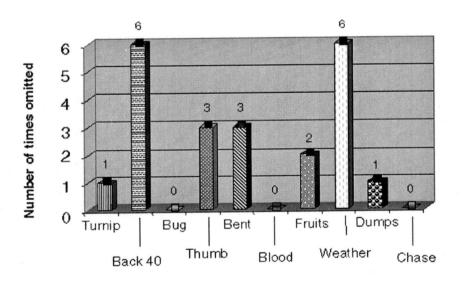

FIGURE 2. *Omissions.*

to exclude "under the weather," it is helpful to look at interpreter lag time during this portion of text. Most of the interpreters had an average five-second lag time, meaning that, as this sentence was presented, they were still completing the previous portion of text. Not only does this sentence mark the start of a new chunk, which began the conclusion of the text, but it was also presented very rapidly.

One possible conclusion is that the interpreters heard the entire chunk and had trouble reconciling "under the weather" with "chase my blues away." The two final clauses—"down in the dumps" and "chase my blues away"—seem to be paired, as the latter resolves the former. An interpreter who was processing on the textual level may have reasoned that "under the weather" was out of place or illogical. Another possibility is suggested by the recency theory (Luchins, 1957), which states that when we are presented with a series of items and our short-term memory begins to overload, the result is the recollection of the most recently heard item first (which is actually the last item on the list). In this case, the items the interpreter heard most recently are "down in the dumps" and "chase the blues away." By the time these concepts have been interpreted, the speaker is delivering the closing sentence. Thus, "under the weather" may be omitted because, once the interpreter has delivered a complete and coherent message consisting of the couplet "down in the dumps" and "chase the blues away," it may have seemed that it was more important to close the presentation along with the speaker rather than to try to fit in the extraneous "under the weather," whose meaning is very nearly conveyed by the phrase "down in the dumps."

FORM AND MEANING

As noted earlier, the only cases in which the unmarked form-and-meaning approach was used occurred in interpretations by the Deaf interpreters. This appears to be attributable to the fact that the English idioms were transliterated rather than interpreted for meaning by the relay interpreter. Moreover, the hearing interpreters, who are not relying on the feed of the relay interpreter to access the source text, never use this option. This indicates that the decision by the feed interpreter to include the form of the English idiom influenced the Deaf interpreters' output.

Importantly, the relay interpreter included the form at the request of the researchers. The relay interpreter was asked to include the form of the English idiom whenever possible, then to add the meaning if needed. Of the seven total cases of the form-and-meaning approach, three occurred for the idiom "blood, sweat, and tears" (see appendix C), three occurred for the idiom "fruits of your labor" (see appendix C), and one occurred for the idiom "chase the blues away" (see appendix C). In four of the seven cases the Deaf interpreter produced a near-exact gloss of the English idiom, followed by a rendering of the meaning (see appendix C, "blood, sweat, and tears"; appendix C, "fruits of my labor"; and appendix C, "chase the blues away").

With regard to form-only interpretations, the Deaf interpreters indicated during the interviews that they often gave the form of the idiom without recognizing it as a marked phrase. In the case of the form-and-meaning interpretations, the Deaf interpreters may have felt they had more time to get clarification from the intermediary interpreter. In the remaining two cases, the Deaf interpreter included aspects of the form embedded in the interpretation. Again, these choices appear to be induced by the feed because there is no indication that they are marked phrases even though they are not native ASL expressions. This may be a variation of the strategy discussed earlier in this section, or it may indicate that the Deaf interpreters decided to produce interpretations that involved some language contact and were comfortable including some of the form of commonly used figurative English in their ASL product.

Whatever the reasoning, the Deaf interpreters tended to give more figurative interpretations of the idioms when employing this strategy than did the hearing interpreters for the same idioms. For example, when interpreting the idiom "blood, sweat, and tears," three of the four hearing interpreters used an intensified version of WORK, while the other hearing interpreter used an intensified version of PLANT (verb) (see appendix C). By comparison, the interpretation of the same idiom by Deaf interpreter D1 contains more figurative aspects of ASL:

RS [wh-CL, 5 -/sh- (IX THAT MY] WORK [wh-CL, 5 -/sh- (IX THAT MY]
ACTION PRO.1 MAKE MCL, 5 "give" MAKE CL, 5 "give" GROW [wh-CL,
5 - /sh- IX] PRO.1 SWEAT, WORK+ TO MAKE NOW GIVE

Examples like this can also been seen in the interpretations of "blood, sweat, and tears" by interpreters D2, D3, and D4 (see appendix C). The same pattern also appears in the interpretations of "fruits of your labor," which hearing interpreters omitted twice and used variations of ENJOY

POSS.3 WORK. In two cases, the interpretations for this idiom (given by interpreters D1, D2, D3, and D4) involve more figurative aspects of ASL.

FORM, MEANING, AND MARKER: ARE THEY EXTERNALLY INDUCED?

Of the five interpretations that fell into this category, three involved cases in which the idiom was embedded in the text in such a way that the interpreters often had no choice but to include its English form. These three cases involved hearing interpreters and their interpretations of the "gardening bug" passage (see appendix A or above in the form, meaning, and marker category). In this passage the concepts expressed in the text, which lead into the idiom, do not indicate that an idiomatic punch line is forthcoming. This is a common humorous device used by native English speakers in the United States (Tray, 2005).

All four hearing interpreters indicated in their interviews that this passage presented difficulty for them. Up to this point the text had been fairly straightforward, so the interpreters predicted that the mention of bug bites would reference literal ones rather than constitute a figurative setup for an idiomatic expression of the speaker's enjoyment of gardening. The four hearing interpreters indicated that, by the time they understood the full meaning of the passage, they had already interpreted much of it literally and had to use the form, meaning, and marker approach in order to build upon what they had already expressed and to avoid having to indicate misunderstanding and start again. In examining the Deaf interpreters' handling of "gardening bug," the figurative meaning was not understood in any of the five cases. Again, the problem appears to be related to the degree to which this particular idiom is embedded and to the time constraints involved in interpreting a text in which the interpreters cannot ask the speaker to pause or clarify remarks.

The other two cases of form, meaning, and marker (one by a hearing interpreter and one by a Deaf interpreter) do not appear to be externally induced. This may mean that the interpreters in this case were consciously attempting to alert the audience to the fact that the speech was marked.

WRONG PATH AND SAVE

"Wrong path and save" represents a common repair technique used by interpreters in a variety of situations. We do not believe this represents a significant idiom-related strategy, and this opinion seems to be supported in that the tactic occurs only once in the data, the least frequently used strategy we noticed.

Limitations

Ours was a rather small study that analyzed the interpretations of nine participants. Each participant was asked to interpret a short text (slightly longer than four minutes) that was heavily idiomatic. Given that most interpreters utilize the first several minutes of a text to warm up and become acquainted with a speaker's style and pace (Ressler, 1999), an exercise involving such a brief text could be challenging.

Also, within the constraints of a research-driven project, aspects of real-world interpreting were lost in the simulation. In a real interpretation, the target audience would not be defined by researchers but would be a reality that the client and interpreter would experience together. Under the conditions of the study, we introduced the target audience via videotape, but it was not present in the room during the interpretation. The absence of an audience could affect an interpreter's ability to convey the nuances of the target language, which are normally coconstructed by active participants (Metzger, 1999). Roy (2000) cites Labov (1972), who stated that, while videotaping research participants for her project, she faced what she called the "observer's paradox." In other words, although the researcher's goal is to answer a question by observing a natural environment, the very presence of an outside party alters the natural environment. We experienced a similar quandary because our research necessitated that a camera be used.

We tried to create the most natural environment possible for the Deaf-hearing interpreting teams. Generally speaking, it is incumbent upon the interpreters to adequately prepare for an assignment and allow plenty of time to meet with their clients. For obvious reasons, during the study the interpreters' only access to the speaker was through a video introduction. Ideally there would be more opportunity to meet with the speaker, obtain preparation materials, and so on.

Another limitation is the fact that not all of the Deaf interpreters had previously worked with the relay interpreter. Each interpreter had only about ten minutes to discuss feeding strategies and techniques for clarification and to develop a working relationship with one another. For each of the five Deaf interpreters, the relay interpreter was kept static and had been exposed to the text multiple times. While we are aware that accessing the text more than once could be considered a translation instead of an interpretation, this decision was not wholly unintentional. Having the same interpreter feeding was a critical part of the stability of the project. Rather than adding more variables, we decided that the benefit outweighed the cost.

To achieve a particular goal, this study involved just one text in a specific genre and register designed to fit a specific audience. There are many possible ways to examine the handling and incorporation of idioms in interpretation. One aspect of the project could be altered to examine the way in which miniscule changes affect the incorporation of idioms. Moreover, in recruiting research participants, the scope could be narrowed so as to analyze across generational, ethnic, gender, and/or regional lines.

SUGGESTIONS FOR FURTHER RESEARCH

As this study progressed, it became increasingly apparent that more questions would be raised than we would have time to address. It would be extremely beneficial to replicate this study and to control for variables such as differences between generations, genres, regions, cultures, and genders. Incidentally, in a profession dominated by women, it is interesting to note that six of nine of our participants were male.

Interpreters are adept at tailoring their interpretation to their specific audience and are careful to analyze for contextual framework. How, then, do variations in setting, power dynamics, and register influence interpreters' handling and incorporation of idioms? This experiment could be replicated to control for these aspects to gain a more global view of the role idioms play in language as seen in interpretations. Simply utilizing a larger group of participants would be more helpful in obtaining a representative sample of the workings of professional interpreters.

Additionally, it would be constructive to survey interpreters with regard to their view on idiomatic interpretations, including whether they consider them necessary or superfluous. Those who feel that idiomatic translations are outside the scope of their "rendering a faithful interpretation" are unlikely to feel at liberty to use them. Interpreters may feel that employing figurative language constitutes a risk and are therefore unwilling to go out on a limb for fear of criticism. Does this belief signify the remnants of the conduit (i.e., the "machine" model of interpreting)?

Are interpreters willing to take a stand toward a culturally and linguistically appropriate interpretation? Since the 1960s the ASL-English interpreting field has grown and come to reject the philosophy that interpreters can render an interpretation apart from the cultural and unique linguistic needs of each assignment. Further research is needed to assess interpreters' views of the way in which idiomatic interpretations aid in the development of a culturally appropriate interpretation.

In the field of ASL linguistics, more research is needed to identify figurative language use among native ASL signers. English uses idioms and other figurative language to make a text more interesting, to mark a portion of text as unique or important, and to avoid monotony. How do native ASL users achieve these same goals? One possible way to determine this is to analyze an audience's perception of two juxtaposing interpretations—one plain language interpretation and one interpretation involving more figurative language use in ASL.

More research is needed to evaluate the intermediary interpretation process with a team of Deaf and hearing interpreters. How do Deaf-hearing interpreting teams normally handle idioms? Is form normally seen as obtrusive and immediately discarded?

CONCLUSION

Interpreters are faced with a problem of two theories in opposition. On the one hand are theorists who espouse the importance of meaning over form. This basic theory is used as a basis for teaching interpreting in numerous ASL-English interpreter training programs throughout the United States. On the other hand are theorists who suggest that, at times, the form is just as important as the meaning; some (Horodecka & Osadnik, 1992) even say that plain language replacement (using nonidiomatic phrases in the target text of a source text idiom) results in zero equivalence. As we have seen, interpreters tend to render plain language target texts when interpreting an English idiom into ASL unless they are compelled to do otherwise by an outside force (such as embedding of the idiom or having the form otherwise overtly presented).

As ASL-English interpreters, we strive for equivalence, yet our working languages present a discrepancy in recognized idioms and idiomatic expressions. Furthermore, when interpreting simultaneously we are forced to decide how to manage our cognitive processes. González, Vásquez, and Mikkelson (1991) suggest that when an interpreter is pressed for time and faces a lack of target text idioms, it is appropriate to render only the meaning of the source text. However, they also propose that this strategy be used as a last resort—when the interpreter cannot think of or produce an interpretation that is idiomatic, proverbial, or otherwise figurative.

When examining the expressive differences between hearing and Deaf interpreters, we found that the latter produced more figurative target texts. This finding is consistent with Ressler's (1999) idea that Deaf interpreters are able to produce more natural-looking ASL interpretations, as well as Tray's (2005) hypothesis that native signers and native English speakers use different strategies when translating a figurative English source text. This finding should alert interpreters for whom ASL is a second language and encourage them to look for ways to improve their grasp of idiomatic and figurative language use in ASL.

Seleskovitch refers to the "kernel of information" that is the essence of every communicative event (1978). However, how is this kernel to be harvested? Agar (1994) maintains that language and culture are inexorably intertwined. Thus, each text is as unique as its speaker, and speakers may choose to express themselves in a variety of ways. Their meaning is generally understood and expressed by interpreters, who are inevitably faced with English speakers who employ idiomatic language. Aside from conveying the information in the form of plain language replacement (Horodecka & Osadnik, 1992), what other options do interpreters have?

We have presented four successful strategies that interpreters employ when working with idioms: meaning only; omission; form and meaning; and form, meaning, and marker. However, the most equivalent interpretation will be the one that conveys the same pragmatic functions as those given in the source language. By clarifying what interpreters do when they encounter idiomatic language, we hope that this research will encourage individual interpreters to think about their work and practice. By developing practical strategies for dealing with idioms, we can make our interpretations more figurative and possibly closer to equivalent. At the very least, by examining and understanding the common tactics used by skilled interpreters from various language backgrounds, we quiet the doubts that sometimes interfere with our interpretations of English idioms.

REFERENCES

Agar, M. (1994). *Language shock*. New York: Morrow.

Battison, R. (1980). Signs have parts: A simple idea. In C. Baker & R. Battison (Eds.), *Sign language and the Deaf community*. Silver Spring, MD: National Association of the Deaf.

Battison, R. (1998). Signs have parts: A simple idea. In C. Valli & C. Lucas (Eds.), *Linguistics of American Sign Language: An introduction* (pp. 231–42). Washington, DC: Gallaudet University Press.

Boatner, M. T., & Gates, J. E. (Eds.). (1966). *A dictionary of idioms for the Deaf*. West Hartford, CT: American School for the Deaf.

Chafe, W. (1968). *English questions*. Washington, DC: ERIC/PEGS.

Cokely, D. (2001). Interpreting culturally rich realities, research implications for successful interpretations. *RID Journal of Interpretation*, 1–45.

Cokely, D., & Baker-Shenk, C. (1980). *American Sign Language: A teacher's resource text on curriculum, methods, and evaluation*. Silver Spring, MD: T. J. Publishers.

Gibbs, R. W., Jr. (2002). A new look at literal meaning in understanding what is said and implicated. *Journal of Pragmatics 34*(4), 457–86.

Gile, D. (1995). *Basic concepts and models for interpreter and translator training*. Philadelphia: John Benjamins.

Giora, R., & Fein, O. (1999). On understanding familiar and less-familiar figurative language. *Journal of Pragmatics 31*(12), 1601–18.

González, R. D., Vásquez, V. F., & Mikkelson, H. (1991). *The fundamentals of court interpreting: Theory, policy, and practice*. Durham, NC: Carolina Academic Press.

Gutt, E.-A. (1991). *Translation and relevance: Cognition and context*. Cambridge, MA: Blackwell.

Hatim, B., & Mason, I. (1990). *Discourse and the translator*. New York: Longman.

Hatim, B., & Mason, I. (1997). *The translator as communicator*. New York, Routledge.

Horodecka, E., & Osadnik, W. M. (1992). A polysystem approach to translation of proverbs and idiomatic expressions from English into Polish. *Journal of Interpretation 5*(1), 25–50.

Ichikawa, S., Mine, T., Inui, R., Kihara, K., & Takaha, S. (1964). *The Kenkyusha dictionary of current English idioms*. Tokyo: Kenkyusha.

Isham, W. (1986). The role of message analysis in interpretation. In M. McIntire (Ed.), *Interpreting: The art of cross-cultural mediation* (Proceedings of the Ninth National Convention of RID, pp. 111–22). Silver Spring, MD: RID Publications.

Keysar, B., & Bly, B. M. (1999). Swimming against the current: Do idioms reflect conceptual structure? *Journal of Pragmatics* 31(12), 1559–78.

Labov, W. (1972). *Sociolinguistic patterns*. Philadelphia: University of Pennsylvania Press.

Larson, M. (1984). *Meaning-based translation: A guide to cross-language equivalence*. Lanham, MD: University Press of America.

Luchins, A. S. (1957). In C. I. Hovland (Ed.), *The order of presentation*. New Haven, CT: Yale University Press.

Lupson, J. P. (1984). *Guide to German idioms*. Lincolnwood, IL: Passport Books.

Metzger, M. (1999). *Sign language interpreting: Deconstructing the myth of neutrality*. Washington, DC: Gallaudet University Press.

Nabokov, V. (1955). Problems of translation: "Onegin" in English. In L. Venuti (Ed.), *The translation studies reader* (pp. 71–83). New York: Routledge.

Norrick, N. R. (1985). *How proverbs mean: Semantic studies in English proverbs*. New York: Moulton.

Palma, J. (1995). Textual density and the judiciary interpreter's performance. In M. Morris (Ed.), *Translation and the law* (219–31). American Translators Association Scholarly Monograph Series, vol. 8. Philadelphia: John Benjamins.

Rawson, H. (1995). *Dictionary of euphemisms and other doubletalk: Being a compilation of linguistic fig leaves and verbal flourishes for artful users of the English language*. New York: Crown.

Ressler, C. (1999). A comparative analysis of a direct interpretation and an intermediary interpretation in American Sign Language. *RID Journal of Interpretation*, 71–97.

Rosenthal, J. (1978). Idiom recognition for machine translation and information storage and retrieval. PhD diss., Georgetown University.

Roy, C. (2000). *Interpreting as a discourse process*. New York: Oxford University Press.

Seleskovitch, D. (1978). *Interpreting for international conferences: Problems of language and communication*, trans. S. Dailey & E. N. McMillan. Washington, DC: Pen and Booth.

Taylor, R., & Gottschalk, W. (1960). *A German-English dictionary of idioms: Idiomatic and figurative German expressions with English translations*. Munich: Hueber.

Titone, D. A., & Connine, C. M. (1999). On the compositional and non-compositional nature of idiomatic expressions. *Journal of Pragmatics* 31(12), 1655–74.

Tray, S. (2005). What are you suggesting? Interpreting innuendo between ASL and English. In M. Metzger and E. Fleetwood (Eds.), *Attitudes, innuendo,* and regulators: *Challenges of interpretation* (pp. 95–135). Studies in Interpretation Series, vol. 2. Washington, DC: Gallaudet University Press.

Tytler, A. F. (1907). *Essay on the principles of translation.* New York: Dutton.

Valli, C., & Lucas, C. (1998). *Linguistics of American Sign Language: An introduction.* (3d ed). Washington, DC: Gallaudet University Press.

Vilar-Sánchez, K. (2002). Functional-communicative grammar (Spanish-German) for translators and/or interpreters: A project. *Babel 47*(2), 109–20.

Virginie, L. (2003). Idiom comprehension and metapragmatic knowledge in French children. *Journal of Pragmatics 35*(5), 723–39.

Winston, E. (1989). Transliteration: What's the message? In C. Lucas (Ed.), *The sociolinguistics of the deaf community* (pp. 147–64). New York: Academic Press.

Wood, M. M. (1986). *A definition of idiom.* Bloomington, IN: University Linguistics Club.

APPENDIX A

Source Text

Good morning, everyone. I'm glad to see so many of you here today. I'm going to be speaking briefly about the benefits of gardening, and then I'm going to open it up to questions.

Let me start out by saying that gardening provides you with nutrition that you might not otherwise get. Studies have shown that nutritionally you are 60% better off if you do home gardening rather than buying your food in a regular grocery store. That's a big, that's a significant increase, um, for your body. And what it means is that most home gardens are done in an organic way. The food—the vegetables and fruit—are grown organically so that your food does not have the chemicals in it that store bought'n vegetables have. Nor do those chemicals then get anywhere near your body.

You also get benefits from the exercise of gardening. Now, most people think, "C'mon, there's not a lot of exercise to gardening." But think about it folks. You're stretching, you're bending, you're hauling, you're lifting, you're digging. So you have both weight-bearing exercises from both the hauling and the digging. You've got stretching exercises from the bending and from the lifting up of things. So the effect on your body of just getting out and doing these things—getting the blood circulating—is a significant increase over those who are not gardening.

But I think that chief among these is the emotional lift you get from gardening. Now, I don't want to sound like I *just fell off the turnip truck,* but until a few years ago I'd never had a garden of my own. I've always lived in apartments in the middle of a big city. So when I moved here, it was a great chance to start planting things in *my own back forty.* Before I moved here I tried all the other pick-me-ups short of Prozac, but now I love gardening, and once you start gardening, I'm sure you will come to love it, too.

Now . . . [dramatic pause] I've had mosquito bites, and I've had spider bites, but I never knew how sweet the itch could feel until I was *bitten by the gardening bug.* Seriously, though, it's really meditative. Even when you garden with other people you find that you can enjoy these times of peace and solitude while at the same time working side by side with a friend! Even pulling weeds become meditative. Putting the seeds in the ground is meditative. Certainly harvesting the goods that you've waited all year for is meditative. It's magic, the way you can take a little bit of dirt and a seed and in a few months you have a flower or something to eat. Oops, I forgot you're not supposed to call it dirt. If you're a real *green thumb,* you call it "soil." Some gardeners get all *bent out of shape* over terminology. Don't ask me why. If you ask me, there's nothing wrong with good old-fashioned dirt. Anyway, the sense of satisfaction you get when you see your friends and family eating food that you coaxed from the ground with your own two hands and put your *blood, sweat, and tears* into . . . It allows you to literally enjoy *the fruits of your labor.* So if I'm feeling *under the weather* or *down in the dumps,* it's there to *chase my blues away.* You start messing around out there, I guarantee you'll feel chipper again—just like that.

APPENDIX B

Context

A local homeowners' association is hosting an annual street fair. The schedule for the day includes brief presentations by members of the neighborhood. You have been requested to interpret from English to ASL for a Deaf member of the neighborhood who is interested in attending the 10:00 A.M. talk on gardening. The Deaf woman uses ASL, and the talk will be approximately five minutes long.

Transcription Conventions

SMALL CAPS	glosses of ASL signs
fs SMALL CAPS	the word in small caps was fingerspelled
#CAPS	the glossed word is lexicalized fingerspelling
+	the sign was reduplicated; each + represents one reduplication.
PRO. 1/2/3	pronoun (first, second, third person, respectively)
*	the sign was emphasized
neg	negation
CL	classifier predicate
WORD-WORD	a single sign that must be represented with a two-word gloss
2h	two-handed sign
hs	handshape
NMS	nonmanual signal
NHS	nonhanded sign
[wh-____/sh-____]	a two-handed sign that shows the action of the nondominant ("weak") hand followed by the action of the dominant ("strong") hand. In this case the actions are performed simultaneously.
IX	indexing
"word"	indicates what a classifier represents or what is being referenced by an IX
(words)	used to clarify various grammatical information
GES-	the following gloss was not taken from a citation form ASL sign but is a gesture that provides the meaning indicated by the gloss

Transcription: H1 (*In the transcription, "terp" indicates "time interpreted."*)

	Form	Meaning	
turnip truck (1:50)	—	—	Omitted
back 40 (2:06)	—	—	Omitted
gardening bug (2:23) (terp: 2:26)	YES	—	have finish get bee bite spider bite #but pro.i finish try fs: gcn (garden) pro.1 never know enjoy will (hand on hip) true good
green thumb (3:18) (terp: 3:22)	—	YES	if true good expert fs: gardening
bent out of shape (3:22) (terp: 3:28)	—	YES	most expert head shake (negative) prefer use word fs: soil
blood, sweat and tears (3:46) (terp: 3:48)	—	YES	work*++ fs: garden
fruits of my labor (3:49) (terp: 3:49)	YES	—	enjoy poss.2 work
under the weather (3:53) (terp: 3:54)	—	NO	pro.1 feel relief (neg)
down in the dumps (3:55) (terp: 3:56)	—	YES	depressed
chase the blues away (3:58) (terp: 4:01)	—	YES	garden will help my emotion improve

Transcription: H2 (*In the transcription, "terp" indicates "time interpreted."*)

	Form	Meaning	
turnip truck (1:50) (terp- 1:55)	—	YES	NO-WAVE+ UNDERSTAND+ PRO.1 DON'T-WANT LOOK-ME (HEAD-TO-TOE) STUPID (2h- hs: 2 "to capacity") NO+
back 40 (2:06)	—	—	Omitted
gardening bug (2:23) (terp-2:29)	YES	YES	RIGHT BEE BITE (face) SPIDER BITE (hand) DIFFERENT++ YES BUT (hand on hip) FEEL THINK PRO.1 INSPIRE (eyes wide) WHAT fs: GARDEN BITE MY . . . MY FEEL MOTIVATE ACTION
green thumb (3:19) (terp: 3:29)	—	YES	SOME PEOPLE WHO SELF USED-TO (lips puckered) fs: GARDEN CALL fs: SOIL
bent out of shape (3:22) (terp: 3:34)	—	YES	UPSET #IF CALL THAT fs: DIRT
blood, sweat, and tears (3:46) (terp: 3:46)	—	YES	PLANT(verb) (NMS: *intense*)
fruits of my labor (3:49)	—	—	Omitted
under the weather (3:53) (terp: 3:56)	—	YES	INFORM PRO.1 FEEL LITTLE-BIT SICK
down in the dumps (3:55) (terp: 3:59)	—	YES	DEPRESSED
chase the blues away (3:58) (terp: 4:01)	—	YES	KNOW-THAT PRO.1 OUTSIDE fs: GARDEN PRO.1 TRUE ALOT FEEL DEPRESS 2h-"what" CHANGE INSPIRE SNAP

Transcription: H3 (*In the transcription, "terp" indicates "time interpreted."*)

	Form	Meaning	
turnip truck (1:50) (terp- 1:55)	—	YES	DON'T-WANT PRO.1 THINK INNOCENT+ KNOW-NOTHING HAND-WAVE "no"
back 40 (2:06)	—	—	Omitted
gardening bug (2:23) (terp: 2:28)	YES	YES	INFORM PRO.2 HAVE MOSQUITO BITE "hand" SLAP SPIDER (1h) BUG BITE BAD BITE WOW NOW (new space) BITE #BY WHAT PAUSE NMS fs: GARDEN fs: BUG QUOTE FEEL HOOK NOW
green thumb (3:19)	—	—	Omitted
bent out of shape (3:22) (terp: 3:26)	—	YES	WOW (2h- shake) SOME PLANT(verb) DON'T-LIKE WORD fs: DIRT
blood, sweat, and tears (3:46) (terp: 3:50)	YES	YES	QUOTE BLOOD SWEAT+ (armpits) CRY PLANT(verb) WORK++
fruits of my labor (3:49)	—	—	Omitted
under the weather (3:53)	—	—	Omitted
down in the dumps (3:55) (terp: 4:01)	—	YES	DEPRESSED
chase the blues away (3:58) (terp: 4:02)	—	YES	HELP INSPIRE FEEL BETTER

Transcription: H4 (*In the transcription, "terp" indicates "time interpreted."*)

	Form	Meaning	
turnip truck (1:50)	—	YES	SEEM CRAZY RIGHT
back 40 (2:06)	—	YES	BIG BACK fs:YARD
gardening bug (2:23)	YES	YES	SOMETIMES BUG BITE SPIDER BITE EXPERIENCE FINISH+ KNOW+ NOW PRO.1 fs:GARDEN BUG BITE PRO.1(head jiggle) FASCINATE fs: GARDEN
green thumb (3:19)	YES	—	fs: GARDEN PEOPLE SELF PREFER CALL fs: GREEN THUMB fs: SOIL
bent out of shape (3:22)	—	YES	DON'T-LIKE THAT WORD
blood, sweat, and tears (3:46)	—	YES	WORK*++
fruits of my labor (3:49)	—	YES	WILL ENJOY POSS.3 WORK
under the weather (3:53)	—	YES	SICK
down in the dumps (3:55)	—	YES	DEPRESSED SAD
chase the blues away (3:58)	—	YES	MEAN PRO.1 FEEL BETTER IMPROVE++

Transcription: D1

	Form	Meaning	
turnip truck (1:50) (terp: 1:58)	—	YES	THINK PRO.1 PEA-BRAIN NO (wave) NOT
back 40 (2:06) (terp: 2:07)	—	YES	WHY-NOT NEW HOME WHY-NOT GO AHEAD PLANT(verb) fs: GARDEN
gardening bug (2:23) (terp: 2:30)	NO	—	HAVE PART NEGATIVE++ WHY BUG BEE PICK-ON PAIN BLOOD FS: BEES CL.1 "sting" NOTHING BUT PAIN REPLACE PRO.2 STILL PLANT(verb) STILL ENJOY ABOVE BEAT NEGATIVE
green thumb (3:19) (terp: 3:35)	—	YES	2h: BIG-BRAIN
bent out of shape (3:22) (terp: 3:25)	—	YES	RESENT
blood, sweat, and tears (3:44) (terp: 3:47)	—	YES	[wh-CL: 5 /sh- IX] THAT MY WORK [wh-CL: 5 /sh- IX] THAT MY ACTION PRO.1 MAKE CL:5 "give" MAKE CL:5 "give" GROW [wh-CL: 5 /sh- IX] PRO.1 SWEAT WORK+ TO MAKE NOW GIVE
fruits of my labor (3:49) (terp: 3:56)	—	YES	2h- GIVE POSS.1 HARD WORK EXPRESS HEART (IX: draw) GIVE
under the weather (3:53)	—	—	Omitted
down in the dumps (3:55) (terp: 4:01)	—	YES	#IF FEEL DEPRESS
chase the blues away (3:58) (terp: 4:04)	—	YES	OUT (topic, nod) FEEL MUCH BETTER FS: FRESH AIR CIRCULATE

Incorporation of Idioms : 37

Transcription: D2

	Form	Meaning	
turnip truck (1:50) (terp: 2:10)	—	YES	hs: Y (modified wave) "goofy" HAND-WAVE (NO) PRO.1 EXPERIENCE
back 40 (2:06)	—	—	Omitted
gardening bug (2:23) (terp: 2:34)	—	NO	UNDERSTAND MOSQUITO STING (BODY) SECOND-ON-LIST BUG CRAWL (on me) BUT NOTHING PSHAW BUG BITE-ME COOL MORE MOTIVATE BUG-BITS (ON ME)
green thumb (3:19)	—	—	Omitted
bent out of shape (3:22)	—	—	Omitted
blood, sweat, and tears (3:44) (terp: 3:58)	—	YES	POSS.3 WORK* + BLOOD CIRCULATE WORK+ INVOLVE ACTION BECOMES-CL:5 FINE-wiggle
fruits of my labor (3:49)	—	—	Omitted
under the weather (3:53)	—	—	Omitted
down in the dumps (3:55)	—	—	Omitted
chase the blues away (3:58) (terp: 4:12)	—	YES	PRO.3 ACTION SICK NONE ACTION FEEL PROCESS MOTIVATE

Transcription: D3

	Form	Meaning	
turnip truck (1:50) (terp: 2:01)	YES	NO–YES	YOU-ALL THINK PRO.1 RECENT FELL FROM fs: TURNIP-TRUCK QUOTE FELL OFF QUOTE THINK PRO.1 AWKWARD CL: "person" FELL SOMETHING NO++ PRO.1 KNOW NEW STUDY
back 40 (2:06)	—	—	Omitted
gardening bug (2:23) (terp: 2:34)	YES	—	UNDERSTAND PRO.1 FINISH EXPERIENCE MOSQUITO BITE (hand) SLAP STING SECOND-ON-LIST SPIDER BITE FINISH SECOND-ON-LIST DON'T-MIND SCRATCH++ QUOTE SWEET ITCH WHY fs: GARDEN BUG IX IMPORTANT INFORM-YOU FINE-Wig
green thumb (3:19) (terp: 3:22)	YES	—	REAL QUOTE GREEN THUMB
bent out of shape (3:22) (terp:	—	—	Omitted
blood, sweat, and tears (3:44) (terp: 3:48)	YES	YES	BLOOD CIRCULATE SWEAT WORK CRY DIFFERENT GATHER THAT
fruits of my labor (3:49) (terp: 3:53)	YES	YES	[wh-CL: 5 /sh- IX] FRUIT POSS.1 WORK* + GATHER NOW BEAUTIFUL [wh-CL: 5 /sh- palm "this"]
under the weather (3:53) (terp: 3:59)	—	YES	SICK
down in the dumps (3:55) (terp: 4:00)	—	YES	DEPRESSED
chase the blues away (3:58) (terp: 4:04)	YES	YES	QUOTE CHASE POSS.1 BLUE AWAY QUOTE EXPRESS CIRCULATE

Transcription: D4 (*The abbreviation "rs" stands for "role shift," which indicates the speaker's use of a blend to represent the speech or actions of a non-present person other than the speaker.*)

	Form	Meaning	
turnip truck (1:50) (terp: 2:06)	—	YES	THINK PRO.1 PEA-BRAIN ACTION PRO.1 KNOW-NOTHING NO+
back 40 (2:06) (terp: 2:11)	—	YES	PRO.1 BUY HOUSE wh:CL.5 sh: CL:claw (on top of) "house" DONE PRO.1 PLANT(verb)+
gardening bug (2:23) (terp: 2:40)	YES	—	PRO.1 HAVE KNOW-THAT (IX= wait) THROUGH CL:x "small flying thing" rs: "FLYING THING" CL: X BITE-ME ITCH-ARM ITCH-BODY BUT PROCESS fs: GARDEN IX BITE-ME PRO.1 DON'T-CARE FLICK-OFF FINE PROCESS LONG fs: TERM WILL WORTH POINT IX "bite" FLICK-OFF NOTHING
green thumb (3:19) (terp: 3:32)	YES	—	THUMBS-UP GREEN fs: THUMB CHANGE GOOD* IX
bent out of shape (3:22)	—	—	Omitted
blood, sweat, and tears (3:44) (terp: 3:54)	YES	YES	POSS.3 WORK SWEAT RAIN WEATHER COMPLETE GIVE-ME #WOW MY SWEAT BLOOD HEART-PUMP EXERCISE COMPLETE FINISH GROW-UP GIVE rs: INSPIRE
fruits of my labor (3:49)	—	—	Omitted
under the weather (3:53)	—	—	Omitted
down in the dumps (3:55) (terp: 4:04)	—	YES	DEPRESS SAD LONELY
chase the blues away (3:58) (terp: 4:12)	YES	YES	MEAN SAD BLUE rs: CHASE SAD NHS-NO DISMISS ACTION-wig CHANGE FEEL MORE ACTION-wiggle NORMAL

Transcription: D5

	Form	Meaning	
turnip truck (1:50) (terp: 2:02)	—	YES	PRO.1 DON'T-WANT PRO.2 THINK PRO.1 2h-PEA-BRAIN PRO.1 WRONG+ NHS-NO INFORM APPROPRIATE GO-AHEAD
back 40 (2:06)	—	—	Omitted
gardening bug (2:23) (terp: 2:32)	YES	—	UNDERSTAND EXPERIENCE SPIDER BITE (hand) KNOW-THAT SAME+ MOSQUITO BITE FINISH SECOND-ON-LIST BUT IMPORTANT IX fs: GARDEN BUG 2h-hs-wiggle: 5 "bugs around" DON'T CARE IMPORTANT INSIDE-SELF FEEL THUMBS-UP
green thumb (3:19) (terp: 3:22)	YES	—	GREEN THUMB
bent out of shape (3:22) (terp: 3:27)	—	YES	INDIGNANT NMS
blood, sweat, and tears (3:44) (terp: 3:52)	YES	YES	POSS.1 BLOOD SWEAT CRY PRO.1 WORK+ EXPRESS
fruits of my labor (3:49) (terp: 3:58)	YES	YES	FRUIT POSS.1 fs: LABOR MEAN POSS.1 WORK RESULT GIVE [wh-CL: 5 /sh- IX] THAT [wh-CL: 5 /sh- IX]
under the weather (3:53)	—	—	Omitted
down in the dumps (3:55) (terp: 4:04)	—	YES	DEPRESSED DEPRESSED (2h- hs: 5) 2h-hs: 5 "DISGUSTED (mixed feelings)"
chase the blues away (3:58) (terp: 4:08)	—	YES	FEEL CIRCULATE RISE-UP FEEL INSPIRE FEEL SNAP GOOD MYSELF

APPENDIX D

Raw Data Analysis

	Turnip truck	Back forty	Garden bug	Green thumb	Bent out of shape	Blood, sweat, tears	Fruits of labor	Under weather	Down in dumps	Chase blues away	Total	Percentage
Meaning Only	3	1	—	2	4	3	1	2	4	4	24	60.0%
Omitted	1	3	—	2	—	—	2	2	—	—	9	22.5%
Form Only (meaning skewed)	—	—	1	1	—	—	1	—	—	—	3	7.5%
Form and Meaning	—	—	—	—	—	—	—	—	—	—	—	0%
Form and Meaning and Marker	—	—	3	—	—	1	—	—	—	—	4	10%
Wrong Path and Save	—	—	—	—	—	—	—	—	—	—	—	0%

(10) idioms × (4) interpretations = 40 possible data points   100%

	Turnip truck	Back forty	Garden bug	Green thumb	Bent out of shape	Blood, sweat, tears	Fruits of labor	Under weather	Down in dumps	Chase blues away	Total	Percentage
Meaning Only	4	2	—	1	2	2	2	1	4	3	**21**	**42.0%**
Omitted	—	3	—	2	3	—	—	4	1	—	**13**	26%
Form Only (meaning skewed)	—	—	5	2	—	—	—	—	—	—	7	14%
Form and Meaning	—	—	—	—	—	3	3	—	—	1	7	14%
Form and Meaning and Marker	—	—	—	—	—	—	—	—	—	—	1	2%
Wrong Path and Save	1	—	—	—	—	—	—	—	—	—	1	2%

(10) idioms × (5) interpretations = 50 possible data points   100%

	COMBINED TOTALS	
Meaning Only	45	50.0%
Omitted	22	24.4%
Form Only (meaning skewed)	10	11.1%
Form and Meaning	7	7.8%
Form and Meaning and Marker	5	5.6%
Wrong Path and Save	1	1.1%
		100.0%

APPENDIX E

Adjusted Data Analysis

Data points		43 points		37 points	80 points
		Deaf percentage		Hearing percentage	Both groups percentage
Meaning Only	21	48.9%	24	64.9%	56.3%
Omitted	13	30.2%	9	24.3%	27.5%
Form and Meaning	7	16.3%	0	0.0%	8.8%
Form, Meaning, and Marker	1	2.3%	4	10.8%	6.3%
Wrong Path and Save	1	2.3%	0	0.0%	1.3%
		100.0%		100.0%	100.0%

Deep and Meaningful Conversation:

Challenging Interpreter Impartiality in the

Semantics and Pragmatics Classroom

Lorraine Leeson and Susan Foley-Cave

This chapter challenges the reality of two related notions that are central to interpreter behavior, namely that interpreters are not actively involved in creating the discourse that they "mediate" and that they are impartial with respect to both the message and the participants in an interpreted event.[1] While much has been said regarding the myth of neutrality vis-à-vis interpreters in medical settings (Metzger, 1999), police interviews (Wadensjö, 1998), and other legal domains (e.g., Brennan & Brown, 1997), we wish to look at the particular challenges that interpreters face in the postgraduate education environment, specifically, in a classroom dedicated to introducing topics in semantics and pragmatics.

We suggest that the challenge of discussing the semantics of one language in interpretation demands that the interpreter make decisions on several levels. We outline some of these and consider the consequences of such decisions. We also discuss the role of consultation with students and staff regarding the appropriateness of message transfer and contrast the practice of active preparation, as well as consulting and decision making both on and off task, with the notion of the interpreter as mediator and impartial bystander.

Finally we suggest that, while the decisions that interpreters make in a semantics or pragmatics classroom are influenced by a metalinguistic framework, similar decisions are made in other interpreted domains, but the nature of interpreter decision making and information management as a necessary component of successful interpretation is typically overlooked. We propose that the highly embedded model of interpreter as conduit continues to influence our understanding of the interpreters' role and that this needs to be challenged in order for us to appreciate more fully the nature of co-constructed interpreted discourse in action.

THE CHALLENGES OF INTERPRETING SEMANTICS
AND PRAGMATICS

In this section we look at some of the challenges that are specific to the interpretation of semantics and pragmatics. We begin by considering interpreting as a three-party exchange, that is, a *triadic interaction* (Wadensjö, 1998), and argue that, while classroom interaction in a traditional lecture session may not be as interactively participatory as other triadic domains, it is nonetheless a situation in which two languages are being used, typically in simultaneous mode, with the potential for communication breakdown. We then examine the ways in which the interpreter's understanding of the function of the interpreting event can aid in preparation and on-task work. Finally we look at how the historic relationship between Irish Sign Language and English presents specific challenges to interpretation, particularly when the focus of the interpreting event is on a metalinguistic discussion of the meaning of words and the ways in which they are contextually driven.

Interpreting: A Triadic Interaction

Interpreting involves a default of two language participants who wish to interact but do not share a common language, along with an interpreter, whose role it is to facilitate the interaction between these parties. In the classroom setting that our discussion focuses on, the main participants are the professor (a hearing man in his 50s); the Deaf students (both in the 30–45 age group; one male and one female), and the two female interpreters (both in their 30s). The hearing students attending the class are also participants, and we could say much about how the interpreters' presence affects their time in class. However, in this chapter we focus on the interpreters, the Deaf students, and the professor. While we are particularly concerned with the issues that arise in a linguistics classroom, many of the topics we raise apply equally to other domains, whether in tertiary education or indeed outside the educational sphere. For example, we believe that interpreting at the tertiary education level and conference interpreting have much in common. Several contextual factors that are relevant to the classroom subject matter can influence interpretation, including the following:

- Both interpreters know the Deaf students and work with them as teaching colleagues in another setting.

- One of the interpreters has known the professor for more than a decade and works closely with him in an academic setting.
- The interpreters have known each other for a decade and have worked closely in a wide range of settings.

As a result, some of the relationships between the participants in this setting extend beyond the actual assignment itself. In an Irish context, it is not unusual for interpreters and Deaf interpreters to know each other, often very well. The Irish Deaf community is very small: Matthews (1996) reports that there are approximately five thousand Deaf Irish Sign Language users in the Republic of Ireland. However, the country has very few interpreters—at present around fifty, but at the time of interpreting this course (2003), only about twenty-four interpreters were available. Given this, we can say that, especially in educational settings, where the same interpreter is working with the same Deaf students over an academic year, relationships evolve. This is reflected to some extent in the informal interaction that takes place between participants. As we will see, this in no way suggests that the interpreters become decision makers in interactions in which they should be impartial. Instead, we maintain that interpreters *do* make decisions about how to frame their target language (TL) output and, as the literature notes, about their responses to other participants in the interaction, the potential consequences of such decisions for the TL, the participants, the dynamics of the situation, their own professional standing, and that of their profession (for example, see Leeson, 2005a, 2005b). These factors interact with the fact that Irish Sign Language (ISL) is an evolving language that has been used in academic classrooms for fewer than twenty years. The consequences of this include lexical gaps for register-specific terminology, which is challenging for interpreters and students alike.

Course Aims and Objectives

When preparing for an interpreting assignment, interpreters draw on the context that they will be working in to frame their preliminary judgments regarding their task. In this classroom situation, the professor is a native English speaker, and the two Deaf students use ISL. The course is an introduction to semantics and pragmatics that is given in the first semester of a master's degree program. The course focuses primarily on the semantics of English, and an English language textbook is used. The terminology that refers to semantic and pragmatic concepts is discussed and debated in class. Students are referred to particular textbook chapters that expand on the ideas discussed in class, and they are expected to read the relevant chapters and complete certain assignments before the following week's class. Thus there is a bridging of expectation between the textbook and the lectures.

For interpreters, this raises the issue of dealing with concepts in interpretation versus transliteration. That is, even if an item can be interpreted into ISL, should the interpreter use the ISL sign, fingerspell the item, use a calque sign (a literal transfer of the morphemes of the source language item), or use a nonce sign (that is, a sign that will be used only for the duration of the interpretation)? For example, the term "logic" can be used in its generic sense in English, but the term is also used as a specialist term in formal semantics. Semanticists differentiate between different kinds of logic, including "propositional logic," in which the truth effects of connectives are studied in formal semantics. This follows from the fact that semanticists call a sentence's truth or falsehood a "truth value" (Saeed, 2003, pp. 89–90). Other logic-related issues discussed by semanticists include modal logic, logical operators, and predicate logic (see ibid., chapter 10, for an overview). Irish Sign Language, however, has a sign that we can gloss as LOGIC, which is typically used in a generic way to mean "logical" or "sensible." But this is articulated in the same manner and at the same location as the ISL sign for SENSE (i.e., "common sense" or "sensible"). This sign is also a tempting equivalent for the semantic notion of "sense" that we discuss later. In these situations, opinions vary on what an interpreter should do: Llewellyn-Jones (1999) and colleagues suggest that transliteration and fingerspelling may work best; Deaf informants in an Irish sample proposed nonce signs as a viable option (Leeson, 2005b), but Stratiy (2005) rejects these.

One problem is that interpreters have no way of guaranteeing that the client will comprehend the TL lexical item that they choose to convey the meaning embedded in the source language (SL). This can lead to a breakdown between the interpreter's intentionality and the audience's understanding of the presenter's point. While this situation may arise in any interpreting setting, a potential for misunderstanding arises when specialist terminology coincides with lexical items that crop up in everyday discourse, where they are used in a different sense. This risk may be greater than is the case when the SL introduces new vocabulary that does not have existing TL collocations or generic uses of the specialist lexical item in the TL (e.g., thematic roles, hyponymy).

The interpreter's decisions are often guided by the fact that the students will have encountered a term in the textbook before class or will do so when they read the relevant chapter after class. Indeed, Sandler (1995, p. 5) made this point when referring to the interpretation of linguistics: "The material is academic: the academic register requires use of the English terminology; and the students have to be able to recognize the English term when they read it."

Other pertinent factors include the following:

- The Deaf students are bilingual.
- A lexical item may or may not exist in ISL.
- The students may express a preference for one lexical sign over another.
- While on task, a nonce sign is agreed upon and maintained throughout the course.

As mentioned earlier, the fact that this particular course focused on the semantics of English also influenced the interpreting decisions. We were constantly conscious of the potential for an interpretation to mislead students into believing that the professor was making universal statements about semantics and pragmatics or implying that the semantics of ISL are the same as those of English. We felt this would be a possible outcome if we interpreted the English sentences that formed the basis of class discussion into ISL. To have done so would have produced very different semantic analyses given verb classification and the attendant semantics of certain polymorphemic or classifier verbs in ISL. The verb "to hit," while something of an "old chestnut" works well here: In English, information about an instrument that is used to hit someone is added after the verb; that is, it is encoded lexically and results in sentences such as "I hit him with the **frying pan**." In ISL, as in other signed languages, this information is encoded in what are usually called "classifier predicates" (although we note the controversy over the naming of such structures. See Schembri [2003] for an excellent discussion of the issue).

Thus, if an example with the verb "hit" was used in class, an ISL interpretation would usually encode information about the fact that the agent (the person doing the hitting) used a fist or a flat hand or held an instrument in a specific way when doing the hitting. Semantic analyses of ISL show that information about the agent is embedded in such a verb, and the path of motion ends at the point in space (the locus) associated with the patient (i.e., the person receiving the action, in this case, the person who is hit). In English, however, while "hit" involves both the agent and the patient of the action, it does not encode information about the instrument. That information must be added by the speaker (e.g., "He hit me with **a hammer**"). The point is that information is packaged differently in different languages. For interpreters in the semantics classroom, this knowledge must guide all of their decisions. They must reflect consciously and extensively on the metalinguistic aspects of their task and the semantic relations between the SL and the TL.

To avoid misunderstandings, we agreed, in collaboration with the Deaf students, to transliterate the English sentences and then interpret the discussion of the example's semantic or pragmatic properties in ISL. This maintained the notion that the discussion was about the semantic or pragmatic properties of English, not ISL. This was successful insofar as the students themselves entered into discussions during break times about the relative similarity or difference in semantic and pragmatic encoding in ISL and English.

However, the use of signed English was embedded in the ISL structures and did not in any way replace ISL. That is, when the interpreters used signed English to establish the SL example, they presented the sentence as if it were printed on a page; in other words, they used signing space to position the sentence.[2] The interpreters then co-referenced the loci established for each argument in order to demonstrate relationships. This use of locus establishment, co-referencing, and placement is typical of signed language interaction, and it makes sense to maximize the usefulness of these structures, even when talking about another language.

ISL as an Evolving Language

As mentioned earlier, ISL is an evolving language that is just beginning to be used in academic environments. Thus, in many domains, lexical gaps exist, typically for concepts or terms that have hitherto not been discussed in ISL, primarily because Irish Deaf people have traditionally not been actively involved in these fields (e.g., law, medicine, finance). One outcome of this is the inappropriate use of established signs in a given context; signers are using certain signs that hold generic meaning to refer to more specific, restricted sets of meanings. Signers choose them apparently because they are glossed with an English word that crops up in an English source language text. For example, although it is possible to say "the store is now in operation," one would not sign SHOP NOW OPERATION. In general, OPERATION refers to a medical operation and is contextually driven (i.e., the context determines where OPERATION is located on the signer's body; for example, was it an operation on the ear, the torso, etc.?). This type of substitution can be considered a miscue (Cokely, 1992).

However, similar literal transpositions of an English SL can also occur in educational contexts and are deliberately chosen by signers as a humorous mnemonic. This use of so-called calque terms, in which the morphemes of the SL are borrowed intact into the TL (where they can strike an observer as being odd contextually) is quite common in ISL, particularly with respect to proper nouns. For example, the place-name Ballsbridge is signed as BALLS+BRIDGE, and the Irish government board established to offer redress to survivors of abuse in educational establishments is referred to (by some signers) as the RED+DRESS BOARD (redress board). While interpreters are trained to avoid such morpheme-for-morpheme or word-for-word replacement in favor of producing equivalent meaning in the TL, it happens nevertheless, either as a conscious decision or as a function of fatigue or processing overload. An example of this occurred during a lecture on the notion of truth and logic in semantics:

Example 1.
SL : As we know, historically speaking, logic springs from an interest in language; it springs from an interest in the correct use of argument. Even before that—the effective use of argument.
TL: LOGIC IDEA LINK INTEREST LANGUAGE//HOW RIGHT WAY USE LANGUAGE//BEFORE HOW BEST USE LANGUAGE FOR **ARGUMENT** ("a quarrel")//DEBATE

In Example 1 the interpreter's fatigue resulted in the use of ARGUMENT, meaning "a dispute between two or more parties." This conveyed a different connotation from the one the SL speaker intended, which was the discussion of logical argumentation. In that context a point (an argument) is presented to support or oppose a proposition. However, the interpreter realized that this lexical choice was contextually inappropriate and added DEBATE/DISCUSS to clarify the meaning.

The use of similarly inappropriate TL lexical choices occurred in this classroom when a metalinguistic term also referred to real-world referents (e.g., an actor, a goal, a patient) or when an SL register-specific item could be used in a more generic way in the TL (e.g., sense, reference, logic, argument).

Additionally, bilingual signed language users play with the relationship between English and ISL. For example, CL.-LEGS (STAND) can be reversed for humorous effect to mean "understand," drawing parallels with the use of the morphological process in English under+stand. Instead of using calque (which would lead to UNDER+STAND), the signer instead plays with the classifier form that represents animate entities. This affects interpretation in the linguistics classroom when a meta-linguistic term can also refer to a real-world referent, for example, an actor or a goal. In the classroom setting we encountered many situations in which one word was used in a range of different or extended senses that exist in English but do not necessarily exist in ISL.

Another issue is homonymy, in which several words share the same form but have a range of meanings. For example, the word "sense" can refer to a physical sense such as touch or taste; it can also indicate common sense. In semantics it can signify the semantic links between elements in the vocabulary (e.g., we talk about a word that is used in a particular "sense"). Yet another example arose in a lecture on word meanings:

Example 2.
1. He felt a python wrap itself around his neck.
2. "I'll drink that Beck's by the neck," he smirked.
3. His idea of a night out was to neck in the car.
   Neck 1: noun; part of the body connecting the head and shoulders
   Neck 2: noun; narrow part of a bottle, near the mouth
   Neck 3: verb; kiss and caress amorously

In ISL, "neck" does not function as a homonym. In translation, interpreters normally seek an equivalent TL meaning that is driven by the context, with the result that the SL form is lost. Yet the reason the professor cited these examples to illustrate homonymy in English. An interpretation, while semantically equivalent, would fail in terms of functionality because it would not capture the crux of the professor's message.

Therefore, one facet of the interpreter's task is to decide when it is appropriate to opt for a literal (Nida, 1964) or a "free" interpretation (Napier, 1998).[3] Of course, in Example 2 the interpreter is constantly mediating aspects of both formal and dynamic equivalence in the TL output and is making conscious decisions about how these aspects interrelate and which approach is most suitable at any particular point in the interpretation. This mirrors Janzen's (2005) view of sophisticated interpretation as that which occurs when the interpreter attends to both form and meaning (thus formal and dynamic equivalence) in every text.

He notes that, for some texts, dynamic equivalence is primary (and perhaps total), whereas in others it is not. Furthermore, as is evident in Example 2, the emphasis on any one approach to interpreting can shift within a single assignment and not only from assignment to assignment, as the literature often implies.

The range of meanings associated with a word (or the range of words that is expressed in the same formal representation) is, of course, an issue for every language. In the semantics classroom we were particularly conscious of this fact as one word was sometimes used in several different senses even within the same lecture. For example, the word "sense," as discussed earlier, was used in a variety of settings, with a range of meanings, often derivable from context. In addition, when two words exist for two concepts in English, there may be only one sign for both of these concepts in ISL (i.e., they are not homonyms in English but are in ISL). An example of this arose in a lecture on word meaning, when the professor was discussing "ambiguity" and "vagueness." In ISL one would normally interpret these concepts using the same sign, but in this context it was necessary to differentiate between the two.

Since these sessions were being interpreted simultaneously, time pressure affected the number of options available to the interpreters. When no word-for-word lexical equivalent exists, interpreters have several strategies to draw on, but a tension exists between maximally utilizing these options (e.g., paraphrasing, describing) and accepting the consequences of such action on subsequent parts of the message. Baker (1992) discusses the choice of options open to translators when seeking TL equivalence at lexical, sentential, and textual levels, while Gile (1995) explains strategies that spoken language interpreters employ and the consequences of their choices. Leeson (2005a, 2005b) discusses the effects of these and other strategies used by signed language interpreters. For example, paraphrasing extends the interpreter's processing time (or lag time, as it is sometimes called in Europe) and may divert attention from the subsequent SL message, leading to a gap in the TL message.

THE INTERPRETER

Interpreter-Created Messages

Interpreters create messages. Although they are not the original author of the source language message, their decisions about the relative weighting to give to an element in a target language are conscious ones. Interpreters make decisions about how SL information is best conveyed in the TL. Modifications are sometimes made in order to clarify a message, including the use of strategic additions, omissions, and substitutions to shape a meaningful and complete TL (Baker, 1992; Leeson, 2005a). Indeed, Jones (1998) states that successful interpreters must "pick up the . . . ideas that make up the backbone of . . . [a] speech and lay sufficient emphasis on them in the interpretation: verbal redundancies should be cut down to a minimum; digressions, extraneous comparisons and rhetoric may be kept in the translation but should have the right relative weight in the overall context of the speech; and the interpreter must not let the form of the speech—quantifying clauses, hesitations, corrections, verbal prevarication—distract them from the substance" (p. 3). All of these activities demand a conscious interaction with the SL message and a series of split-second decisions by the interpreter.

Beyond the fact that interpreters make decisions about meaning, the appropriate transfer of message, and the weighting to give to portions of the message (for example, Is this the central point? Is this redundant?), the interpreter's degree of involvement in interpreting events has also come under scrutiny. In contrast to approaches that see the interpreter as an uninvolved "machine" or "conduit," Wadensjö (1998) sees interpreter-mediated interaction as "sustained activity" or, specifically, as "an *instance of a particular kind of three-party interaction*" (p. 18). She states that participant status conditions the organization of talk in interpreted events at a global level (i.e., the police interrogation or, for us, the semantics and pragmatics lecture) and at a local level (i.e., how the interaction is structured on a turn-by-turn basis). She says that the interpreter's task involves a "coordination" aspect and presents an overview of the "distribution of knowledge and responsibility amongst speakers, and interdependencies between speakers and between communicative activities in interpreter-mediated interaction" (ibid., p. 279).

These findings are generally mirrored by Metzger (1999), who challenges the notion of interpreter "neutrality": "Interpreters are *participants within interactive discourse and not mere conduits to it*" (p. 204). She considers both the fact that interpreters are ethically guided to be neutral and the notion that, at the same time, they do not have an impact on the interpreted discourse as a paradox. This leads her to pose the question with which she ends her book: "Should interpreters pursue full participation rights within interpreted encounters? Or should interpreters attempt to minimize, where possible, their influence within interpreted interaction?"

Despite the fact that the interpreted classroom we are discussing does not entail much turn taking among participants (because of the lecture format, the interpretation is mostly from English to ISL, with only a little student participation during question-and-answer sessions), evidence suggests that, even in less interactive frameworks, interpreters are participants on many levels.

Interpreters as Impartial Participants

Robinson (1997) sees interpreters as pretenders: "Translators and interpreters make a living out of pretending to be (or at least to speak or write as if they were) licensed practitioners of professions that they have typically never practiced" (p. 148). He goes on to cite Paul Kussmaul (1995), who says that expert behavior is "acquired role playing" (p. 33). In this interpreted classroom, the interpreters' knowledge and training mean that they are not neutral bystanders: One of the interpreters has a PhD in linguistics and is an active linguistics researcher, while the other has a BSc in anthropology and has completed some sign linguistics courses. The interpreters make judgment calls with respect to the professor's intention when discussing a point, and these calls are informed by their understanding of the lecture. Interpreters construct meaning by drawing on their own knowledge of the world. This fact is far removed from the idea that words contain meanings; thus, so as long as one knows the words of a language, one understands. Thus, a cognitive, constructionist view of communication can inform our understanding of what interpreters do (see Wilcox & Shaffer, 2005).

Add to this the fact that we each bring our own understanding of the world to bear on everything we observe (Turner, 2005) and that interpreters are obliged to make choices given what we understand a message to mean (Turner & Harrington, 2001). This individual response to communicative events is clearly variable and suggests that in highly specific topic domains, interpreters who have expertise in that domain will be best skilled to make the most sense of what is being discussed. In this instance, one interpreter held a PhD in linguistics, while the other had some basic knowledge of linguistics: This meant that the interpreter with the postgraduate linguistics background was better able to interpret, given that she readily understood the content, while the interpreter without a postgraduate linguistics background was conscious of working with greater attention on understanding than in domains in which she had an established knowledge base.

Since both interpreters were also university lecturers, their decision making was also informed by their knowledge of classroom interaction, such as knowing when it is appropriate to interrupt a speaker and when doing so would not facilitate interpretation or would even alienate the Deaf students from the speakers. This scenario might occur when a shy hearing student does not speak clearly when responding to a question from the professor. The interpreter may ask the professor to ask the student to repeat the point, but if it remains unintelligible to both the interpreter and the co-interpreter, then the interpreter may, in agreement with the Deaf students, not seek a third repetition. An alternative and a more successful means of accessing the SL content in such a situation occurred when the professor paraphrased the student's response. This benefited not only the interpreters and Deaf students but also the other hearing students, who also could not hear the original speaker.

Such partiality vis-à-vis the message, guided by knowledge about the subject, the course structure, and the participants in an event, is useful in helping the interpreter make decisions. That is, interpreters can use all of the information at their disposal when deciding how to best present an appropriate TL. Thus, interpretation is not just about how the interpreter deals with the individual words and sentences of the SL as they arise in a lecture. Interpreters must think contextually. For example, Leeson (2005b) discusses how ISL/English interpreters deal with sociolinguistic variation. Knowing the audience and predicting its preferences are key factors for success. Preferences include gendered signs, regional variants, frequency of fingerspelling, and use of signed English.

Interpreter Participation in Banter: Participant Status Acknowledged

The idea of interpreter neutrality can be questioned with respect to collaboration with Deaf students, even while on task. For example, both students and interpreters played on the relative relationship between lexical terms used in semantics and in the literal translation of these terms to ISL. For example, "patient"—the recipient of an action—became SICK PERSON, and "goal" (the entity toward which something moves) became FOOTBALL (soccer) GOAL. The presence of humor between the interpreters and the Deaf students promoted a relaxed working relationship.

These wordplays were not maintained as nonce signs throughout the course: They were simply a bit of light (linguistic) relief that built on the shared bilingual status of the students and the interpreters. The data we recorded showed a number of such incidences. Some were initiated by the interpreter, as the following example shows:

Example 3.
Before class, the interpreter and the Deaf students good-naturedly discussed the professor, who habitually signed the ISL sign NOW with an incorrect orientation of the hands. When the professor arrived, the first thing he said was "Now . . ." In light of the preceding discussion, the interpreter intentionally misarticulated NOW, using the incorrect orientation of the palms as previously discussed by the students.

Other humorous events were instigated by the Deaf students or the professor but referred to the interpreter in some way. This indicates an awareness of the interpreter's presence and hints at how the participants view the interpreter's role:

Example 4.
One of the Deaf students had received funds for a laptop computer and a note taker who took notes on the laptop during class. Another student did not receive money for a laptop computer but had funds for signed language interpretation. In reality, both students had shared access to both the transcribed notes and the interpretation, but the notion of *not* sharing access to these supports was jokingly mentioned. Following a scenario in which the note taker was unable to access the computer because she did not know the password, there was a discussion about the fact that at least interpreters did not require passwords in order for users to get them to work. This was followed by other exchanges that drew on the concept of "interpreter as machine." For example, the Deaf student who did not own the laptop pretended to be offended and, in collusion with the interpreter, insisted that the interpreter move to a position where her fellow student could not see the interpretation. When the fellow student moved to see the interpretation, the first student responded by "switching off" the interpreter with the REMOTE-CONTROL.

In this example humor was embedded in a literal mapping between the fact that machines are not autonomous and can be turned on and off at will (i.e., they can be controlled) and the "machine model of interpreting" (i.e., interpreters are machines; they are not autonomous; they do only what the client wishes them to do; thus, the client controls the interpreter). This merges with the fact that, at that moment, the students were "fighting" over access to a real machine (i.e., the laptop computer) and the interpreters ("the interpreting machines"). The metaphoric mapping of concepts (i.e., machines have remote controls and can be switched on and off when they are not needed; interpreters are machines; therefore, we can switch them off when they are not needed) is highly effective. While the students would not consider the machine model of interpreting to accurately reflect the interpreter's role, they were aware of its existence and drew on it very successfully. Indeed, the comparison was so successful that it was maintained throughout the course and always raised a laugh from both the Deaf students and the interpreters.

The interpreter's presence was also playfully referred to in class dialogue between the professor and the class:

Example 5.
When the professor realized that the interpreters would not participate by responding to questions from the textbook during the question-and-answer sessions, he advised those students who were struggling with questions that, if they wanted to be excused from answering, they could simply state, "I'm an interpreter."

This example illustrates the visibility of the interpreter in the classroom setting and the fact that the interpreter's participation is recognized as having certain boundaries that do not constrain the interaction of other participants.

In summary, the amusing exchanges about the interpreter reflect an awareness of the interpreter's role in the classroom interaction while recognizing the constraints that limit the interpreter's degree of participation. Significantly, such references, which acknowledge the interpreters as professionals who play a novel role in the classroom environment, serves to ratify them (Metzger, 1999), something typically reserved for participants in an event. The fact that the interpreters are ratified by each other, the Deaf students, the professor, and some of the hearing students (who would occasionally try out the "I am an interpreter" line in an attempt to avoid answering a question) demonstrates just how far from the interpreter as invisible conduit we are, even though our participation remains, of necessity, in the background.

CONSULTATION AS STRATEGY

In the course of interpreting these sessions, the interpreters consulted with a wide range of parties. Each facet of consultation has specific characteristics that are governed by what the interpreter hopes to achieve in maximizing access in an interpreted classroom using the metalanguage of linguistics. Individual consultation, when necessary, took place both prior to and after each session with the professor, Deaf students and the co-interpreter.

The Hearing Professor

The interpreters consulted with the professor regarding the course plan and class content. Preparatory notes were forwarded to the interpreters ahead of time to aid in their preparation for class. We also discussed the management of the information the professor planned to present: We needed clarification from the professor that this class would deal with the semantics of English in particular, though, in places, general statements on semantics would be made. Such clarification was necessary in order for us to consider how to frame our interpretation of specific examples.

Consultation also took place when problems arose (e.g., when overlapping talk in the question-and-answer sessions made it impossible to interpret effectively, the interpreters asked the professor to remind the students that only one person could contribute at a time, which he duly did). The interactive nature of the classroom setting meant that, during the question-and-answer sessions, there was obligatory contribution from the floor (i.e., the professor required the students to answer the questions that he had posed the previous week). Some comments were difficult to hear due to overlapping discourse, as well as students who mumbled or spoke too quietly. The interpreters indicated to the professor that this was an issue, which he responded to by repeating the question clearly and allowing for interpretation. This was a "universal" adjustment insofar as, when the professor reiterated a question or comment from the floor, the hearing students (who otherwise could not hear the remarks) could hear the questions and comments from their fellow students, and the interpreters could work them into ISL.

The Deaf Students

A number of environmentally driven issues arose, including where the interpreter would sit and the appropriateness of lighting. Linguistic consultation also took place on the challenges of handling register-specific lexical gaps in ISL for the fields of semantics and pragmatics. Nonce signs were often agreed to both before and during the interpreted discourse. Typically students would negotiate a sign among themselves and then inform the interpreters of their preference so that these nonce items could be incorporated into the TL output. One such example is the sign for "pragmatics," DEPEND SITUATION. This sign derived from an earlier form for pragmatics, DEPEND CONTEXT, but because the discussion of pragmatics entails discussion of contextual cues (e.g., for inferencing), the nonce sign was modified to DEPEND SITUATION.

This use of nonce signs relates to Sandler's (1995) discussion of linguistic settings. She states that such signs remain active for the duration of an event but do not automatically become established signs. What is interesting in the Irish context is that, over the course of the past fifteen years (when the first Deaf students began studying linguistics), a number of signs that had originally emerged as nonce signs have become the established lexical items in ISL for these concepts. Examples include the sign for "semantics" (a compound, MEAN^DEEP) and the sign for "cognition" (a compound, THINK^WELL-OILED-MACHINE), both of which Deaf students originally coined as nonce signs but which, with the evolution of a small but robust sign linguistics community, have entered into the register-specific lexicon of ISL.

As mentioned earlier, the use of signed English for transliterating SL English examples was agreed on when the professor was discussing semantic issues relevant to English specifically. For discussion of the specific semantic issues that arose from these examples, ISL was used.

Consultation with the Co-Interpreter

The co-interpreter's role was central to the successful interpretation of this module. Consultation between colleagues dealt with preassignment issues such as the preferred means of giving and receiving support from a colleague while on task and clarification of the best approaches to dealing with certain concepts in the target language. During the assignment, the co-interpreters monitored each other's use of spatial referencing in order to ensure that information flow was maximally maintained across interpreter changes. Post-assignment consultation allowed for mutual feedback on performance during the session. The degree of trust between the interpreters meant that absolute honesty was possible, which in turn allowed for real sharing and professional growth.

Methods of support were governed by an understanding between the interpreters of how each one liked to receive support while on task. The interpreters took the opportunity to discuss how they would interpret each session, including dealing with more complex conceptual distinctions demanded by the subject matter. They brainstormed solutions to working around lexical gaps in the TL and—in consultation with the Deaf students—frequently reviewed their progress. The off-task interpreter also served as a monitor for the on-task interpreter. For example, the former would identify an unclear interpretation or one that was based on a misunderstanding by the on-task interpreter.

Example 6.
The on-task interpreter has misheard "bush" for "push" and therefore used the sign HEDGE. The off-task interpreter signaled to the on-task interpreter that she had misheard and offered her the appropriate sign or word instead.

Importantly, these levels of support are viable only where co-interpreters are comfortable in accepting direct on-task feedback from a colleague. Both interpreters and clients have to be aware that such support is not a criticism by the off-task interpreter and that the on-task interpreter must view the support as a successful collaboration toward the maximal transfer of information to the TL. Only when these conditions are met can co-interpreting of this kind be truly effective. Otherwise the danger exists that interpreters will view the assignment as a competition of some sort, in which each must outperform the other to avoid losing face at all costs, even to the extent that they may refuse to acknowledge errors or continue to work through segments that they do not understand in order to avoid having to seek clarification (see Gile, 1995 and Leeson, 2005a for further discussion of these issues with respect to spoken and signed language interpreters, respectively). In our opinion, this sort of reaction is detrimental and does nothing to improve collegiality and mutual respect between colleagues in the interpreting profession, nor does it improve the way in which both Deaf and non-Deaf clients perceive the interpreting profession as a whole.

Because one of the interpreters had a linguistics background, the clarification of register-specific terminology could be dealt with locally; that is, the interpreters could consult with each other in order to clarify the meaning of register-specific terms rather than having to seek ongoing input at this level from the professor. Thus, the interpreters shared their knowledge and understanding of particular linguistic concepts such as those relevant to the field of pragmatics (e.g., implicature, Grice's maxims). This supports the idea that background knowledge of a subject enables interpreters to focus their attention on the production of the TL message since they do not have to struggle with the comprehension of meaning in the SL to the same degree, which would take processing attention away from the coordination and output of the TL message. Thus the distribution of effort (see Gile, 1995 and Leeson, 2005a) is geared more toward a deeper-level analysis of meaning (e.g., the functionality of the message, the relationship between segments of the message, the relative weighting given to a specific aspect of the discourse) and the production of the TL.

Feedback on performance was another facet of co-interpreting that worked well in this series of assignments. The off-task interpreter offered a critical appraisal of the on-task interpreter's performance, and this was then discussed at class break times and at the end of each session. Register, cohesion, TL equivalence (whether functional, dynamic, or literal), grammaticality and problematic issues were among the main issues the co-interpreters addressed. This peer review allowed for continual assessment of performance and directed focus to areas that needed further attention. It also created an environment of constructive dialogue that fostered sharing and learning between the interpreters. This degree of collaboration also demonstrates a high degree of involvement with the event, underpinned by notions of professionalism.

Another issue that demands attention in co-interpreting situations is the way in which the expectation to monitor one's co-interpreter's performance may affect the quality of performance over an extended period of time. The rationale for having two interpreters when an assignment is particularly complex or runs beyond a specific time frame is that quality is maintained longer with a rotation of interpreters (e.g., see Brennan & Brown, 1997). We therefore need to determine how the monitoring of a colleague (often in an intense manner) may in fact impede the co-interpreter's performance when that person's turn to interpret comes, given that the co-interpreter has been actively listening to the SL and assessing the TL output on the part of the colleague. In essence, the co-interpreter has been mentally carrying out the interpreting task, albeit with a lesser degree of effort.[4] We have not had an opportunity to look at this aspect of co-interpreting, but this area calls for empirical research.

DECISION MAKING IN SUCCESSFUL INTERPRETATION

While linguistic classrooms make significant use of metalinguistic discussion, which influences interpreters' decisions in this context, decision making is a factor in *all* interpreting domains. Our awareness of the factors that prompt successful decision making for interpreters is not empirically based. Researchers must investigate the contextual factors that guide interpreters' decision making (e.g., what are they, what common questions specific contexts prompt, and what common strategies interpreters respond with). These may be culture- or language-specific (e.g., influenced by the participants' gender or age, regional variations, clients' familiarity regarding how to work with an interpreter).

PERSISTENCE OF THE INTERPRETER AS CONDUIT NOTION

Interpreting texts discuss a host of models that influence interpreters (e.g., Mindess, 1999; Humphrey & Alcorn, 1996; Wilcox & Shaffer, 2005). However, it is the conduit model that persistently informs perceptions of what interpreters do (Wilcox & Shaffer, 2005; Allsop & Leeson, 2002). Wilcox and Shaffer (2005) note that our basic concept of communication as entailing the simple transfer of messages from one person to another is problematic. They also state that interpreters must become conscious of the fact that, while the conduit model is a powerful construction for explaining communication metaphorically, it is a too literal account of how communication occurs. Instead, communicators are involved in constructing meaning. Given this, viewing interpreting as the simple transfer of information from one language to another is problematic. Yet, as Allsop and Leeson (2002) have shown, the conduit model is pervasive, even among those who train signed language interpreters and even when they are aware of alternative approaches to framing and discussing the interpreter's task and role (e.g., the participant-interaction model, the bicultural model).

One of the clearest-cut problems occasioned by the embedded conduit model is that it creates expectations of interpreters as uninvolved mediators of messages. This contrasts with the reality of situations in which, as we have seen, interpreters are highly involved in the interpreting event—constructing meaning for themselves (on the basis of the SL message) and then transferring this message to the TL. In these instances, their intentions are for their own comprehension to be in concert with the SL presenter's message and for the TL client to understand the message in the same way. This closely aligns with Hatim and Mason's (1990) suggestion that, by making assumptions about their audience, interpreters can make considered choices throughout their translation, leading them to make inferences about their cultural and linguistic understanding of the topic and transpose cultural meaning appropriately. However, it leads us very far away from Neumann-Solow's (1981) view of interpreter as an unobtrusive, passive conduit.

SUMMARY

This chapter has outlined specific issues for interpreters in linguistics classrooms. We have pointed out the problem of lexical gaps and outlined several solutions. Most successful were the solutions that were formulated in consultation with Deaf students and co-interpreters. The co-interpretation relationship was central to the successful handling of this task. The analysis of the interaction between interpreters and other core participants clearly demonstrates that interpreters are not mere conduits, even in settings that are less interactive than those explored by others who have looked at the issue of interpreter neutrality, most notably Metzger (1999). We are not suggesting that class-based lectures are wholly uninteractive but rather that they are less interactive than the situations that Metzger (ibid.) and Wadensjö (1998) examined when investigating the notion of interpreters as participants in interpreted triads.

Interpreters interact with participants and build relationships over time. This necessarily affects the nature of the interaction by prompting familiarity, which to a degree exceeds the distance that a rigid interpretation of a demand for impartiality by a code of ethics might imply. Indeed, one of the Deaf students remarked that interpreters could not be expected to be machines and that, if they were, Deaf students would feel somewhat less engaged in the classroom interaction. For this student, "good interpreters" are those who interact with clients and are human rather than distant and cold.

In terms of further research, we suggest that successful interpretation needs to be systematically examined in order to derive an understanding of the process that guides appropriate decision making and the view of these decisions when judged postperformance. Co-interpreting practices ought to be examined to identify good practice in such interactions, and benchmarked practices should be incorporated into training programs. Collaboration with Deaf clients must be promoted: This not only maximizes the interpreter's linguistic knowledge but, perhaps more importantly, establishes good working relationships, which serve to bring the Deaf community and the interpreting profession closer together. In the past decade, both groups in Ireland have advocated the latter outcome at almost every collaborative event that has made reference to interpreting. This issue of relative positionality is not unique to Ireland; the issue of how and why interpreters and the Deaf community have moved away from one another and on occasion been polarized is one that is also documented in the international literature, most notably in Cokely (2005).

In closing, we submit the following practical recommendations:

- Before the interpretation begins, discuss with the lecturer the importance of using visual aids when referring to examples and terminology.
- To enable maximum use of background knowledge, match the assignment to the interpreter's skills where possible.
- Because a team interpreting approach can work very efficiently, utilize it where possible. It will provide a positive learning environment and assist interpreters in developing both their knowledge and interpreting skills, especially in highly complex subjects.
- Develop a working relationship with your clients, and draw on their expertise as language users, whether of the spoken or the signed language of the interpreting domain.

ACKNOWLEDGMENTS

We offer our sincere thanks to the Centre for Language and Communication Studies, School of Linguistic, Speech and Communication Sciences, Trinity College Dublin, for allowing us to record the 2003 session of "An Introduction to Semantics and Pragmatics." Particular thanks go to J. I. Saeed, Dee Byrne-Dunne, and Senan Dunne.

NOTES

1. An earlier, shorter version of this chapter was presented at the Supporting Deaf People online conference in 2004.

2. Cognitive analyses of this phenomenon would allow for discussion of mental space theory (Fauconnier, 1985).

3. A literal interpretation is also referred to as formal equivalence; a free interpretation is also referred to as dynamic equivalence.

4. We thank Jim Kyle at Bristol University for his thoughts on this topic. Thanks also go to Anna-Lena Nilsson of Stockholm University for her willingness to debate this issue.

REFERENCES

Allsop, L., & Leeson, L. (2002). Professionalism, philosophy, and practice. Paper presented at the Association of Sign Language Interpreters (ASLI) Conference. *Newsli* 42, 4–6.

Baker, M. (1992). *In other words: A coursebook on translation*. New York: Routledge.

Brennan, M., & Brown, R. (1997). *Equality before the law: Deaf people's access to justice*. Durham, UK: Deaf Studies Research Unit.

Cokely, D. (1992). *Interpretation: A sociolinguistic model*. Burtonsville, MD: Linstok.

Cokely, D. (2005). Shifting positionality: A critical evaluation of the turning point in the relationship of interpreters and the deaf community. In M. Marschark, R. Peterson, & E. A. Winston, (Eds.), *Sign language interpreting and interpreter education: Directions for research and practice* (pp. 3–28). New York: Oxford University Press.

Davis, J. (1989). Distinguishing language contact phenomena in ASL interpretation. In C. Lucas (Ed.), *The sociolinguistics of the Deaf community* (pp. 85–102). San Diego: Academic Press.

Fauconnier, G. (1985). *Mental spaces*. Cambridge, MA: MIT Press.

Gile, D. (1995). *Basic concepts and models for interpreter and translator training*. Philadelphia: John Benjamins.

Hatim, B., & Mason, I. (1990). *Discourse and the translator*. New York: Longman.

Humphrey, J. H., & Alcorn, R. J. (1996). *So you want to be an interpreter? An introduction to sign language interpreting*. Amarillo, TX: H & H Publishers.

Janzen, T. (2005). Interpretation and language use: ASL and English. In T. Janzen (Ed.), *Topics in signed language interpreting* (pp. 69–106). Philadelphia: John Benjamins.

Jones, R. (1998). *Conference interpreting explained*. Northampton, MA: St. Jerome.

Leeson, L. (2005a). Making the effort in simultaneous interpreting: Some considerations for signed language interpreters. In T. Janzen (Ed.), *Topics in signed language interpreting* (pp. 51–68). Philadelphia: John Benjamins.

Leeson, L. (2005b). Vying with variation: Interpreting language contact, gender variation, and generational difference in Ireland. In T. Janzen (Ed.), *Topics in signed language interpreting* (pp. 251–92). Philadelphia: John Benjamins.

Leeson, L., & Foley-Cave, S. (2004). MEAN-DEEP BUT DEPEND CONTEXT. Interpreting, semantics, and pragmatics at postgraduate level: Challenges to interpreter notions of impartiality. Paper presented at the "Supporting Deaf People" online conference.

Llewellyn-Jones, P. (1999). *Three interpretations* (video). SLI. Kavana Ltd.

Matthews, P. A. (1996). *The Irish Deaf community*, vol. 1. Dublin: ITE.

Metzger, M. (1999). *Sign language interpreting: Deconstructing the myth of neutrality*. Washington, DC: Gallaudet University Press.

Metzger, M., Fleetwood, E., & Collins, S. (2004). Discourse genre and linguistic mode: Interpreter influences in visual and tactile interpreted interaction. *Sign Language Studies* 4(2), 118–37.

Mindess, A. (1999). *Reading between the signs: Intercultural communication for sign language interpreters*. Yarmouth, ME: Intercultural Press.

Napier, J. (1988). Free your mind—The rest will follow. *Deaf Worlds* 14(3).

Napier, J. (2002). *Sign language interpreting: Linguistic coping strategies*. Coleford, UK: Douglas McLean.

Neumann-Solow, S. (1981). *Sign language interpreting: A basic resource book*. Silver Spring, MD: National Association of the Deaf.

Nida, E. (1964). *Toward a science of translating*. Leiden, Netherlands: Brill.

Robinson, D. (1997). *Becoming a translator: An accelerated course*. New York: Routledge.

Saeed, J. I. (2003). *Semantics* (2d ed). Malden, MA: Blackwell.

Sandler, W. (1995). I can't get no constraint satisfaction: The linguistics interpreter's lament. *International Sign Linguistics Association* 8(1), 4–6.

Schembri, A. (2003). Rethinking "classifiers" in signed languages. In K. Emmorey (Ed.), *Perspectives on classifier constructions in sign languages* (pp. 3–34). Mahwah, NJ: Erlbaum.

Stratiy, A. (2005): Best practices in interpreting: A deaf community perspective. In T. Janzen (Ed.), *Topics in signed language interpreting* (pp. 231–50). Philadelphia: John Benjamins.

Turner, G. H. (2005). Toward real interpreting. In M. Marschark, R. Peterson, & E. A. Winston (Eds.), *Sign language interpreting and interpreter education: Directions for research and practice* (pp. 29–56). New York: Oxford University Press.

Turner, G. H., & F. J. Harrington. (2001): The campaign for real interpreting. In F. J. Harrington & G. H. Turner (Eds.), *Interpreting interpreting: Studies and reflections on sign language interpreting* (pp. vi–xiv). Coleford, UK: Douglas McLean.

Wadensjö, C. (1998). *Interpreting as interaction.* New York: Longman.

Wilcox, S., & Shaffer, B. (2005). Toward a cognitive model of interpreting. In T. Janzen (Ed.), *Topics in signed language interpretation: Theory and practice* (pp. 27–50). Philadelphia: John Benjamins.

Part II Sociolinguistic Considerations

Initial Observations on Code-Switching in the

Voice Interpretations of Two Filipino Interpreters

Liza B. Martinez

The Republic of the Philippines is an archipelago of more than seven thousand islands located in Southeast Asia. It lies at the western edge of the Pacific Ocean, south of Taiwan, east of Viet Nam, and north of Indonesia. The major islands are Luzon in the north, Mindanao in the south, and the Visayan island group in between. The country is culturally diverse, with numerous languages and dialects belonging to the Austronesian family. Ninety percent of the inhabitants speak one of the following: Cebuano, Tagalog, Ilocano, Hiligaynon, Bicol, Waray, Kapampangan, and Pangasinan.

The language policy of the Philippines is rooted in three constitutional milestones. Spanish was once widely spoken because the country was under Spanish rule for more than three centuries. Thus, the 1935 constitution identified both Spanish and English as the official languages. Today Spanish is rarely used except in areas of the cities of Zamboanga and Cavite. In 1973 the constitution mandated the continuation of Pilipino and English as the official languages. In addition, it decreed that "the National Assembly shall take steps toward the development and formal adoption of a common national language to be known as Filipino; this language is to be composed of the existing languages of the Philippines" (González, 1981, p. 51). In 1987 Filipino was adopted as the national language (University of the Philippines, 2004, p. xi).

This historical odyssey is evident in the continuing vigorous debate over bilingualism and language policy and the nature of the Pilipino and Filipino lexicon, particularly as they draw from Tagalog and other Philippine languages (Constantino, 2005; Bautista, 1999a). Domains such as government, media, commerce, education, and science and technology continue to reflect the strong influence of English (González, 1981). The lingua franca is characterized by a code-switching variety, Taglish (from Tagalog and English) (Sibayan, 1991).

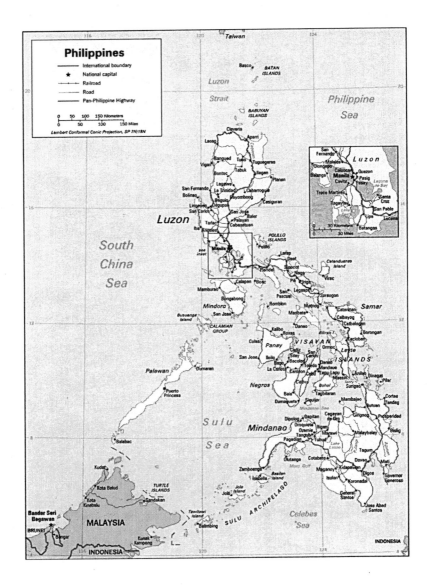

LANGUAGE SITUATION OF THE FILIPINO DEAF COMMUNITY

Recent milestone studies on the visual-spatial language of the Filipino Deaf community (i.e., Filipino Sign Language, or FSL) have been initiated by Filipinos themselves. In the seventies and eighties, publications by American writers drew largely from American Sign Language and artificial sign systems to disseminate highly prescriptive material (e.g., Shaneyfelt, 1979).

The pioneering research of Martinez on linguistic structure and socio-linguistics (Martinez, 1993, 1994, 1995a, 1995b, 1996) comprise the earliest descriptive works on Filipino Sign Language. To date, the most comprehensive linguistics reference is *An Introduction to Filipino Sign Language,* for which Martinez was the writer and primary contributor (Philippine Deaf Resource Center and Philippine Federation of the Deaf, 2004). This four-volume publication presents an overview of sign linguistics as a discipline in the context of the phonology, morphology, and discourse characteristics of FSL. It also documents traditional and emerging signs (in information technology and mobile phone communications) and tackles the issues of Deaf culture, education, signed language instruction and interpreting, and language policy.

The current project of the Philippine Federation of the Deaf—Practical Dictionaries for Asian-Pacific Sign Languages—has already yielded "Filipino Sign Language: A Compilation of Signs from Regions of the Philippines (Part 1)," which documents regional variation and the history of the use of signed language in ten regions of the country. The Part 2 publication of the project is forthcoming in 2007 and includes lexico-statistical findings proposing regional varieties of FSL. It also demonstrates the strong linguistic pressure that American Sign Language has had on FSL and its resulting endangering presence on the latter. This project has produced a core group of nine Deaf linguistics and field researchers in the federation, trained by sign linguists Martinez and James Woodward (the latter is currently based in Viet Nam) and Deaf sign linguist Yutaka Osugi of the World Federation of the Deaf and the Japan Institute for Sign Language Studies.

Recent papers presented at the Ninth Philippine Linguistics Conference covered several topics on FSL in a special plenary: phonology and regional variation (Apurado & Agravante, 2006), language contact and lexicalization (Puson & Siloterio, 2006), early signed language history (Abat & Martinez, 2006), education (Bustos & Tanjusay, 2006), language processing and instruction (Tiongson, 2006), and legal interpreting (Martinez, 2006a). Reports on the National Sign Language Committee (Andrada & Domingo, 2006) and the Dictionaries Project (Corpuz, 2006) were also included. The presentation of these eight papers at this conference, held at the premier academic institution of the country (the University of the Philippines), brought FSL into the mainstream of Philippine linguistics research for the very first time.

Subsequent lectures by Woodward at the University of the Philippines in coordination with the Philippine Deaf Resource Center and the Philippine Federation of the Deaf (Woodward 2006a, 2006b) have been significant events for academicians and policy makers. Also noteworthy is the comprehensive field study of the National Sign Language Committee (under the Philippine Federation of the Deaf), which documents the use of signed language in education, interpreting, signed language instruction, and media in fifteen regions throughout the country. The *Status Report on the Use of Sign Language in the Philippines* is forthcoming in 2007 as well. Among the important findings of the report are the extremely low numbers of interpreters throughout the country in comparison to the estimated 121,000 deaf Filipinos. Self-assessments of interpreting skills also reveal weakness in voice interpreting (as opposed to sign interpreting).

In 2006 the compilation of multisectoral position papers on the signed language targets of the National Plan of Action (i.e., the standardization of signed language and the establishment of an interpreting system) also provided numerous insights on the problems of interpreting in the Philippines (Philippine Deaf Resource Center, 2005). Advocacy work by the Philippine Deaf Resource Center in women's health, rights, and other issues (Martinez, 2006b) has also been part of the impetus for continuing applied linguistics research. Flagship projects Equal Access to Communication for the Deaf in Legal Proceedings by the Philippine Deaf Resource Center, the Philippine Federation of the Deaf, the Filipino Deaf Women's Health and Crisis Center, and Pagsasalin at Pagbuo ng Talatinigang Pambatas sa Wikang Senyas ng mga Binging Pilipino ("Translation of legal terms and creation of a glossary in Filipino Sign Language") will contribute to the establishment of an interpreting system. To date, despite the efforts of a handful of private enterprises and faith-based organizations (mostly in the national capital) to provide interpreting services for Deaf people, there is still no organized, nationally mandated system.

Awareness of Filipino Sign Language, its structure, and issues concerning its use has been spreading largely through efforts of the Philippine Deaf Resource Center and the Philippine Federation of the Deaf. Since the printing and dissemination of "An Introduction to Filipino Sign Language" in January 2005, twenty lectures and lecture forums led by Martinez throughout the Philippines (Baguio, Angeles, Naga, Cebu, Davao, Tacloban, and Cotabato, as well as several in Metro Manila) have been presented to universities, public schools, developmental pediatricians, local government agencies, parents of deaf children, and advocacy organizations for deaf people and persons with disabilities. In addition, the Japanese Deaf community has taken an interest in the language situation of Deaf Filipinos (Martinez, 2005a, 2005b).

Code-Switching

Romaine (1989, p. 111) defines *code-switching* from a classic Gumperz perspective as "the juxtaposition within the same speech exchange of passages of speech belonging to two different grammatical systems or subsystems." She describes this behavior as distinct from diglossia and as occurring in both monolingual and bilingual communities. The following are some of her examples from different parts of the world:

Kodomotachi liked it. (Japanese/English bilingual adult; Nishimura 1986)
"The children liked it." (Romaine, 1989, p. 2)

Will you *rubim* off? *Ol' man* will come. (Tok Pisin/English bilingual child from Papua New Guinea)
"Will you rub [that off the blackboard]? The men will come." (ibid., p. 1)

Have *agua*, please. (Spanish/English bilingual child; Kessler, 1984)
"Have water, please." (Romaine, 1989, p. 2)

This morning I *hantar* my baby *tu dekat* babysitter *tu lah*. (Malay/English bilingual adult; Ozog, 1987)
"This morning I took my baby to the babysitter." (Romaine, 1989, p. 2)

Poplack (1980) initially identified tag-switching, as well as intrasentential and intersentential types of code-switching. In 1988 Poplack and Sankoff enumerated four mechanisms in code-switching. Bautista described samples from Tagalog-English code-switching with the following framework:

SMOOTH SWITCHING
Smooth switching is a term that describes a sentence change at syntax boundaries in both Tagalog and English:

1. switching between a main clause and a subordinate clause
   Buti na lang hindi sila nagtagal because they had put a damper on our *salu-salo*.
   "Good that they did not stay because they had put a damper on our gathering" (Bautista, 1999b, p. 19).

2. switching between coordinate clauses
   They tried Alabang Hills, *pero hanggang bewang daw sa tapat ng Benedictine.*
   "They tried Alabang Hills, but it was waist deep in front of the Benedictine" (ibid.).
3. switching to a prepositional phrase
   Wala pa rin kaming nakitang sofa for the family room.
   "We still did not find a sofa for the family room (ibid.).

NONSMOOTH/FLAGGED SWITCHING

Nonsmooth or *flagged* switching is motivated by hesitation, meta-linguistic commentary, or pauses to call attention to the code switch.

CONSTITUENT INSERTION

Constituent insertion is the inserting of a grammatical constituent in one language into a sentence of another language:

1. tag expressions
   Oo nga pala, is anyone traveling around September 10–14?
   "By the way, is anyone traveling around September 10–14?"
   (Bautista, 1999b, p. 19).
2. enclitic adverbials
   Jakarta *naman* is so different *na.*
   "Jakarta, on the other hand, is so different already" (ibid.).

NONCE BORROWING

1. nouns
   We got a note from our MIS saying that the reason for the *kapalpakan* was a lightning strike in analog devices.
   "We got a note from our MIS saying that the reason for the fiasco was a lightning strike in analog devices" (ibid., p. 20).
2. adjectives
   And the same personality, too—very *malambing* and *mabait.*
   "And the same personality, too—very affectionate and good" (ibid.).
3. English "make" + Tagalog verb
   If I didn't make *kulit,* for sure we won't have the phone yet.
   "If I didn't persist, for sure we won't have the phone yet" (ibid.).
4. English words with Tagalog affixes
   To make things worse, *naflatan pa kami.*
   "To make things worse, we even got a flat tire" (ibid.).

Bautista (ibid.) says that code-switching appears to be a natural mode of discourse in the Manila community and that smooth code-switching appears to be the norm, whereas nonsmooth switching rarely occurs.

Since the first study on mixing patterns in Tagalog and English (Azores, 1967), various studies on the sociolinguistics, cognitive basis, language attitudes, and teaching implications of code-switching and bilingualism have accumulated (Bautista, 1999b; Chanco, Francisco, & Talamisan, 1999; Fuentes & Mojica, 1999; Martin, 1999; Castillo, 1999). Bautista (1999b, p. 21) reviews the functions of code-switching as enumerated by Gumperz (1982, pp. 75–84) as follows:

quotation/reported speech
addressee specification
interjection/sentence filler
reiteration (message repetition in the other code)
message qualification (e.g., sentence and a verb complement; predicate after a copula)
personalization vs. objectivization (speaker involvement; opinion/fact)

Code-switching is observed among Filipinos of different genders, ages, educational levels, and professions. The following are some conversation samples from individuals from Metro Manila:

1. Filipino/English/Bicol multilingual seventy-six-year-old housewife (college graduate)
    1Tungkol sa . . . sa car. 2Na 'yun daw agent, bukas ko na . . . bukas na daw makakausap. 3Kasi she is out, selling three cars . . . delivering three cars. 4Maybe he has an interest we don't know. 5Baka girlfriend niya yung si Nilda. 6O maybe dahil the bank is part owner of that branch kaya he is interested. 7I don't know. 8He called, tinatanong ang address ni Mr. Garcia. 9Eh sabi ko he is no longer the assistant manager. 10At the time he called me last year, he was promoted to the Head Office. 11Yung gamot ko sa Manila Doctor's, last tablet na ngayong eight o'clock. 12The other one is up to the end of the month, once a day.
    1About the . . . the car. 2That the agent (according to him), tomorrow is when . . . tomorrow I can talk to her. 3Because she is out selling three cars . . . delivering three cars. 4Maybe he has an interest we don't know. 5Maybe Nilda is his girlfriend. 6Or maybe because the bank is part owner of that branch, that's why he is interested.

7I don't know. 8He called, asking for the address of Mr. Garcia. 9Eh I said he is no longer the assistant manager. 10At the time he called me last year, he was promoted to the Head Office. 11My medicine from Manila Doctor's, the last tablet is this eight o'clock. 12The other one is up to the end of the month, once a day.

2. Filipino/English bilingual fifty-two-year-old male (physician)
   *1*Merong race sa. . . windsurf race sa **Puerto Galera.** *2*Libre lahat! *3*There will be a boat na pupunta sa **Anilao.** *4*Susunduin lahat ng mga **windsurf equipment.** *5*Tapos there's another boat na susunod, yun namang windsurfers ang susunduin. *6*Supposed to be nung **December.** *7*Pero may mga 'binalik na furniture kaya na-occupy yung **boat.** *8*So sa next week na. *9*Mga pinaglumaan sa El Nido. . . na kayak lahat. *10*Walang idea kung anong klase pero mga used na.

   1There's a race. . . a windsurf race at Puerto Galera. 2Everything's free! 3There will be a boat that will go to Anilao. 4It will fetch all the windsurf equipment. 5Then another boat will follow, the windsurfers' turn to be fetched. 6Supposed to be last December. 7But some furniture was returned so the boat was occupied. 8So it will be next week. 9Old beat-up stuff from El Nido. . . all kayaks. 10No idea what kind but used already.

3. Filipino/English/Masbateno twenty-eight-year-old female house helper (high school graduate)
   *1*Pinalitan yung ano . . . yung **fire extinguisher** namin kasi paso na. *2*Umiikot kasi dun papunta sa. . . yung ano. . . yung parang **com-pass.** *3*Umiikot. . . dapat na palitan. . . *4***August two thousand one.** *5*Dapat kasi, **every year.** *6*Tatanggalin muna yung pin, hi'ila'in, saka hahawakan sa **handle.** *7*Saka doon ii-**spray** sa ano. . . malapit sa apoy. . . hindi talaga sa apoy, medyo malapit lang.

   1Changed the uhm . . . our fire extinguisher because it's expired already. 2The whatchamacallit was turning toward . . . the uhm . . . the compass-like thing. 3It was turning . . . (it) must be changed . . . 4August two thousand one. 5That's a must, every year. 6Remove first the pin, pull, then hold the handle. 7Then spray the . . . near the flame. . . not really right at the flame, just a little near it.

Another abundant source of code-switching data among Filipinos is mobile phone text messages. Filipinos are well known for being avid texters, and texting in the Philippines as discourse and cultural behavior has been the subject of two studies (Pertierra et al., 2002; Pertierra, 2006). The following are examples of code-switching:

1. a Filipino/other Philippine language/English multilingual house-wife in her thirties, originally from Mindanao (southern island of Philippines), settled in Metro Manila ten years ago
   1Good morning 2mother po 2 ni gigi 3tnong ko po san puwede bumili ng books n sign language
   1**Good morning. 2Mother** po 'to ni Gigi. 3Tanong ko po s(a)an puwede bumili ng **books on sign language?**
   1*Good morning. 2This is the mother of Gigi. 3May I ask, where can we buy books on sign language?*

2. a Filipino/English bilingual in his thirties, academic (PhD)
   1Pwd sa lunes. 2Magte-text nga sana ako para kumustahn paper mo. 3Nangako ako ng materials pero di ako nakapagbgay. 4Hatid ko nanay ko bukas sa airport. 5Kung makablik ako agad, pwd rin siguro sa hapon. 6Pero ang mas sure ako, sa lunes. 7Sensiya ka na sa atraso ko. 8Katabi rin pala ng pottery collection ko ang cactus. 9Raming salamat.
   1Puwede sa lunes. 2Magte-text nga sana ako para kumustahin paper* mo. 3Nangako ako ng **materials** pero di ako nakapagbigay. 4Hatid ko nanay ko bukas sa airport*. 5Kung makabalik ako agad, puwede rin siguro sa hapon. 6Pero ang mas **sure** ako, sa lunes. 7(Pa)sensiya ka na sa atraso ko. 8Katabi rin pala ng **pottery collection** ko ang **cactus.** 9(Ma)raming salamat.
   1*Monday is possible. 2I was really about to text you to ask how your paper was. 3I promised materials but I was not able to give you. 4I am bringing my mother tomorrow to the airport. 5If I get back right away, maybe tomorrow afternoon is possible. 6But I am more sure on Monday. 7 I hope you understand. 8Beside my pottery collection also is the cactus. 9Thank you very much.*

RATIONALE

This study was conducted as an exploratory inquiry into the difficulties that Filipino interpreters have with voice interpreting. Prior interactions with and observations of a number of signed language interpreters point to a complex set of factors affecting the multilingual

Filipino when the interpreter is voice interpreting. Communicative competence and language attitudes in particular seem to influence the outcome of voice interpretation. Thus, describing demonstrable behavior during code-switching may provide valuable insights into more extensive research into the underlying roots of interpreters' difficulties with voice interpretation.

DATA GATHERING

Two interpreters of comparable experience were selected and asked to view video clips of deaf dyads engaged in free-flowing discourse (videos from the field data collection of the Philippine Federation of the Deaf). The Deaf informants from the Visayas were more than forty years of age. The data were elicited through the use of pictorial visual aids by a Deaf researcher.

Prior to viewing the video footage, the interpreters were given instructions. They were shown the three pictorial visual aids that the field researcher had used to elicit the dyad discourse. They were also informed of the kind of hearing consumer the interpretation was intended for: (1) monolingual Filipinos from a Tagalog-speaking province, (2) English-speaking foreigners, and (3) professionals (mostly teachers) in Metro Manila (the nation's capital). Video clips for each Deaf signer were interpreted for the three kinds of consumers in different order. The simulated voice interpretation for each of the four Deaf signers on video was recorded. A total of twelve voice interpretations (thirty-second excerpts for each Deaf signer) per interpreter were collected.

Additional data included the following: responses to a questionnaire on background, experience, and language use; recorded informal conversation discourse (interpreter B only); mobile phone text messages, and brief postinterpretation interviews. The following were observed for transcription and translation of the voice interpretation and other data (these are reflected in the samples shown in this chapter):

Variant forms and contractions in Filipino were transcribed in the original form as used in the interpretation:

Example.
meron, mayroon   "have"
ta(po)s, tapos   "then"

ni-, ini-	(prefix)
yan, iyan; yung, iyong	"that"
do'n, doon	"that/there"

For simplicity, accents for Filipino were not included. Code switches in the samples are as follows:

- Uncertain use of words (e.g., baby, school, paper) as either nonce borrowing from English or lexicalized loanwords in Filipino are marked (see discussion).
- Cultural phrases, colloquialisms, and slang in Filipino were translated idiomatically:

| Pasensiya na sa atraso ko. | "I hope you understand my shortcoming." |
| apir | "high five" |

Mobile Phone Text Excerpts

The samples include the original form of the text (with contractions, etc.), followed by the expanded form (full spelling) showing any code switches and finally by the full English translation. For easier understanding, some of the English translations show inserted subjects in parentheses (deleted in the Filipino sentences). Use of the polite form *po* in Filipino was reflected in the English translation. After transcription and translation, the resulting voice interpretations were compared with the intended consumer language needs. We examined the data for code switches and noted their characteristics. Possible explanations for the unexpected code switches are discussed in the context of other data from the interpreters' profiles, questionnaire and interview responses, and other language use (conversation, mobile phone text excerpts).

RESULTS

Interpreter Profiles

Table 1 is a summary of highlights from the profiles of the two interpreters who participated in the study. The data are from a written questionnaire.

Voice Interpretation

Table 2 shows the results from eight of the twelve voice interpretations by each of the two interpreters. It indicates the language need of the intended (monolingual) consumer and the language of the voice interpretation. The results show an expected consistent match between language

TABLE I. *Profiles of Interpreter Informants in This Study*

	Interpreter A	Interpreter B
Age	33	42
Languages		
most fluent	English (E), (Taglish)	English
second most fluent	English, Filipino Sign Language	Filipino (F)
third most fluent	Filipino	Filipino Sign Lang.
fourth most fluent	Cebuano	
Place of residence (languages spoken in school)		
elementary school	Laguna (E, F)	Metro Manila (E, F)
high school	Metro Manila (E, F)	Metro Manila (E, F)
college	Metro Manila (E, F, Visayan, Taglish)	Metro Manila (E, F)
Father		
age	70	65
profession	engineer	supervisor
residence during		
elementary school	Capiz	Metro Manila
high school	Iloilo	Metro Manila
college	Iloilo	Metro Manila
Languages		
most fluent	E	F
second most fluent	Capiznon	Taglish
third most fluent	F	E
Mother		
age	62	66
profession	teacher	trainer
residence during		
elementary school	Dumaguete	Metro Manila
high school	Dumaguete	Metro Manila
college	Dumaguete	Metro Manila
Languages		
most fluent	Cebuano	F
second most fluent	E	Taglish
third most fluent	Cebuano mixed with Tagalog Spanish	E
fourth most fluent	Spanish	

TABLE 1. *Continued*

Years of signing	eight years	ten years
Years of interpreting	eight years	nine years
Learning of signed language	interactions with Deaf people	class instruction
Learning to interpret	interactions with Deaf people	formal training
Past Deaf interactions/ involvement	Deaf dance group interpreter; office interpreter	work; conversations
Current Deaf interactions/ involvement	classroom interpreter; friends; dating	teacher of Deaf children; interpreter; Deaf spouse

need and the language of the interpretation by both interpreters (i.e., for the intended monolingual Tagalog consumers, the interpretation was in Filipino, while for the monolingual English speakers, the interpretation was in English).

Table 3 shows the results of four of the twelve voice interpretations by each of the two interpreters. For these, the interpreters received instructions to interpret for intended Filipino/English bilinguals. The resulting interpretations of Interpreter A were all consistently in Filipino. For Interpreter B, however, all but one were in Filipino.

TABLE 2. *Languages of Eight Voice Interpretations by Two Interpreters Compared to Languages of Intended Monolingual Consumers*

Signer on video	Languages of intended consumer		Language of voice interpretation			
			Interpreter A		Interpreter B	
	English	Filipino	English	Filipino	English	Filipino
Signer #1	√		√		√	
		√		√		√
Signer #2	√		√		√	
		√		√		√
Signer #3	√		√		√	
		√		√		√
Signer #4	√		√		√	
		√		√		√

TABLE 3. *Languages of Four Voice Interpretations by Two Interpreters Compared to Languages of Intended Bilingual Consumers*

Signer on video	Languages of intended consumers		Language of voice interpretation			
			Interpreter A		Interpreter B	
	English	Filipino	English	Filipino	English	Filipino
Signer #1	√	√		√	√	√
Signer #2	√	√		√		√
Signer #3	√	√		√		√
Signer #4	√	√		√		√

Table 4 indicates the presence or absence of code switches in twelve voice interpretations each by the two interpreters.

Interpretations with unexpected code switches are shown in table 5. Note that the unexpected code switches all took place in Filipino interpretations (i.e., the intended consumers were monolingual Tagalog speakers). Thus, the direction of code-switching was virtually always

TABLE 4. *Languages and Code-Switching in Twelve Voice Interpretations by Two Interpreters Compared to Languages of Intended Consumers*

Signed on video	Languages of intended consumers	Interpreter A		Interpreter B	
		Languages of voice interpretation	Code switches	Languages of voice interpretation	Code switches
Signer #1	F	F	—	F	√
	E	E	—	E	—
	F/E	F	—	E, F	√
Signer #2	F	F	—	F	√
	E	E	—	E	—
	F/E	F	—	F	√
Signer #3	F	F	√	F	√
	E	E	—	E	—
	F/E	F	√	F	√
Signer #4	F	F	√	F	√
	E	E	—	E	—
	F/E	F	√	F	√

√ Unexpected code switches
F = Filipino; E = English

TABLE 5. *Voice Interpretations with Unexpected Code Switches by Two Interpreters*

		Interpreter A		Interpreter B	
Signed on video	Languages of intended consumer	Languages of voice interpretation	Code switches	Languages of voice interpretation	Code switches
Signer #1	F	F	—	F	√[c]
Signer #2	F	F	—	F	√[d]
Signer #3	F	F	√[a]	F	√[e]
Signer #4	F	F	√[b]	F	√[f]

F = Filipino

Filipino to English and not vice versa. One seeming exception occurred in an interpretation by Interpreter B (see table 5, Interpreter B with Signer 4). Interpreter A showed unexpected code switches in only two out of four interpretations, whereas Interpreter B demonstrated these in all. The superscripts indicate sample excerpts of the unexpected code switches (see [a]–[f] in table 5).

Table 6 is also a subset of the results of table 4 and focuses on the presence of code-switching by the two interpreters for those interpretations where the intended consumers were bilingual. Interpreter B code-switched for all four, whereas Interpreter A showed code-switching for only two of the four tasks.

TABLE 6. *Languages and Code-Switching in Voice Interpretations for Intended Bilingual Consumers*

		Interpreter A		Interpreter B	
Signed on video	Languages of intended consumer	Languages of voice interpretation	Code switches	Languages of voice interpretation	Code switches
Signer #1	F/E	F	—	E, F	√
Signer #2	F/E	F	—	F	√
Signer #3	F/E	F	√	F	√
Signer #4	F/E	F	√	F	√

F = Filipino; E = English

Code Switches

The following are samples of the code switches by the two interpreters in their simulated voice interpretations for Metro Manila Filipino/English bilinguals:

(1)

After several months, <u>nabuntis.</u> (Signer #3)

After several months, (she) got pregnant.

(2)

They didn't give me money . . . money . . . <u>pang</u> . . . <u>pang saan?</u> (Signer #4)

They didn't give me money . . . money . . . for . . . for what?

(3)

<u>Pagkatapos, uwi</u> **then** <u>at natulog; nagpahinga.</u> (Signer #4)

After that, go home then . . . and sleep, rest.

(4)

1And I climbed up the tree and it was so cold! 2There was nothing to eat. 3<u>Hayaan mo na!</u> **4Be patient.** 5<u>Tinulungan mo sana.</u> 6<u>Sa bahay lakas ng hangin so </u>**ni-lock** <u>ko agad.</u> (Signer #1)

1And I climbed up the tree and it was so cold! 2There was nothing to eat. 3Never mind! 4Be patient. 5You should have helped. 6At home the wind was so strong so I locked (it) immediately.

(5)

<u>Nag-</u>**row** <u>ako ng </u>**b(oat).** . . <u>Nag-</u>**row** <u>ako nang nag-</u>**row.** (Signer #2)

I rowed a boat . . . I rowed and I rowed.

(6)

<u>Buntis ngayon – mga</u> **two months** . . . (Signer #3)

Pregnant now – about two months.

(7)

<u>O,</u> **so** <u>iba-iba 'yung mga</u> **prostitutes.** (Signer #4)

Oh, so there are many kinds of prostitutes.

(8)

<u>Nag-apir</u> (**"appear"**) <u>pa kami.</u> (Signer #4)

We even gave each other a high-five.

The following are the unexpected code switches by the two interpreters in their voice interpretations intended for monolingual Tagalog speakers:

[a]
(9)
Tiningnan ko 'yung bata . . . may baby*.   (Signer #3)
   I looked at the child . . . there was a baby.

[b]
(10)
Doubt – sabi sa akin na meron daw ibang babae.   (Signer #4)
   I was doubtful – (he) told me there was another woman.

(11)
Sinabi ko sa kanya "hoy, 'di ako nagpupunta sa mga **bar,** nag-iibang babae.
                                                   (Signer #4)
   I told him, "hey, I don't go to bars, and go with other women."

(12)
Ikaw, gusto mo magka-**AIDS** ka?
   You, you want to get AIDS?

[c]
(13)
Na-**disturb** nga ako do'n.   (Signer #1)
   That disturbed me.

(14)
Nagwowork ako dito tapos . . .   (Signer #1)
   I was working here then . . .

(15)
Eh 'yung **pa(rents)** . . . **parents*** . . . 'yung asawa mo?   (Signer #1)
   What about your pa(rents) . . . parents . . . your wife?

(16)
Eh papa'no **baby*** mo?   (Signer #1)
   Eh, how about your baby?

[d]
(17)
Eh di nag . . . 'yung nag . . . **row** ako ng **boat.**   (Signer #2)
   Eh then . . . then . . . I rowed the boat.

[e]
(18)
Tapos nu'ng nakita ko nga 'yung **wife** ko, umalis na siya. (Signer #3)
   Then when I did see my wife, she left.

(19)

Ta(po)s nakita ko 'yung **baby**.   (Signer #3)
   Then I saw the baby.

(20)

Siguro mga **one month . . . two months**.   (Signer #3)
   Maybe about one month . . . two months.

(21)

Tanung sa 'kin nu'ng **wife** ko "Ano, maysakit ba?"   (Signer #3)
   My wife asked me "Well, (is he) sick?"

(22)

So nag-intay. . . ta(po)s nagbayad.   (Signer #3)
   So (I) — waited . . . then paid.

[f]
(23)

Baka mahawa ka ng **AIDS**.   (Signer #4)
   You might get infected with AIDS.

Other Discourse

Other data on the use of Filipino and English by the interpreters are
as follows (data from conversation was available for only one interpreter):

C O N V E R S A T I O N
Interpreter B

(24)

1NARECEIVE KO YUNG MESSAGE MO LATE NA EH, MGA ONE O'CLOCK
GANON. 2TA(P)OS NAG-E-EMAIL AKO. 3TA(P)OS NASA SCHOOL PA KO
HANGGANG TWO DI BA? 4HANGGANG TWO. 5TA(P)OS TINULUNGAN KONG
MAG-TYPE YUNG CLERK. 6KINUHA KO YUNG ISANG RESEARCH. 7YUNG
GRADES DAW I-TA-TYPE . . . NAWALA YUNG ANO YUNG COPY SA COMPUTER.

1Nareceive ko 'yung message mo late na eh, mga one o'clock gano'n.
2Ta(p)os nag-i-email ako. 3Ta(p)os nasa school* pa 'ko hanggang two 'di
ba? 4Hanggang two. 5Ta(p)os tinulungan kong mag-type 'yung clerk*.
6Kinuha ko 'yung isang research. 7'Yung grades daw ita-type . . .
nawala 'yung ano . . . 'yung copy sa computer*.

   *1I received your message late already, about one o'clock. 2Then I was
   doing email. 3Then I was in school until two right? 4Until two. 5Then*

I helped the clerk type. 6I got one research. 7(He) said the grades were to be typed . . . lost the . . . the copy on the computer.

(25)

1PERO MAY NADISCOVER AKO. 2MARAMI DIN PALA DON NA CHRISTIAN CHURCHES! 3MGA APAT ANG NANDUN. 4OVER OVERNIGHT YUN. 5WALA KA NAMAN MAPASYALAN! 6SAKA WALA SILANG INTERNET. 7KASI. . . OO, TALAGA! 8HINDI . . .NAGTWENTY MINUTES RIDE PA KAMI SA BANGBANG. 9DOON MAY INTERNET CONNECTION RAW. 10OK YUNG EXPERIENCE KASI IBA NAMAN DI BA?

1Pero may na-discover ako. 2Marami din pala do'n na Christian churches! 3Mga apat ang nandu'n. 4Over.. overnight 'yun. 5Wala ka naman mapasyalan! 6Saka wala silang internet. 7Kasi. . . oo, talaga! 8Hindi . . . nag-twenty minutes ride pa kami sa Bangbang. 9Doon may internet connection raw. 10Okey yung experience kasi iba naman, 'di ba?

1But I discovered something. 2Turns out there are many Christian churches there! 3About four are there . . . 4That's over.. overnight. 5There's nowhere to take a walk! 6And they don't have internet. 7Because . . . yes, really! 8No . . . had to take a twenty-minute ride to Bangbang. 9There, they said they had internet connection. 10The experience was okey because it was really different, right?

MOBILE PHONE TEXT EXCERPTS
Interpreter A

(26)

1Its ok, ll try 2 call u 2nyt po. 2As far as I can remembr, I visualizd d respctv audncs. 3My fault was, I didn't cnsdr dpossblty dat t wud b hard 4 me 2 undstd their signs.

1It's OK, I will try to call you tonight po. 2As far as I can remember, I visualized the respective audiences. 3My fault was, I didn't consider the possibility that (it) would be hard for me to understand their signs.

1It's OK, I will try to call you tonight (polite form). 2As far as I can remember, I visualized the respective audiences. 3My fault was, I didn't consider the possibility that (it) would be hard for me to understand their signs.

(27)

1D AFTN B4 NEW YEAR EVERY MEMBER OF MY FAMILY WAS BC PREPN 4 A SUPPSDLY SIMPLE FEAST. 2T TURND OUT OTHRWYS COZ T WAS ALMST

MDNYT YET WE WER STUK CHOPPN, TOSS'N ANDBREW'N. 3TWAS KNDA CHA-OTIC 4 AWYL COZ D DOGS WER N A FRENZY. 4WE WERE RUSHN EVRYTHN N D KTCHN PLUS D ENDLESS PUTOK. 5WHEN ALL WAS ALMST PEACFUL, WE HAD OUR FIRS PRAYR AND FEAST AS A FAMILY 2GDR 4 2007. 6WE DOWND 3 BOTTLES OF WYN 2.

1The afternoon before New Year, every member of my family was busy preparing for a supposedly simple feast. 2It turned out otherwise because it was almost midnight yet we were stuck chopping, tossing and brewing. 3It was kind of chaotic for awhile because the dogs were in a frenzy. 4We were rushing everything in the kitchen plus the endless <u>putok</u>. 5When all was almost peaceful, we had our first prayer and feast as a family together for 2007. 6We downed three bottles of wine too.

1The afternoon before New Year, every member of my family was busy preparing for a supposedly simple feast. 2It turned out otherwise because it was almost midnight yet we were stuck chopping, tossing and brewing. 3It was kind of chaotic for awhile because the dogs were in a frenzy. 4We were rushing everything in the kitchen plus the endless exploding sounds. 5When all was almost peaceful, we had our first prayer and feast as a family together for 2007. 6We downed three bottles of wine too.

(28)

1havnt sent d 3rd 1 yet. 2yan cguro ung kanina. 3so others no nid 2 send agen? 4complete na?

1Haven't send the third one yet. 2'<u>Yan siguro 'yung kanina.</u> 3So others no need to send again? 4Complete <u>na</u>?

1Haven't send the third one yet. 2That's probably the earlier one. 3So, (for the) others no need to send again? 4Complete already?

(29)

1Yaiks! 2Sad namn. 3Que haba2 p naman nun. 4nwei. . . priorityz my health and go bk 2 schl. 5Save, save, save. 6And focus on servng pwds.

1Yikes! 2Sad <u>naman</u>, 3<u>Kay haba-haba pa naman nu'n</u>. 4Anyway . . . priority is my health and going back to school. 5Save, save, save. 6And focus on serving PWDs.

1Yikes! 2What a pity. 3That was even the really long one. 4Anyway . . . priority is my health and go back to school. 5Save, save, save. 6And focus on serving PWDs.

Interpreter B

(30)

14x? 2guess ko wala ako mahagilap na fil word o kaya d pa sapat conscious effort

14x? 2**Guess** ko wala ako mahagilap na **Filipino** word o kaya di pa sapat **conscious effort.**

> *1Four times? 2My guess is I couldn't find a Filipino word or maybe (I) lacked conscious effort.*

(31)

puede rin I was more focused on d content of d signs than on d lang

Puwede rin **I was more focused on the content of the signs than on the language.**

> *That's possible also (that) I was more focused on the content of the signs than on the language.*

(32)

1In general boring kc wala mga malls. 2Exciting lang 'yung trip to & from Isabela. 3We passed thru Dalton Pass and medyo zigzag. 4Ang ganda ng view ng mga bundok at valleys.

1**In general, boring** kasi walang mga **malls.** 2**Exciting** lang 'yung **trip to and from** Isabela. 3**We passed thru** Dalton Pass **and** medyo **zigzag.** 4Ang ganda ng **view** ng mga bundok at **valleys.**

> *1In general, boring because there are no malls. 2Only the trip to and from Isabela was exciting. 3We passed thru Dalton Pass and it was somewhat of a zigzag. 4The view of the mountains and valleys was beautiful.*

(33)

1Galing kami sa Doulos ship. 2haba pila dami tao mga bata. 3marami buks 4 kids. 4mainit sa loob. 5d last time nakapunta ako was 6 yrs ago. 6masarap cookies nila pero ice cream mas masarap dati. 7wala rin masyadong academic bks. 8nasa pier 13 pa cya til jan 22. 9enjoy c mario sa ship & sa bks.

1Galing kami sa Doulos **ship.** 2Haba pila, dami tao - mga bata. 3Marami **books** for **kids.** 4Mainit sa loob. 5The last time nakapunta ako **was 6 yrs ago.** 6Masarap cookies nila pero ice cream mas masarap dati. 7Wala rin masyadong **academic books.** 8Nasa **pier 13** pa siya (un)til **Jan 22.** 10(Nag)-enjoy si Mario sa **ship and** sa **books.**

> *1We came from the Doulos ship. 2The line was long, there were many people – kids. 3There were many books for kids. 4It was hot inside.*

5The last time I was able to go was six years ago. 6The cookies were delicious but ice cream was better before. 7There also weren't many academic books. 8It's there at pier 13 until Jan. 22. 9Mario enjoyed the ship and the books.

DISCUSSION

The Interpreters

The two interpreters for the study are active freelance interpreters in Metro Manila. Their experience in signed language learning and their interpreter skills are typical of those of other frequently sought-after interpreters in the nation's capital. They also assessed themselves as having better sign than voice interpretation skills. Both felt that the signing of the four Deaf informants in the video presented to them for interpretation was quite difficult because of the speed of signing and some unfamiliar signs.

Despite the differences in the interpreters' years of experience and training, their language background may be the more influential factor in their interpretation performance. Interpreter A (with multilingual parents) is also multilingual for spoken languages in Filipino, English, and Cebuano. Interpreter B, on the other hand, has parents who are bilingual in Filipino and English bilingual and is thus strongly bilingual. This is likely related to the greater use of code-switching by Interpreter B, which is evident in conversation, text, and interpretation.

The two interpreters also differed in their definitions of language and code-switching (i.e., Taglish). Initially, Interpreter B viewed language as only Filipino and English. As the interview progressed, Interpreter B's views shifted toward including Taglish as a language, which was used not only in mobile phone text messages but also in conversation and even interpretation. On the other hand, it was evident at the outset that Interpreter A viewed Taglish as a language on a par with English and Filipino. It is still unclear how these attitudes influence actual performance among bilingual and multilingual Filipino interpreters.

Voice Interpretation

The results of table 2 are expected. The language of interpretation consistently matched the language of the intended monolingual consumers. Both interpreters voiced in Filipino when they were instructed that the intended consumers were monolingual Tagalog speakers, while the interpretation was in English for monolingual English speakers. However, one interpretation by Interpreter B for intended Filipino/English bilinguals stood out as different (table 3). For Deaf Signer #1, Interpreter B used entire sentences in both English and Filipino. The start of the interpretation was in English and the end was in Filipino. In all other interpretations by both interpreters for this intended bilingual group, the language of the interpretation was Filipino. In the postvideo interview Interpreter B was surprised at the output of this particular interpretation. Interpreter B ascribed this behavior to either his being engrossed in understanding the signing and/or nervousness, as this was the very first video presented. In any case, the language of interpretation for the intended bilinguals was basically consistent. Consciously or not, both interpreters veered toward essentially Filipino interpretations.

With these intended bilingual consumers, both interpreters said in the postvideo interviews that they felt least anxious about the interpretation (for all four Deaf signers). For the intended monolingual consumers (whether Tagalog or English speakers), they both said they had to prepare themselves more consciously. Presumably the strategy was to avoid code-switching and keep the interpretation comprehensible by using *only* Filipino or English, respectively. Both interpreters commented that, since the instructions for the intended bilingual consumer indicated that they were professionals from Metro Manila, they both considered the intended consumers to be similar to themselves (in terms of language use, attitude, and preference). Thus, their virtually consistent interpretation in Filipino perhaps reflects their view of their own language needs and competence.

Code-Switching

My observations of the two interpreters' use of language are consistent with Bautista's statement (1999b, p. 20) that code-switching is a natural form of discourse in the Metro Manila community. Interpreter B's pausing and phrasing patterns in the majority of code switches coincide with those of free-flowing discourse. Despite the lack of data on conversational discourse with Interpreter A, pausing and phrasing also appeared to be smooth code-switching (see samples 1–23). Some examples of the less frequent flagged or nonsmooth code-switching are shown in sample 2 of Interpreter A and samples 5, 15, and 17 of Interpreter B. Ellipses were added in transcription to denote pauses. Repetitions with these pauses indicate pauses or points of hesitation.

(2)

They didn't give me money . . . money . . . <u>pang</u> . . . <u>pang saan?</u> (Signer #4)

They didn't give me money . . . money . . . for . . . for what?

(5)

<u>Nag-row</u> <u>ako ng b(oat)</u>. . . <u>Nag-row</u> <u>ako nang nag-row.</u> (Signer #2)

I rowed a boat . . . I rowed and I rowed.

(15)

<u>Eh 'yung</u> **pa(rents)** . . . <u>_parents*</u> . . . <u>'yung asawa mo?</u> (Signer #1)

What about your pa(rents) . . . parents . . . your wife?

(17)

<u>Eh di nag</u> . . . <u>'yung nag</u> . . . **row** <u>ako ng</u> **boat.** (Signer #2)

Eh then . . . then . . . I rowed the boat.

There has always been vigorous discussion about the difficulty of determining the base language of a sample of bilingual discourse (Romaine, 1989, p. 134). Because of the number of items in the sample, both interpreters' decision to assign Filipino as the base language was straightforward. Only one interpretation (by Interpreter B) proved problematic, and this was the sole divergent interpretation shown below (also in table 4):

(4)

*1*And I climbed up the tree and it was so cold! *2*There was nothing to eat. *3*<u>Hayaan mo na!</u> *4*Be patient. *5*<u>Tinulungan mo sana.</u> *6*<u>Sa bahay lakas ng hangin so ni-lock</u> **ko agad.** (Signer #1)

1And I climbed up the tree and it was so cold! 2There was nothing to eat. 3Never mind! 4Be patient. 5You should have helped. 6At home the wind was so strong so I locked (it) immediately.

The interpretation begins with English (sample 1), ends in Filipino (sample 6), and has three sentences in English only (samples 1, 2, and 4) and three in Filipino only (samples 3, 5, and 6). The only intra-sentential code switches are in the last Filipino sentence; the first one occurs between clauses, and the second one is a nonce borrowing of an English verb with a Tagalog prefix (*ni*-lock). Borrowing in relation to the corpus of Filipino and other Philippine languages is a complex subject that is under continuing investigation (G. Zafra, personal communication, 2007; Baklanova, 2005).

Samples a–f and table 5 show unexpected code switches since the intended consumers were monolingual Tagalog speakers. Thus, one would not expect any code switches to English items since these would be incomprehensible to the monolingual Tagalog consumer. These code switches appear to be motivated differently. The nonce borrowing of "AIDS" in sample b, S12 is clearly to fill a lexical gap since the Filipino corpus has no equivalent. The use of "bar" and "doubt" in sample b, S10 and S11 could be in the same category, although these have been designated as loanwords (Almario 2001).[1] The use of "disturb" in sample c, S13 is a nonce borrowing of the English verb with a Filipino prefix. Though the Komisyon sa Wikang Filipino dictionary lists *abala* as "disturb," it is not included as an entry in the *UP Diksiyonaryong Filipino* (ibid.). Thus, it is not likely in frequent use as a loan equivalent.

The use of "parents" in sample c, S15 is probably a case of flagged or nonsmooth code-switching because of the hesitation pause and repetition. Since the plural form is used, it is an English element in this switch. The frequent use of "parent" in general, however, has led to its inclusion in the *UP Diksiyonaryong Filipino* (ibid.) as a loanword. The same holds for "row" and "boat" in sample d, S17 and for "so" in sample e, S22. Other words used as loan equivalents are the following (ibid.):

"baby"   sample a, S9; sample c, S16; sample e, S19
"work" (nonce-borrowing verb with Filipino prefix) sample c, S14
"one, two month(s)"   sample e, S20 (note plural form)
"wife"   sample e, S18, S21

For both interpreters, code switches for intended bilinguals (see table 6) show that Interpreter B code-switched for all of the interpretations, while Interpreter A did so for only half of the interpretations. This has interesting implications if analyzed in the context of a previous study. Bautista (1999b, p. 30) proposes the classification of code-switching in the Philippines as either deficiency driven (i.e., the speaker is not competent in the second language [L2] and thus reverts to the first language [L1]) or competence driven (i.e., the speaker is competent in both the L1 and the L2 and displays communicative efficiency by choosing the best way of expressing an idea in one language).

Thus, Bautista views bilingualism as providing resources in two languages to those who can flexibly utilize them with different interlocutors, topics, and situations for greater efficiency. Despite the limitations that she recognizes, Bautista still concludes that competence is the fundamental impetus for the extensive and popular code-switching behavior observed among Filipinos. Interpreter B, who has bilingual parents and clearly displays stronger code-switching behavior in conversation, texting, and interpretation, appears to belong to the category of bilinguals that Bautista describes.

The fact that Interpreter B code-switched in all four of the interpretations for intended bilinguals (because it was allowable anyway) seems to confirm that code-switching is a strategy that bilinguals employ to take advantage of the resources at their disposal, according to Bautista. Interpreter A, on the other hand, who could have code-switched when it was allowed (since the intended consumers were bilingual), opted to (or could) code-switch only half of the time. This appears to imply that Interpreter A is more limited in Filipino/English code-switching. If so, this may be attributable to the multilingual background of Interpreter A's parents (English/Capiznon/Filipino; Cebuano/English/Tagalog), as well as to spoken languages during Interpreter A's formative years (English/Filipino/Visayan). Interpreter A would conceivably have strengths in code-switching in other Philippine languages (Visayan/Tagalog), however, that Interpreter B would not have at all.

If this analysis is accurate, it demonstrates the enormous challenges that a bilingual or multilingual Filipino interpreter faces. Similarly, interpreter training program administrators and policy makers need to bear in mind that interpreters must be prepared to deal with a wide range of consumers (monolingual Filipino, monolingual English, monolingual non-Filipino language/dialect; bilingual Filipino/English, bilingual non-Filipino/English, bilingual Filipino/non-Filipino) whom they will encounter throughout the archipelago.

Moreover, interpretation to monolingual consumers of course requires solid competence in that language. Such skill development must be carefully integrated into current and future interpreter training programs. On the other hand, for interpretation to bilingual consumers, training programs will need to recognize the legitimate use of code-switching by *fluent* bilinguals as a strategy for communicative efficiency. The potential difficulty for interpreter training programs is whether to allow code-switching by *nonfluent bilinguals*.

The significance of code-switching in a country that is just developing its interpreting system and whose pool of interpreters resides mostly in the national capital region is tremendous. It is inextricably linked to classic questions concerning bilingualism: "Is code-switching random linguistic behavior? . . . Is it always indicative of poor competence?" (Romaine, 1989, p. 2). However, code-switching even among fluent bilinguals is well documented, and, in fact, switching often occurs for items that are known in both languages (ibid., p. 132). Bautista's (1999b) analysis of competence-driven code-switching by Manila speakers is an important one.

The ideal Filipino interpreter must then demonstrate both monolingual competence (in Filipino, English, or another Philippine language) and bilingual fluency. The latter (and the inevitable code-switching) will then be a carefully honed skill that is part of the Filipino interpreter's repertoire. This versatility enables the interpreter to communicate efficiently and appropriately with consumers with a range of language fluencies.

Bilingualism and multilingualism among Filipino Sign Language interpreters must be considered as strengths—not as weaknesses. To consider them otherwise would be counterproductive. Interpreters must understand and accept their unique linguistic background and pursue definite language career goals. Training programs need to build on these natural assets, while testing and evaluation policies must distinguish between and assess specific performance indicators appropriately. Furthermore, prospective clients and consumers should understand the portfolio of skills of the interpreter they are hiring.

This chapter has dealt with situations and issues that confront Filipino interpreters today. However, these considerations may also apply in other developing countries that face similar challenges in developing an interpreting system in a linguistically diverse environment.

CONCLUSION

The Filipino is typically at least bilingual and not uncommonly multilingual. This simple inquiry has revealed the challenges and complexity of language use among Filipino interpreters:

1. That both of the interpreters in this study interpreted virtually consistently in Filipino to an intended group of Filipino/English bilinguals is indicative of a strong tendency. Future studies need

to probe the reason for such behavior and determine whether it is rooted in competence, language attitude, or both.

2. The tendency of both interpreters to code-switch to English for intended monolingual Filipino consumers (which would surely result in incomprehensible segments) is another striking finding.

It is imperative for us to investigate and understand the mechanisms at work in code-switching among Filipino bilingual and multilingual interpreters because of the profound impact they have on interpreting performance. Training programs, national standards for testing, evaluation, and certification must take into consideration these natural behaviors of interpreters.

The linguistic environment of the Philippines is in a perpetual state of flux because of political agendas, academic and educational philosophies, and popular sentiment. Yet it is essential to overcome these challenges so that an interpreting system may deliver effective and efficient services to the thousands of deaf Filipinos who are fighting for their right to language and justice.

ACKNOWLEDGMENTS

I would like to thank Galileo Zafra and Ruby Alcantara for their valuable assistance. Moreover, I am indebted to Rommel Agravante and the Philippine Federation of the Deaf Practical Dictionaries for Asian Sign Languages project, which is supported by the Nippon Foundation, for their contribution. The Asia Foundation and USAID are also gratefully acknowledged for partnering with the Philippine Deaf Resource Center, the Philippine Federation of the Deaf, and the Filipino Deaf Women's Health and Crisis Center for the related Equal Access to Communication for the Deaf in Legal Proceedings project.

NOTES

1. The current edition of the *UP Diksiyonaryong Filipino* (Almario, 2001) includes entries in their original spelling, as well as their respelled form (e.g., "school" and *iskul).* The revised edition will omit the former and include only the latter as the main entry (G. Zafra, personal communication, 2007).

REFERENCES

Abat, R., & Martinez, L. (2006). The history of sign language in the Philippines: Piecing together the puzzle. In *Proceedings of the Ninth Philippine Linguistics Congress*. University of the Philippines, Quezon City, January 27. http://web.kssp.upd.edu.ph/linguistics/plc2006/papers.

Almario, V., (Ed.). (2001). *UP Diksiyonaryong Filipino*. Pasig City: University of the Philippines, Sentro ng Wikang Filipino.

Andrada, J., & Domingo, R. (2006). Key Findings for language planning from the national sign language committee. In *Proceedings of the Ninth Philippine Linguistics Congress*. University of the Philippines, Quezon City, January 27. http://web.kssp.upd.edu.ph/linguistics/plc2006/papers.

Apurado, Y., & Agravante, R. (2006). The phonology and regional variation of Filipino Sign Language: Considerations for language policy. In *Proceedings of the Ninth Philippine Linguistics Congress*. University of the Philippines, Quezon City, January 27. http://web.kssp.upd.edu.ph/linguistics/plc2006/papers.

Azores, F. (1967). A preliminary investigation of the phenomenon of language change in the Philippines. Quoted in M. L. Bautista, Code-switching studies in the Philippines, *International Journal on the Sociology of Language 88* (1991), 19–32.

Baklanova, E. (2005). Typological classification of borrowings in Tagalog. In *Proceedings of the Ninth Philippine Linguistics Congress*. University of the Philippines, Quezon City, January 27. http://web.kssp.upd.edu.ph/linguistics/plc2006/papers.

Bautista, M. L., (Ed.). (1999a). *The Filipino bilingual: A multidisciplinary perspective*. Proceedings of the Centennial Congress on Philippine Bilingualism from a Multidisciplinary Perspective. Manila: Linguistics Society of the Philippines.

Bautista, M. L. (1999b). An analysis of the functions of Tagalog-English code-switching: Data from one case. In M. L. Bautista (Ed.), *The Filipino bilingual: A multidisciplinary perspective* (pp. 19–31). Proceedings of the Centennial Congress on Philippine Bilingualism from a Multidisciplinary Perspective. Manila: Linguistics Society of the Philippines.

Bustos, M. T., & Tanjusay, R. (2006). Filipino Sign Language in deaf education: Deaf and hearing perspectives. In *Proceedings of the Ninth Philippine Linguistics Congress*. University of the Philippines, Quezon City, January 27. http://web.kssp.upd.edu.ph/linguistics/plc2006/papers.

Castillo, E. (1999). Alternative assessments of language ability. In M. L. Bautista (Ed.), *The Filipino bilingual: A multidisciplinary perspective* (pp. 163–65). Proceedings of the Centennial Congress on Philippine Bilingualism from a Multidisciplinary Perspective. Manila: Linguistics Society of the Philippines.

Chanco, A., Jr., Francisco, E., & Talamisan, T. (1999). A look at the code-switching patterns of some television hosts in metro Manila. In M. L. Bautista (Ed.), *The Filipino bilingual: A multidisciplinary perspective* (pp. 32–35). Proceedings of the Centennial Congress on Philippine Bilingualism from a Multidisciplinary Perspective. Manila: Linguistics Society of the Philippines.

Constantino, P. (Ed.). (2005). *Filipino at ang pagpaplanong pangwika.* Manila: Sentro ng Wikang Filipino, University of the Philippines Diliman, Sanggunian sa Filipino, Pambansang Komisyon para sa Kultura at mga Sining.

Corpuz, M. R. (2006). Ang kahalagahan ng Proyektong Diksiyonaryo ng Philippine Federation of the Deaf sa edukasyon ng Bingi sa Pilipinas. In *Proceedings of the Ninth Philippine Linguistics Congress.* University of the Philippines, Quezon City, January 27. http://web.kssp.upd.edu.ph/linguistics/plc2006/papers.

Fuentes, G., & Mojica, L. (1999). A study of the language attitudes of selected Filipino bilingual students toward Filipino and English. In M. L. Bautista (Ed.), *The Filipino bilingual: A multidisciplinary perspective* (pp. 50–55). Proceedings of the Centennial Congress on Philippine Bilingualism from a Multidisciplinary Perspective. Manila: Linguistics Society of the Philippines, 1999.

González, A. (1981). Language policy and language-in-education policy in the Philippines. *Annual Review of Applied Linguistics 2,* 48–59.

Gumperz, J. (1982). Discourse strategies. In M. L. Bautista, (Ed.), *The Filipino bilingual: A multidisciplinary perspective* (p. 21). Manila: Linguistics Society of the Philippines, 199b.

Kessler, K. (1984). Language acquisition in bilingual children. In S. Romaine, *Bilingualism,* 2. Oxford: Basil Blackwell.

Komisyon sa Wikang Filipino. (2000). Diksyunaryong Filipino/English. Manila: Author.

Martin, M. I. (1999). Language and institution: Roots of bilingualism in the Philippines. In M. L. Bautista (Ed.), *The Filipino bilingual: A multidisciplinary perspective* (pp. 132–36). Proceedings of the Centennial Congress on Philippine Bilingualism from a Multidisciplinary Perspective. Manila: Linguistics Society of the Philippines.

Martinez, L. (1993). Eye-gaze as an element in Filipino Sign Language discourse. *Communication Forum 2,* 99–112.

Martinez, L. (1994). A linguistic study of some aspects of Filipino Sign Language in Manila and Cebu. Unpublished manuscript, Department of Linguistics and Interpreting, Gallaudet University, Washington, DC.

Martinez, L. (1995a). Filipino Sign Language: May kaugnayan at kabuluhan ba sa Deaf Education? Tan Chi King Professorial Chair Lecture. Manila: De La Salle University.

Martinez, L. (1995b). Turn-taking and eye gaze in sign conversations between deaf Filipinos. In C. Lucas (Ed.), *Sociolinguistics in Deaf Communities* (pp. 272–306). Washington, DC: Gallaudet University Press.

Martinez, L. (1996). Understanding the Deaf student: Phonological modifications in Filipino Sign Language. Unpublished manuscript, University Research Coordination Office, De La Salle University, Manila.

Martinez, L. (2005a). Determining the historical relationship of Filipino Sign Language and American Sign Language. Paper presented at a meeting of the Japan Association of Sign Linguistics, Kyoto, Japan, June 12.

Martinez, L. (2005b). Filipino Sign Language: Understanding the past, looking to the future. Keynote speech at a meeting of the Japan Institute for Sign Language Studies, Kyoto, June 12. *Sign Language Communication Studies* (June), 2–11 (publication is in Japanese).

Martinez, L. (2006a). Institutionalizing linguistically based measures in legal interpreting: A focus on the rights of Deaf women. In *Proceedings of the Ninth Philippine Linguistics Congress*. University of the Philippines, Quezon City, January 27. http://web.kssp.upd.edu.ph/linguistics/plc2006/papers.

Martinez, L. (2006b). Where do the Deaf women belong? Reproductive health policy considerations for a language minority. Paper presented at the International Conference on Reproductive Health Management, Manila, May 3.

Nishimura, M. (1986). Intrasentential code-switching. In S. Romaine, *Bilingualism*, 2. Oxford: Basil Blackwell.

Ozog, A. C. K. (1987). The syntax of the mixed language of Malay. In S. Romaine, *Bilingualism*, 2. Oxford: Basil Blackwell.

Pertierra, R. (2006). *Transforming technologies and altered selves: Mobile phone and internet use in the Philippines*. Manila: De La Salle University Press.

Pertierra, R., Ugarte, E., Pingol, A., Hernandez, J., & Dacanay, N. (2002). *Txt-ing selves*. Manila: De La Salle University Press.

Philippine Deaf Resource Center. (2005). Preliminary sectoral position papers for an initiative in language planning for sign language policy for the Republic of the Philippines: A compilation. Unpublished manuscript, Quezon City.

Philippine Deaf Resource Center and Philippine Federation of the Deaf. (2004). *An introduction to Filipino Sign Language*. Quezon City: Author.

Poplack, S. (1980). Sometimes I'll start a sentence in English y terminó en español. In S. Romaine, *Bilingualism*, 112. Oxford: Basil Blackwell.

Poplack, S., & Sankoff, D. (1988). Code-switching. In M. L. Bautista (Ed.), *The Filipino bilingual: A multidisciplinary perspective* (pp. 19–20). Manila: Linguistics Society of the Philippines.

Puson, M. J., & Siloterio, M. (2006). Language contact and lexicalization in Filipino Sign Language: A focus on fingerspelled signs. In *Proceedings of the Ninth Philippine Linguistics Congress.* University of the Philippines, Quezon City, January 27. http://web.kssp.upd.edu.ph/linguistics/plc2006/papers.

Romaine, S. (1989). *Bilingualism.* Oxford: Basil Blackwell.

Shaneyfelt, W. (1979). *Love signs: The sign language in English and Pilipino.* Valenzuela, Philippines: D&M Print.

Sibayan, B. (1991). The intellectualization of Filipino. *International Journal of the Sociology of Language 88*, 69–82.

Tiongson, P. (2006). Making texts more meaningful to the Deaf reader for deeper levels of information and language processing and language instruction. In *Proceedings of the Ninth Philippine Linguistics Congress.* University of the Philippines, Quezon City, January 27.

University of the Philippines, Sentro ng Wikang Filipino and Pambansang Komisyon para sa Kultura at mga Sining. (2004). *Pambansang Direktoryo ng mga Alagad ng Wika.* Manila: University of the Philippines, SWF and NCCA.

Woodward, J. (2006a). Endangered Asian sign languages: Universal and unique characteristics of sign languages. Lecture, Philippine Federation of the Deaf, Philippine Deaf Resource Center, Linguistics Department, University of the Philippines, February 21.

Woodward, J. (2006b). Sign linguistics as an emerging field. Lecture, Linguistics Society of the Philippines, Komisyon sa Wikang Filipino, Philippine Deaf Resource Center, University of the Philippines, September 19.

Indirectness Strategies in American Sign

Language Requests and Refusals:

Deconstructing the Deaf-as-Direct Stereotype

Daniel Roush

Professional interpreters must constantly grapple with deficiencies and exuberances in understanding and expressing the meaning of the languages they work between (Becker, 1995).[1] This task can be especially daunting when dealing with languages that are as divergent as English and American Sign Language (ASL). Interpreters must set aside the exuberances and fill in the deficiencies by looking at language itself and taking into consideration both the conscious and unconscious broad-based perceptions of the speakers and signers with whom they work. In doing so, they consider not only their own native language but also the language and culture of those with whom they have cross-cultural contact; interpreters may even take into account their own perceptual deficiencies and exuberances. One example of the latter is social stereotyping, and interpreters should strive to become conscious of stereotypes that they themselves may harbor. Self-examination of one's stereotypes is part and parcel of the omissive ethic of doing no harm, as well as the commissive ethic of respect, which has become central to the *Professional Code of Conduct* of the Registry of Interpreters for the Deaf (RID, 2005). This chapter outlines a research-based process of deconstructing the prevailing folk stereotype that views the ASL-using Deaf community as being direct or blunt.

BACKGROUND AND STRUCTURE OF THE STUDY

As a hearing person raised by Deaf parents in the Deaf community of the United States, I have intuitively noticed that my style of conversation varies depending on whether I am conversing in English or ASL.

(The notions of style and strategy are defined later.) While signing in ASL, I do not use particular indirectness strategies that I would use when saying the same thing in English. In a sense, I detect a more direct bias in ASL. However, the folk stereotype of Deaf conversation as being blunt or direct does not adequately describe the style I use in ASL conversational interactions. I believe that the issue is much more complex than this, and the Deaf people I have consulted concur. One cannot be direct in every situation. Although some situations call for directness, they do not neatly fit the "having no tact" interpretation that English speakers often mention. These intuitions helped me to form a hypothesis and to articulate my need to deal with the apparent exuberances and deficiencies in my own understanding, which constituted the motivation for this study.[2]

Although I have summarized several themes on the use of directness in the ethnographic interviews section of the analysis, this study ironically approaches the directness issue in a backhanded way by providing a preliminary discussion and description of indirectness strategies that are evident in a videotaped series of two speech acts: requests and refusals. I use certain theoretical notions borrowed from the literature of formal pragmatics, linguistic politeness, and conversational analysis to elucidate the data on the relative use of indirectness in the ASL community. The data reveal that the Deaf-as-direct stereotype does not adequately characterize the complexity and diversity of conversational styles and strategies that members of the ASL Deaf community use. Although many of these indirectness strategies are unique to ASL, their functions and the theoretical dynamics that explain them parallel the conversational interaction in many other language communities. It is, however, beyond the scope of this study to provide a full catalogue of the conversational styles of the ASL signing community. Certainly more ethnographic and sociolinguistic research is needed in this area.

This study is structured as follows: To begin, I briefly expand on the stereotype in question. I then review the literature and provide a theoretical framework for the inquiry. Next I present a discussion of the methodology and a thematic summary of the ethnographic interviews. The analysis section addresses the two speech/social activities of requests and refusals and includes a discussion of the politeness strategies found in each. The conclusion presents suggestions for future research.

In many minority groups and subcultures throughout the world, misperceptions and stereotypes proliferate and become reinforced not only between but within groups as well. Kochman (1981) provides a classic study of these misperceptions and stereotypes—namely that white people perceive black argumentation as less objective due to personal involvement and emotional expression. In the United States, the community of ASL-using Deaf people is not without its own stereotypes, which come from both within and without. To begin with, before William Stokoe's work in the early 50s, the general view was that Deaf people used an iconic gesture system that was not subject to linguistic analysis. Unfortunately, many uninformed people in the hearing community in the United States and even in pockets within the Deaf community still hold this view. The Deaf community continues to struggle with pejorative perceptions about themselves, especially in relation to the pathological/disabled versus language and cultural minority debate and the academic potential of Deaf children (Lane, 1992).

This study focuses on the stereotype that the quintessential style of conversation among ASL-using Deaf people is direct or blunt.[3] This view is frequently brought up in relation to the contact between the English-speaking majority and the ASL Deaf community or in discussions of the differences between the two communities. Even within the Deaf community the ASL phrase in example 1 is often repeated (see appendix B for ASL transcription conventions):

Example 1. KNOW-THAT DEAF TEND DIRECT
"You know, Deaf people tend to be direct."

Some of the most cited examples of this directness focus on comments about changes in the addressee's physical appearance (see discussion under Analysis: Ethnographic Interview). They also seem to be related to speaker-focused disclosures (expression of opinions and complaints) or other-focused advisements (see discussion under Related Signed Language and Interpreting Studies). This chapter does not investigate the directness phenomena in these areas. Rather, it discusses indirectness strategies within the speech activities of requests and refusals. While providing descriptions of indirectness strategies, I also present evidence that the Deaf style of talk is constrained by cross-linguistic metacommunication principles of human interaction.

LITERATURE REVIEW AND THEORETICAL BASE

This section devotes considerable space to a review of related literature in order to build a theoretical framework for the analysis. The literature reviewed falls under two main areas of inquiry. The first is formal
pragmatics, which is rooted in Anglo-American philosophy, as well as a
subfield of generative linguistics. Although this chapter works from an
overall sociolinguistic perspective, relevant notions have been selected
from formal pragmatics. The second area draws salient points from a
combination of literature on linguistic politeness and conversational
analysis. Also included is a brief section on related signed language and
interpreting studies. A final section describes the relativity and benefits
of indirectness.

Formal Pragmatics

Levinson (1983) discusses the difficulty of providing a simple definition of pragmatics; his discussion is not irrelevant. However, for our
purposes, I propose a working definition taken from his discussion:
"Pragmatics is the study of the relations between language and context
that are basic to an account of language understanding" (p. 21). This
definition emphasizes context-dependent pragmatic phenomena. The
theories of formal pragmatics that I review inform us of the importance
of these issues in developing a typology of conversational styles and strategies within ASL interaction.

Conversational Implicature

The widely influential theory of conversational implicature was set
forth by philosopher Paul Grice (1975). In developing this theory, he
proposed a governing principle for conversations:

Cooperative Principle (CP): Participants in a conversation cooperate
with each other.

He further postulated that the CP consists of four conversational
maxims:

- Maxim of Quantity: Participants' contribution to a conversation
  should be just as informative as is required.
- Maxim of Quality: Participants' contribution should be truthful
  and based on sufficient evidence.

- Maxim of Relation: Participants' contribution should be relevant to the topic.
- Maxim of Manner: Participants' contribution should be clear.

If participants choose to flout one or more of these maxims, they raise an implicature (meaning an implication or a suggestion is flagged). The following ASL example demonstrates the effect of flouting the maxims of quantity and manner on its interpretation:

Example 2.

<pre>
           y/n-q
</pre>
A: PRO-1 KNOW A-P-R-I-L
   "Do you know April?"
B: (nods)

<pre>
                 y/n-q
</pre>
A: POSS-3++, NEED PRO-1 SAY MORE
   "Her ways! Need I say more?"

Speaker A's utterance related to April is minimal and therefore not clear. This flouting raises the possible implied proposition in example 3:

Example 3. If you know April, then you can commiserate with me about her annoying personality quirks.

Raising an implicature—in other words, being indirect, as in this example—depends on the participants' ability to identify flouted maxims and infer the speaker's meaning. This example supports the hypothesis that the principle of conversational implicature is applicable in ASL conversation.

The universal application of Grice's CP has drawn criticism in the literature (Watts, 1992). Specifically, not all styles of conversation work from a principle of maximized clarity, as the CP and related maxims posit. Attempts have been made to supplement the CP (Leech, 1983). I do not intend to support or reject the universality of the CP in this study. I simply posit that, as a theory, it informs our understanding of indirectness with regard to ASL conversation. The CP and its maxims will become one interrelated component of the overall theoretical base that I am developing. These notions are discussed in the analysis section, as what is actually said informs the theory and how the theory might inform what is actually said.

Speech Act Theory

Austin (1962) originally proposed that language is rule-governed behavior that entails the performance of speech acts (i.e., using particular words and sentences within particular contexts). He proposes that there are three kinds of acts:

locutionary act: the utterance of a sentence with a particular sense and reference—a proposition
illocutionary act: a conventionally recognized social act that has associated with it an illocutionary conventional force, or intention
perlocutionary act: the effect of the utterance upon the addressee

The illocutionary effects or acts have been further categorized by Searle (1976) into the following typology:

representatives: utterances that commit the speaker to the truth of the expressed proposition (asserting, concluding)
directives: utterances that are attempts by the speaker to get the addressee to do something (requesting, questioning)
commissives: utterances that commit the speaker to some future action (promising, threatening, offering)
expressives: utterances that express a psychological state (thanking, apologizing, welcoming, congratulating)
declarations: utterances that effect immediate changes in the institutional state of affairs and that tend to rely on elaborate extra-linguistic institutions (declaring war, firing from employment)

The following ASL example will help to clarify these categories of acts and illocutionary effects:

Example 4. FINISH!
        "Quit it!"

This locutionary utterance has the structure, sense, and reference of an imperative sentence. Within the Deaf community the illocutionary force of example 4 can be categorized as a conventionally recognized directive or request. The perlocutionary effect of example 4 upon the addressee would be the stopping of whatever that person was doing.

The validity of these acts is based on felicity conditions that Austin originally developed (1962) and Searle expanded (1969, 1976). These conditions are as follows:

preparatory conditions: existing antecedent to the utterance, including the speaker's beliefs about the addressee's physical capabilities and state of mind
sincerity conditions: relating to the speaker's state of mind

essential conditions: requiring that the utterance be recognizable as an instance of the illocutionary act in question
propositional content conditions: relating to the state of affairs predicated in the utterance

As this study focuses on requests and refusals, I specify the particular felicity conditions of the illocutionary act of a request:

preparatory: 1. S believes A is able to do IA; 2. IA is something A would not normally do.
sincerity: 1. S wants A to do IA.
essential: 1. counts as an attempt to get A to do IA
propositional content: 1. future IA of A
Key: S = speaker, A = addressee, IA = illocutionary act

If all of the correct felicity conditions are in place, then the utterance would be a valid performance of the requestive act. To illustrate further, the felicity conditions for the utterance FINISH may be as follows:

preparatory: 1. S believes A is able to "stop." 2. "Stop" is something A would not normally do.
sincerity: S wants A to "stop."
essential: counts as an attempt to get A to "stop"
propositional content: future "stop" of A

Any condition not satisfied would reduce the validity of the utterance. The effect of contextualization cues and conversational frame upon these conditions is discussed later.

Indirect Speech Acts

Having provided a minimal review of Austin's and Searle's speech act theory (SAT), I now turn to the area within SAT that is most salient to this study: indirect speech acts (ISA). Searle (1975) noted that speech acts can be carried out indirectly by appearing to carry out another illocutionary act. In the following example, the speaker appears to be asking a question:

Example 5.

```
     y/n-q_____
```
A: MUST LIGHT CL: "dimmed lights"
   "Must the lights be turned down?"
B: (addressee turns up the lights)

The speaker is not only asking a question but also issuing a directive. The hearer responds by following the speaker's directive (perlocutionary) force and turns up the lights. Direct speech acts (DSA) are carried out when an illocutionary act is issued directly rather than being carried out by way of another act. An ISA or a DSA can be recognized by comparing the syntactic form of the locutionary act and the conventional force of the illocutionary act. If the illocutionary force matches its usual syntactic form, it is a DSA (directive IA with an imperative syntactic form); if it does not match (as in example 5), it is an ISA (directive IA with a yes/no question syntactic form).

From data such as in example 5 we can conclude that the notion of an ISA informs this type of phenomenon in ASL conversation. (The use of ISAs is discussed later.) The question of whether ASL parallels other languages that use ISAs primarily to carry out directives needs further investigation.

The original works of Austin and Searle have received much criticism and revision in the literature. Interestingly, Searle (1969) himself noted, that although he drew his data from English sentences, he was not primarily interested in the actual structures of natural human languages. His conclusions were not about languages but about language. He admits that many of his claims are based simply on his intuitions as a native speaker of English. Since the focus of this study takes a descriptive rather than a theoretical approach, I leave the development of the theory in its classic form and simply alert the readers to other SAT studies that have helped shape my understanding of the current state of the art and have had a peripheral influence on this study: Bach and Harnish (1979), Nira Reiss (1985), Michael Geis (1995), and Anna Wierzbicka (1991).

In review, the notions of locutionary, illocutionary, and perlocutionary force, as well as felicity conditions within SAT, form one stratum of the theoretical base of this study. I find this theory useful only to the extent that it informs the analysis of my data and vice versa. It not my intent to paint a formal or reductionist picture of speech acts within ASL but to allow the details of what is actually said in the data to be painted on a theoretical canvas.

Style, Strategy, and Linguistic Politeness

Before proceeding to a review of the literature on linguistic politeness, I discuss two key terms: style and strategy. Tannen (1984) develops a comprehensive discussion of the notion of style and strategy. Drawing primarily from the work of Hymes (1974), Ervin-Tripp (1972), Sapir (1958), and Lakoff (1973, 1979), Tannen defines style as "ways of speaking" and "a way of doing something":

> It is crucial to make clear that style does not refer to a special way of speaking, as if one could choose between speaking plainly and speaking with style. Plain is as much a style as fancy. Anything that is said or done must be said or done in some way, and that way constitutes style. . . . Anything you say must be said at a certain rate, at a certain pitch and amplitude, in certain intonation, at a certain point in interaction. All these and countless other choices determine the effect of an utterance in interaction and influence judgments that are made both about what is said and about the speaker who says it. All these and countless other necessary choices determine a speaker's style. (p. 8)

Style can both display an individual's personality and reflect a group's social differences. It is difficult to make a clear differentiation between these. The analysis of the videotaped data may well be a commentary on the participants' individual styles and on the style of Deaf interaction.

Lakoff's notion of stylistic strategies was first introduced in her discussion of the "logic of politeness" (1973). She notes that speakers often do not say what they mean (indirectness) because of the higher goal of politeness, which in her sense broadly means the social function of language. She develops three governing principles, originally called rules of politeness:

Don't impose.
Give options.
Be friendly.

When each principle is applied to a particular utterance in an interaction, it creates a particular stylistic effect. Giving preference to one of these principles results in a communicative strategy that makes up style, and style is made up of the habitual use of linguistic devices motivated by these metastrategies.

This study looks at particular linguistic devices in the data that may constitute strategies within a style. In the analysis, based on the consistency of the strategies used in each videotaped situation, as well as the textual coherence of the conversations, I suggest that the participants, as members from the same social group, share the conventional stylistic strategies of indirectness and mitigation that are under study.

Lakoff (1979) further develops her notion of communicative style by positing a grammar of style that is analogous to Chomskian generative grammar and the concomitant surface and deep levels of linguistic structure. The grammar of style entails implicit rules that guide behavior in a descriptive manner. Lakoff postulates that these intuitions are based on metastrategies of communicative competence. The idealized strategies are evolved from her original rules of politeness, with the addition of clarity. These strategies include clarity (Grice's maxims), distance (do not impose), deference (give options), and camaraderie (be friendly). These are interrelated in a dynamic continuum (see figure 1).

The targeting of a particular strategy (or combination of strategies) and the interpretation of such in particular contexts varies from culture to culture, as well as from individual to individual. This model informs and is informed by the stereotypical distinctions between men's and women's personal styles. Men typically target clarity and distance styles, whereas women target deference and camaraderie styles. Lakoff states that women are often negatively viewed for their other-than-male personal styles.

Lakoff mentions that her argument for a stylistic grammar has been based on the principal example of the distinction between men's and women's typical personal styles. She goes on to say that the argument can hold for the behavior of any individual or group that is felt by its members and outsiders to function as a cohesive unit. I suggest that, by analogy to Lakoff's argument, Deaf people have their own stylistic strategies. In a later section I discuss the targeting of camaraderie and concomitant sincerity in the use of direct devices by members of the Deaf community. I also discuss the use of indirectness strategies as targeting not only camaraderie but distance and deference as well.

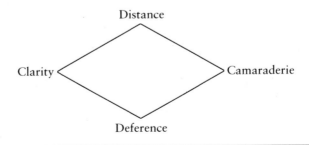

FIGURE 1. *Lakoff's dynamic continuum of metastrategies.*

Apart from Grice's maxims, one of the most developed discussions of universal politeness phenomenon has been provided by Brown and Levinson (1978, 1989). Drawing from the work of Goffman (1967) on presentational rituals and avoidance rituals evolved from Durkheim's (1915) positive rites and negative rites, they posit—on the basis of what has been termed "face"—two major categories of politeness:

negative face: the want of all competent adult members that their actions be unimpeded by others
positive face: the want of all members that their wants be desirable to at least some others

It is in the interest of the participants in a conversation to cooperate in maintaining each other's faces. As some speech acts are intrinsically face threatening (FTA), the speaker may either decline to perform the FTA or go ahead and do the FTA (see figure 2). If the speaker has decided to do the FTA, then that person may choose to go off record (indirect speech act; an ambiguous attributable intention would allow the speaker to avoid commitment to one intent). Alternatively, speakers can go on record and make their intention clear. If the speakers are on record, then they may communicate their intentions with or without (baldly) redressive action (minimizing/mitigating face-threatening strategies).[4] Stating the utterance baldly can be seen as conforming to the Gricean maxims. Redressive action can be taken in two directions: negative politeness strategies, which recognize the addressee's personal territory and personal freedom of action, and positive politeness strategies, which show recognition and appropriate validation of the addressee's self-image, that is, that person's wants are appreciated and approved of in social interaction.

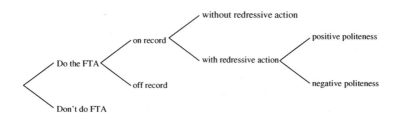

FIGURE 2. *Politeness strategies for doing FTAs (Brown and Levinson, 1987).*

The choice of strategies depends on the speaker's estimation of face loss. The weightiness of the imposition is evaluated on the basis of three culture-specific factors:

P: the relative power relationship between the speaker and addressee
D: the social distance between the speaker and the addressee
R: the ranking of the imposition in the social context in which it is used

Upon determining the unique weightiness combination of these factors, the speaker selects various strategies to counteract it. Successful communication then entails a constant awareness and maintenance of the self-image and face of both the addressee and the speaker by the utilization of various politeness strategies.

An illustration of the FTA and the P, D, and R factors here would take considerable space. Given the lack of contextual information about the participants in my data in relation to the P, D, and R factors, it would be difficult to demonstrate how these affect the use of strategies in the data. For this reason I make some assumptions about these factors in the analysis section. Both of the speech and social acts of requests and refusals that I analyze later fall under the rubric of FTAs since they threaten the speaker's and the addressee's negative and positive faces.

Just as there are arguments against the universality claims of SAT, there are also critics of the universal claims of Brown and Levinson's politeness theories. The field of linguistic politeness has blossomed and come to full maturity in the last thirty years. Hundreds of works have been published in this area, including several books that have attempted to provide some cumulative review, critique, and revision of the state of the art in politeness theory (Eelen, 2001; Watts, 2003; Lakoff & Ide, 2005). Lakoff and Ide (ibid.) have grouped politeness studies into several categories: theoretical, descriptive, comparative, and historical. Since my study has more of a descriptive and comparative flavor and since none of the critiques of this theory have completely invalidated it (except for the contribution of Tannen, discussed later), I leave my review of Brown and Levinson's theory in its classic form at this point. I simply alert the reader to some of these additional works that have influenced my understanding and have a cursory relation to the present study: Trosborg (1995), Watts, Ide, and Ehlich (1992), Scollon and Scollon (1981), Hickey and Stewart (2005), and Land (2003). It is my hope that future signed language politeness studies will help shape the evolution of politeness theory.

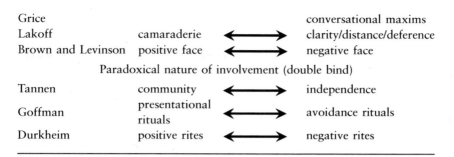

FIGURE 3. *Tannen's paradoxical nature of involvement: Community and independence.*

Tannen (1984 and class lecture) outlines a schema in which the power and solidarity—or positive and negative face dynamics—in the theoretical paradigms outlined earlier should not be viewed as a binary distinction or a polarity. Rather, she suggests that these dynamics can be summarized into the paradox of community and independence that always presents itself in conversational interaction (see figure 3).

In demonstrating that these theoretical paradigms are not opposite poles, Tannen states that:

> Human beings are always balancing the paradoxical fact that they are simultaneously individuals and social creatures. They need each other and yet they need to be separate. . . . That is why all communication is a double bind, as Scollon (1982, p. 344) points out, in the sense that participants receive and send a double and contradictory message, and a bonding that makes it difficult to leave the situation. Scollon observes, too, and this I think is crucial, that it is not that each message must service either one or the other need, but that any message must be a carefully concocted blend of the right amounts of deference and solidarity. (1984, p. 17)

The double bind principle is evident in many instances within the analyzed data. Since the terms "independence" and "community" are more lucid, I give preference to their use in this study over the terms "negative" and "positive" face, respectively. I refer to the notion of the independence-community paradoxical double bind in the analysis of the data.

Contextualization Cues

Gumperz (1982) proposes the development of a theory that explains both the way in which social knowledge is stored and retrieved in the mind and its interaction with grammatical and lexical knowledge during conversation. He briefly surveys and critiques the current theories that deal with contextual factors in interpretation, namely, ethnography of communication and discourse analysis. Bolstering what these theories downplay, he asserts that the suprasegmental and other surface features of speech are often crucial to identifying the meaning of an interaction. Contextualization is the process of matching the message meaning with these surface "cues." This process is based on culture-specific, learned co-occurrence expectations that enable us to associate styles of speaking with contextual presuppositions.

To illustrate what these cues might be in ASL, I return to the example of the directive FINISH. The following examples are the four interpretations that are based on surface features, including sign production and nonmanual signals:

Example 6. FINISH (one steady rotation movement)
　　　　　"Done"

Example 7. FINISH (small oscillating movements and contained laughter)
　　　　　"Stop making me laugh."

Example 8. FINISH (small oscillating movements, head nod, and flat expression)
　　　　　"That's enough, I'm warning you."

Example 9. FINISH (one snapping motion pointed at the addressee, as well as FE lip configuration)
　　　　　"Quit it!"

Attention to the contextualization cues in ASL is imperative for a correct interpretation of an utterance.

Gumperz (1992) builds upon his previous discussion of contextualization cues and conventions to investigate the implications of his approach for views of how language and linguistic and cultural variability enter into situated understanding. He asserts that participants signal the way that the interaction is to be framed (activity type) through various contextualization cues (including postural and gestural moves) that can be empirically verified. He succinctly states his basic assumption: "All understanding is framed understanding, that it ultimately rests on contingent inferences made with respect to presuppositions concerning the nature of the situation, what is to be accomplished and how to be accomplished. The term activity can be seen as a cover term to suggest what these presuppositions are" (pp. 43–44).

In the analysis I propose that several contextualization cues signal the activity type in the transcribed data. I argue that certain politeness markers that take the form of manual and nonmanual signs (NMS) help to frame the conversation as a face-threatening act within which certain inferences are drawn. Referring once more to Becker's (1995) deficiencies and exuberances in cross-linguistic contexts (e.g., the work of interpreters), I maintain that these subtle cues, which take different forms in other languages, may often be overlooked by the nonnative and thus present themselves as classic cases of deficiencies in understanding.

Related Signed Language and Interpreting Studies

The history of the ASL-using Deaf community has been in documented existence for more than 150 years. However, beginning with the work of William Stokoe in the late 1950s, ASL and other signed languages have only recently become recognized as legitimate natural human languages with their own structure, which both parallels and differs from various spoken-language structures. Likewise, the recognition of the community that uses ASL has been established in the literature. However, much of the linguistic research on ASL has focused more on its syntax, phonology, morphology, and so on and less on sociolinguistics and pragmatics.

At the present time, much of the literature on signed language pragmatics focuses on the use of eye gaze (Mather, 1996) and turn-taking behavior (Baker & Padden, 1978). Celo (1996) investigated the pragmatic and syntactic markers that indicate the signer's interrogative intention in Italian Sign Language (LIS). Although Celo briefly mentions the potential for yes/no questions to imply an imperative intention (p. 141), he does not explicitly state whether this occurs in LIS and whether the interrogative markers differ if the intention is an imperative one.

In order to outline the conventions of politeness and etiquette of conversations in ASL, Hall (1989) conducted an ethnography of communication study in a Deaf club. She posits two underlying social attitudes in the politeness conventions of ASL: One should facilitate communication, and one should promote unity among Deaf people. Hall further states that:

> One basic principle of etiquette seems to be clear despite its complex manifestations: one should always act in a way that facilitates communication and access to information. . . . This basic rule also explains why some behavior that is rude among hearing people, blunt

speech or telling a secret, is not rude among the Deaf. Another underlying principle of verbal politeness suggests that people must act in a way that will promote unity among the Deaf. . . . Maintaining unity is related to the principle of facilitating communication because sharing information and keeping the lines of communication open are also ways of promoting group unity.

Although Hall's generalized principles are the very thing that I am arguing against, they lend insight into the overall targeting of strategies within some ASL conversations. Both principles seem to be related to the strategies of camaraderie, community, and solidarity. What is lacking in her discussion is the interplay between these strategies and the independence (negative face) needs of Deaf speakers and hearers—in other words, the paradoxical double bind of human communication discussed earlier.

Hoza (1999) expands the model and metaphor of the role of the signed language interpreter to include considerations of interactional sociolinguistics and politeness strategies. In cross-cultural communication between Deaf and hearing people, conflicts of unconscious politeness approaches (negative vs. positive vs. a mix of the two) often occur. Interpreters should expand their role to include mediation between conflicting politeness needs. Within the scenarios that Hoza uses to illustrate these conflicts and in the pursuant analysis, he alludes to the tendency of Deaf speakers to use directness in positive politeness (emphasizing community) and negative politeness (emphasizing independence and its concomitant indirectness), which the hearing interlocutor expects. Even though Hoza's focus is on typical cross-cultural conflicts, he does not assume that Deaf individuals always use negative politeness, and he provides insight into the relativity of politeness; that is, for Deaf individuals, directness in positive politeness is just that—polite.

Pietrosemoli (2001) has conducted another study that focuses on the cross-cultural conflicts of politeness between hearing and Deaf communities in Venezuela. The conflict under study concerns the fact that Deaf Venezuelans take a positive politeness approach by borrowing or code-switching to certain "cultural sign" gestures that the mainstream hearing community uses. She proposes that, because Deaf Venezuelans do not have access to spoken Spanish, they are not aware of the taboo nature of these cultural sign gestures. Rather than effecting positive politeness, the use of these taboo gestures constitutes an on-record, bald, face-threatening act for the hearing person; thus a negative conflict arises and perpetuates due to the underlying politeness dynamics. According to Pietrosemoli's study, it appears that Venezuelans also have a Deaf-as-direct stereotype, but its basis is different from that of its counterpart in the United States.

Mindess (1999) argues that directness is more polite in American Deaf culture. She cites Katriel (1986), who contends that straight talk in the Sabra culture of Israel parallels the polite function of direct speech—or "straight talk" in American Deaf culture. Essentially, Katriel argues that the motivation for direct speech is a strong sense of personal sincerity and a desire to signal solidarity. This seems to reinforce Hall's principles. However, Katriel delimits the distribution of Israeli direct speech to the speech act categories of speaker-focused disclosures or other-focused advisements. The approach taken in both of these face-threatening acts is a bald one wherein the speaker's personal display of sincerity and integrity are protected (negative face). In displaying sincerity within the Israeli Sabra culture, one signals one's solidarity (thus positive face/community needs are also maintained) within a group that detests fanciful speech. Likewise, Mindess parallels these speech act categories and the underlying dynamics by highlighting the typical directness used in personal comments and the sharing of personal information in ASL discourse.

Tray (2005) identifies strategies for interpreting English innuendo (a type of indirectness) into ASL. The ASL Shakespeare Project (2006) also speaks to the challenges and strategies used in translating/interpreting innuendo in an ASL performance of Shakespeare's *Twelfth Night*. Clearly more research is needed on direct and indirect speech within the American Deaf culture not only from a descriptive perspective but also from a comparative/cross-cultural perspective. In conducting research, one must bear in mind the distribution of direct and indirect speech in relation to specific speech acts or social activities, the potential for threat to face needs, and the double bind of human communication.

The Relativity and Benefits of Indirectness

Tannen (1994) has demonstrated the relativity of the linguistic strategies of directness and indirectness. She argues against the idea that indirectness is exclusively used to express deference or defense by those in lower positions of power (i.e., women). She posits the existence of payoffs in both defensiveness (i.e., you cover yourself if the other rejects) and rapport (i.e., the satisfaction of understanding without having to say something directly). Tannen's research in comparing indirect and direct interpretations by American, Greek, and Greek American men and women supports the relativity view: "I found that whereas American women were more likely to take an indirect interpretation of a sample conversation, Greek men were as likely as Greek women, and more likely than American men or women, to take an indirect interpretation. Greek men, of course, are not less powerful vis-à-vis women than American men" (p. 34). She further cites the work of Keenan (1974), which shows that Malagasy speakers on the island of Madagascar consider women as direct and men as indirect. This contrasts with the view of women's style in the United States.

METHODOLOGICAL ISSUES

In this section I describe some of the problems encountered in collecting natural data and several alternative approaches to studying speech acts cross-culturally. I provide a review and criticism of one study that used a written English discourse completion test with Deaf students. I then discuss the specific methodology used in this study.

Naturalness Issue

Some debate has arisen in the literature regarding the best methodology for collecting data for sociolinguistic analysis. Particular to this study are the data of speech acts and conversational style. Regardless of approaches, there will always be what has been termed the "observer's paradox" (Labov, 1972); that is, the mere presence of a researcher affects the naturalness of the situation (see Lucas & Valli, 1989 for a detailed discussion). Although participant observation may yield the most natural ethnographic data, attempting to study a particular speech act (requests and refusals in this case) or phenomenon (direct and indirect conversation) can be problematic since it may take years to collect the data in question. Conducting a series of ethnographic interviews may be more productive but less natural and may not capture native speakers' tacit knowledge. Compounding the difficultly of presence is the need to record the data in order to analyze subtle linguistic and communicative behavior. The additional presence of an audiotape recorder further detracts from the naturalness of the situation. The use of video equipment, which is necessary in signed language research, poses even more problems with regard to naturalness. Although a perfectly natural situation is impossible to achieve in ethical data collection, the researcher can take certain measures to increase the relative naturalness of the situation.

Cross-Cultural Speech Act Realization Project (CCSARP)

To collect a large corpus of data on speech acts for cross-cultural comparison, several researchers (Blum-Kulka, House, & Kasper, 1989) have established the CCSARP, which uses written discourse completion tests (DCT) that have been translated into various languages. Written surveys such as these are not without their problems. The validity of this approach has been addressed in the literature (Wolfson, Marmor, & Jones, 1989). Beebe and Cummings (1996) have found no significant difference in a comparison of refusal data collected through "natural" phone conversation and written discourse completion tests. One of the benefits of using DCTs is that the CCSARP has been able to collect a great deal of data that have yielded much information in the comparisons of languages.

Following the DCT model, Keenan (1993) has elicited written English data of Deaf students' apologies. Results of the study show that both word choice and word order give a routinized feel to the apologies, which she attributes in part to influences from ASL. Keenan also ascribes the observed flavor of bluntness of the responses to the students' reduced control of English.

In a critique of this study Keenan mentions the efforts of examining apologies cross-linguistically and cross-culturally although she does not appear to see the value of conducting a similar study using Deaf students' native or primary language—ASL. It would seem that once a baseline understanding of ASL apology strategies was established, influences in written English apologies could then be more clearly delineated. The bluntness she attributes to reduced control of English could additionally have roots in a different cultural understanding of directness and indirectness.

In general, one of the greatest limitations of written DCTs is their inability to capture the Gumperzian contextualization cues that help frame the interpretation of utterances. This method limits one's ability to collect and analyze the use of intonation and nonverbal communication in spoken languages. Using written DCTs for signed languages is a moot point as there is no widely used writing system for ASL. Even if one used written English glosses, much would be missing in the way of nonmanual signs and body postures. The use of video technology in designing a DCT for signed languages (and spoken language, for that matter) holds better promise.

Methodologies in the Present Study

I use a two-pronged approach in collecting data for this study. The first consisted of a series of five informal ethnographic interviews that were guided by a questionnaire that I developed (see appendix A). Not all of the questions were answered in every interview. Presented in the next section is a thematic summary of the informants' reactions to the questions. The second approach involved using a segment from *Signing Naturally* (Lentz, Mikos, & Smith, 1992) titled "Language in Action: Asking to Borrow a Truck." This videotape was developed for ASL learners using a functional-notional approach to language instruction. The actors in the videotape are all native Deaf ASL signers. The segment that I analyze is a series of four situations in which a character named Anthony asks several Deaf people to borrow their truck to transport a dresser he recently bought from a furniture store. His first three attempts are met with refusals. His fourth try is successful—although conditional.

I selected this segment because of the face-threatening content: Anthony's requests threaten the face wants of those whom he has asked (maintaining their personal possessions, i.e., their independence, as well as a sense of community with Anthony). The refusals are a threat to Anthony's face wants (his personal need to transport his dresser—independence and power—and to maintain community and solidarity). (See appendix C for the full transcript and contextual information.)

Although the situations were contrived for the videotape, the actors assumed their real names in this segment, thus enhancing the validity of the data. While this segment focuses on requests and refusals, the video was not specifically intended for the analysis of direct-indirect speech and the mitigation of strategy phenomena. Additionally, I asked a Deaf native ASL signer to review this segment of the video for validity and feedback. She commented that, although the signers were slightly stilted, possibly due to being videotaped, the data accurately depict the way in which Deaf people interact in these specific speech acts. She also provided valuable feedback on the indirectness strategies in the videotaped data, which is incorporated in the analysis.

In this section I summarize the responses of the ethnographic inter-view participants under the headings of use of directness, cross-cultural contact, and use of indirectness.

Use of Directness

One of the most frequently cited examples of directness has to do with comments about appearance. These might include statements about weight loss or gain, change in hairstyle, clothes, aging, or just about anything that has changed since the last time the interlocutors saw each other. When asked about this form of directness, most of the interviewees replied that these sorts of statements would be directed only at acquain-tances. Some said that the practice harkened back to school days, when, as children, they would reunite after being apart for the summer. It was a welcoming back to the "family" that the schoolmates had become. They kept each other in line, and direct talk was a sign of community and sincerity (see the earlier discussion of Mindess's 1999 and Katriel's 1986 work). After going out into the world, some continued to use the direct style with hearing or Deaf people, while others used it only with Deaf people, and a few never used it again. One participant mentioned that Deaf people can be downright "raw" with each other in the club-room. Several of the interviewees mentioned that Deaf people who have been mainstreamed in a hearing school do not acquire the direct style of Deaf talk.

Cross-Cultural Contact

Many of the participants related that directness is most often an is-sue of conflict only in relation to situations involving hearing people. When communication options and time are limited, one must get to the point quickly. One Deaf interviewee commented that the use of into-nation is important in conveying politeness in English. She felt that Deaf people would never arrive at perfect English intonation. Additionally, to some hearing people the use of "gestures" is not seen as subtlety. At parties or the dinner table, stories always crop up about difficulties in communicating with hearing people. Because of some hearing people's lack of ASL skills, directness in cross-cultural contact is considered the only resort. Sharing stories about these conflicts builds a sense of community. Conversely, one of the Deaf participants mentioned that many hearing people do not know how to use the subtleties of ASL facial expression, which can also be considered a form of bluntness.

Use of Indirectness

Some of the interviewees related that, at times, ASL conversation indeed lends itself to indirectness, such as when one is trying to keep a surprise or relate something that might cause embarrassment. On several occasions after beginning this study, I observed the way in which criticism is offered at times. Rather than assert oneself as an individual authority, an interlocutor would emphasize community. This is evident in comments that are translated as "This is not the Deaf way" or "I've never seen Deaf people do that." Another participant pointed out that many Deaf people are bilingual and may use English-like politeness. One of the participants mentioned that using a less direct way of putting things when it comes to taboo topics is sometimes more appropriate. Here are some of the indirect terms that were compiled during the interview:

Example 10. MONTHLY   "menstrual period"
Example 11. NOW   "currently having a menstrual period"
Example 12. PRO-3 ONE #OF US   "he/she is gay/lesbian"
Example 13. BROTHER/SISTER   "he/she is gay/lesbian"
Example 14. GONE   "deceased"

Speakers who use these terms may experience the benefits of defensiveness—they can deny the taboo inference if it is considered offensive and at the same time establish rapport with the addressee through mutual sense making of private language. This lends support to Tannen's thesis of the relativity and benefits of indirectness strategies.

In summary, it appears that, although conversational ASL may employ directness, it is not without rules of use. This style appears to reflect the politeness of community and sincerity. When used in the correct frame of interaction (e.g., greetings, certain Deaf gatherings), directness is not considered rude or inconsiderate. Moreover, the use of a direct style appears to vary with the participants and the context of the conversation. Much of the stereotyping regarding the bluntness or directness of Deaf people may stem from cultural contact with hearing people. An indirect style of conversation is also prevalent and appropriate in certain frames of interaction. Indirectness in ASL appears to serve the purposes of both defensiveness and rapport.

Using the conventions in appendix B, I present relevant lines from the transcription of the data for analysis and discussion. The full transcription and description of context can be found in appendix C. Because it is not possible to transcribe in full detail every linguistic and non-linguistic behavior, I focus primarily on the manual signs and nonmanual grammatical markers. Additionally, I transcribe certain contextualization cues that seem to serve a politeness function, including mouth and head behavior. The Deaf native ASL signer mentioned previously pointed out that important signals are also conveyed by eye gaze, eye squint, and relative height of the shoulder. These cues are reserved for future research.

The video provides little information regarding Brown and Levinson's power (P), social distance (D), and ranking (R) of the imposition factors. We can assume that the actors are relatively equal in their power relationships. With regard to social distance, they all seem to be intimates or at least friends. The ranking of imposition appears to be quite high in light of the request to borrow a truck. The high imposition of the request and the desire to maintain intimate relations seem to create a need for indirectness and mitigating strategies for both speakers and hearers in these face-threatening acts.

My thematic analysis called for three passes through the data in order to focus on different aspects. The first pass dealt with the identification and description of contextualization cues or what I call politeness markers. The second and third pass singled out requestive and refusal strategies respectively. As part of this analysis, I provide an exegesis, or an interpretation of the forms and strategies in the data. I base these interpretations on the consistency of strategies seen in each videotaped situation, the textual coherence of the conversations, and the corroboration of comments from native informants who viewed the data.

Politeness Markers

The politeness discourse markers I identify and discuss are essential elements that the interlocutors added to the conversation in order to bid for cooperative behavior. These serve as contextualization cues to frame the utterances in polite terms. In this preliminary analysis, I have focused on four markers that serve this function. One is a manual sign/gesture, while the other three are nonmanual signs. Nonmanual signs (NMS) in

ASL have been classified as syntactic markers and lexical NMSs, which must be produced simultaneously with certain manual lexical signs and modifiers (adverbials). (See Bridges & Metzger, 1996 for a discussion of research on NMSs in ASL.) Because these markers are frequently used in concert with each other in the data, I first discuss each marker, its form, and general function. I then introduce excerpts from the data that show how the participants used these markers, either alone or in combination. Further research that incorporates all of these levels of cues is necessary.

Manual Item 5HPU

The manual item 5HPU (WELL, /well-what/, OPEN HAND, part:indef, and PU in other literature), which occurred frequently in the conversation, seems to serve an important politeness function. I use this gloss based on the phonetic production (5 handshape, palm up, made with one or two hands) because of the difficulty in finding an English equivalent with the same range and scope of meaning. In fact, its ambiguous semantics appear to serve its politeness function as an indirectness marker. Because of this, its status in the lexicon as a content word is called into question. Emmorey (1999) proposes that it may not be a sign at all but a gesture. Interestingly, its ambiguity in function and meaning may explain why it has received little attention in the literature despite its pervasiveness in ASL discourse. Because of its lack of attention, one might hypothesize that nonnative signers are not aware of the deficiency in their understanding of this cue and the role that it plays in downgrading face-threatening acts. This may provide more insight into the roots of the Deaf-as-direct stereotype.

Other studies treat the function of 5HPU in various ways. Winston and Monikowski (2003) and Van der Kooij, Crasborn, and Ros (2006) analyze it as an extralinguistic discourse marker that essentially functions to mark topic boundaries. Conlin, Hagstrom, and Neidle (2003) have classified 5HPU as a particle of indefiniteness (part:indef) and propose that it serves to express uncertainty and can have a domain-widening effect on the discourse.

In looking at the overall texture of the conversations in the data, I found that 5HPU appears to cluster around utterances in which the threat to the participants' face is the greatest and does not appear to be used only for indicating the speaker's propositional uncertainty. In the data, 5HPU serves several discourse functions, especially indirectness and positive politeness strategies. In the cases in which 5HPU may be interpreted as an indefinite particle, it seems more likely (given the context and the explanatory power of politeness dynamics) that the speaker is certain about the propositional content but is using 5HPU as a politeness marker. What may be uncertain to the speaker in these instances is how the interlocutor will accept the face-threatening act. Certainly more complete research is needed on the function of 5HPU in varied contexts and discourse genres. The following is a proposed typology of the way this marker is used in the transcribed data:

1. 5HPU "I'm done. Go ahead." "The floor is yours." "It's your turn."
2. 5HPU "Continue." "Keep talking."
3. 5HPU "What can I say?" "I don't know." "Well . . ."
4. 5HPU "I don't mean to impose." "I know this is a lot to ask."
5. 5HPU "What do you think?" "How does that sit with you?"
6. 5HPU "I accept." "I agree."

The implication of these meanings is based on the utterances before and after these markers, the additional nonmanual cues that frame its interpretation, and the general context and social activity at the time. If phonologically possible, the weak (nondominant) hand of 5HPU sometimes continues through the production of the next sign. This marker appears to be semantically and phonologically related to ASL verbs that denote conversational acts, including CONVERSE, INTERACT, SUGGEST, BRING-UP-TOPIC, CONVINCE, and INTRODUCE. It also appears to be related to the honorific pronoun.

Nonmanual Politeness Markers

The first nonmanual modifier I describe is the polite grimace (*pg*) (Bridges & Metzger, 1996 use the generic *IS*), which is made with a tight symmetrical smile (with or without teeth showing). It seems to add the meaning "Sorry, can't do it," "I don't think it can be done," or "I don't agree" and is sometimes used with a head shake (*neg*) nonmanual marker or a head/body teeter (*bt*), which are discussed later. This strategy appears to soften the manual NO sign in ASL. The use of the polite grimace is apparently an important marker in mitigating the face threat of an ASL utterance.

The second nonmanual marker that adds important politeness information is the polite pucker (*pp*), which is made with pursed lips (sometimes with the jaw lowered) and appears to mean "Not bad," "It's a good idea/possibility," "Why don't you/I try that?" or "You/I'll think about it." It is used when one does not want to state a strong opinion or suggestion or wants to avoid making a commitment to do something. The third nonmanual marker involves a side-to-side head movement or a shifting of one's weight from one foot to the other. I label this modifier body teeter (*bt*), which seems to impart a meaning similar to the politeness grimace (and is sometimes produced simultaneously with it): "I don't think this is going to work." Again, because these NMSs have received little attention in the literature, one could hypothesize that a nonnative speaker's deficiency in this area may lead to the conclusion that ASL lacks a sufficient repertoire of conventional indirectness and mitigating strategies and thus may be one source of the Deaf-as-direct stereotype.

Politeness Markers in the Data

I now turn to a discussion of how these markers and cues are used in my data (in the embedded excerpts, they are in boldface type). Beginning with the first situation, Anthony approaches Joe about using his truck. After explaining that he has bought a new dresser, he states that the store has told him that he has to haul it himself. He adds that his car is too small and then uses a combination of *bt* and 5HPU (numbers 3 and 4 in the typology proposed above) with the accompanying *pg* marker to send a prefacing cue before requesting the truck. Clearly, this cue gives the sense of "I don't mean to impose" or "I know this is a lot to ask." After giving this cue, Anthony uses an appealer, which is glossed DON'T-MIND, and a yes/no question construction to mitigate the face threat of the request (this strategy is discussed more fully in the request section):

Example 15.

	tm	**bt, pg**
Anthony:	POSS-1 CAR, SMALL. STUCK	**5HPU(3,4)**

head forward y/n-q		hn

DON'T-MIND PRO-1 BORROW POSS-3 #TRUCK.

"My car is too small. I'm out of luck. I know it's a lot to ask. Would you mind if I borrowed your truck?"

The combination of these strategies is decidedly indirect. The payoff of using this approach can be understood in terms of defensiveness and rapport. Anthony can deny the request or reap the benefit of rapport when Joe interprets his indirect request successfully.

After explaining that the truck is a company vehicle, Joe states that he is not permitted to loan it to anyone. He does not actually express the lexical NO in his refusal but uses 5HPU(5) with the weak hand con-

tinuing throughout his statement of regret—SORRY—produced with both
the nonmanual *neg* marker (head shake) and the polite grimace (example
16). Combined with these cues, this utterance can be interpreted to mean
"Sorry, I can't. I hope that's okay":

Example 16.

<u>**neg/pg**</u>

    Joe: **5**HPU(**5**) SORRY

Example 17.

    Anthony: **5HPU**(6) #OK PRO-1 TRY ASK OTHER **5HPU**(6) (shrug shoulder)
                "That's okay. I'll try to ask someone else."

Again a combination of indirect strategies is used. The threat to
Anthony's independence and community needs seems quelled by these
cues. This success of Joe's strategy seems ensured when Anthony responds with 5HPU(6) #OK . . . 5HPU(6) in an affirming way (example 17).
The use of these strategies appears to be conventionalized in the Deaf
style of talk and to promote self-protection and rapport. From these data
and at least in situations like these, indirectness strategies appear to be
preferred over direct strategies that emphasize integrity and sincerity.

In the next situation Anthony approaches Shane, who is on a bench
at a baseball game. Despite the time constraints of the situation (Shane
is waiting to bat), there is nevertheless enough time for indirectness strategies. Shane is not able to loan Anthony his truck because he has already
loaned it out. However, he seems obligated to offer an alternative. He
suggests that Anthony see Pat, who also has a truck. He adds the po-
tentially negative qualifier that her truck is old, which is accompanied
by 5HPU(5) in example 18. Anthony, at first resistant to this suggestion,
as indicated by *pg*, then uses the *pp* marker to show his openness (example 19). He continues to use *pp* in lines 21 and 23, indicating through
the use of this cue that he is willing to accept Shane's alternative:

Example 18.

<u>hn</u>

    Shane: **5HPU**(5) OLD **5HPU**(5)
          "It is old though."

Example 19.

<u>**pg pp**</u>

    Anthony: OLD! SO-SO
            "No, it's old? Well, that might not be too bad."

Example 20.

Shane: REALLY NOT-YET ENGINE-DROP STILL GOOD++ PRO-3 GO SEE++

5HPU(5)

"The motor isn't dead yet. It's still pretty good. Why don't you give it a try?"

Example 21.

<u>   pp   y/n-q   </u>

Anthony: 5HPU(6) SEE++ . . . PAT STILL LIVE NEAR P-A-R-K

"I might see about that. . . . Does Pat still live near the park?"

Example 22.

Shane: STAY-SAME++

"Yeah, the same place."

Example 23.

<u>   pp   </u>

Anthony: FINE PRO-1 GO   :

"Fine. I think I'll go."

In the midst of suggesting and accepting alternatives there seems to be tension with regard to the participants' community and independence needs. The use of the politeness markers gives recognition to these conflicting needs and helps facilitate the interaction. The concluding use of the *pp* marker in example 23 resolves the threat to each other's independence and community needs.

In the next segment Anthony takes Shane's suggestion and seeks out Pat, who shows her indirect resistance to loaning out the truck by using a combination of the *pg* and *bt* markers because of the distance Anthony must travel with it (example 24). She uses the *pp* marker along with the manual DON'T-MIND to show that she is willing to loan him the truck; however, her message seems conflicted since she counterbalances this with a very negative tone and a combination of descriptors both manual (OLD, TROUBLE, and SO-SO) and nonmanual *th* ("careless"; adverbial modifier). Finally, using the *pg* and *neg* markers, she says that she does not trust the truck. This is followed by 5HPU(5) (example 24). Anthony picks up on her indirect refusal and, utilizing the *pg* marker, declines to use it (example 25). He then attempts to make something positive out of the situation by stating that he will look elsewhere and employing the *pp* marker. Pat offers a statement of regret with the *pg* marker (example 26):

Example 24.

<u>pg/bt   pp/hn</u>

Pat: REALLY PRO-1 DON'T-MIND LOAN-OUT POSS-1 CAR BUT

                     <u>hn   th</u>   <u>pg/neg</u>

REALLY POSS-1 #TRUCK, OLD, TROUBLE++ AND ENGINE SO-SO.

<u>pg/neg</u>

PRO-1 NOT TRUST, 5HPU(5)

"I don't mind lending you my car but my truck is old and often gives us trouble, and the engine is not running great, I don't trust it."

Example 25.

<u>pg</u>

Anthony: REALLY++ PSHAW. PRO-1 BETTER NOT BORROW

                  <u>hn/pp</u>

PRO-1 GO LOOK OTHER

"It's really that bad? Forget it. I'd better not borrow it. I'll look somewhere else."

Example 26.

<u>pg</u>

Pat: SORRY

"I'm really sorry about that."

Attention to the use of politeness markers is crucial to understanding the indirectness strategies used in this segment. One could easily misinterpret the full use of indirectness and mitigation strategies if these cues were disregarded.

In the final segment, Anthony succeeds in borrowing Cinnie's and Lon's truck; however, the negotiation is not without hitches. When Anthony first approaches Cinnie, she—like Pat—expresses her willingness to let Anthony use her truck. However, she adds that the truck bed has an oily spot (which might stain Anthony's new dresser). She leaves it at that, punctuated with the use of 5HPU(5) and the *pp* marker (example 27). Cinnie's response may be interpreted as an indirect refusal that gives Anthony an opportunity to opt out because the truck is dirty. This ambiguity is further fostered by the use of *pp* and 5HPU(5). Anthony expresses mitigated resistance by the use of 5HPU(3) and the *pg* marker (example 28). Anthony's strategy here may be to indirectly establish Cinnie's true intentions by giving her a safe option to support his proposal to look elsewhere.

His decline is predicated on the condition that, if he is not able to find another truck, he will come back. However, she makes her intentions to loan the truck clearer by suggesting that he have a seat and wait until Lon comes back with the truck, which is punctuated again by the use of 5HPU(5) (example 29). Since Anthony's indirect test of Cinnie's ambiguous remarks leads to a satisfactory result, he accepts her insistence (example 30):

Example 27.

Cinnie: FINE++ #BUT IX (thumb) "points right" DIRTY
IX (thumb) "points right" BACK OIL CL:"spot".
BEFORE MOTOR PRO-1 CL:"put engine in bed, then take out".

<u>pp</u>
PRO-1 NOT-YET CLEAN 5HPU(5)
"That's fine, but the truck is dirty. There's an oil spill in the back from when we hauled an engine. It's not clean yet. What do you think?"

Example 28.

<u>pg</u>
Anthony: 5HPU(3) SEE TRY ASK OTHER PRO-3++
<u>cond</u>   <u>hn</u>   <u>pp</u>
SUPPOSE 5HPU(4) FAIL, PRO-1 USE POSS-3 #TRUCK 5HPU(4)
"Well, I'll see if I can borrow someone else's truck. If I can't find one, I'll be back to use your truck."

Example 29.

<u>pp</u>
Cinnie: FINE PSHAW WHY NOT SETTLE-DOWN WAIT L-O-N COME ANY TIME.
<u>pp</u>
PRO-3 HAVE #TRUCK PRO-3 5HPU(5)
"Come on, why don't you stick around. Lon will be back at any minute. He will have the truck."

Example 30.

Anthony: 5HPU(6) FINE (sits down)
"All right."

Because of Cinnie's ambiguous use of 5HPU(5) and the *pp* marker in example 27 and Anthony's indirect test in example 28, we might conclude that, in interactions such as these, the use of these markers leads to an ambiguous interpretation, which is useful in indirectness strategies.

The second hitch in this situation occurs when Lon expresses his willingness to loan Anthony the truck (example 31) with the use of *pp* and 5HPU (functions 4 and 6). Here these cues fulfill several functions. First, they indicate that, despite the imposition to his independence, Lon is willing to lend the truck for the sake of community. The cues are also a sign that the loan comes with a condition: a request to fill the gas tank—which would be a threat to Anthony's independence. Lon asks Anthony whether he will fill it up, and Anthony eagerly accepts this condition (example 32). Lon then reconfirms their agreement by the standalone use of 5HPU(6) (example 33):

Example 31.

> pp/hn
> Lon: 5HPU(6) FINE 5HPU(4) UNDERSTAND #GAS ALMOST RUN-OUT ON-"E."
> DON'T-MIND GAS FULL
> "That's fine. The only thing is that it's almost out of gas it's on 'e.' Would you mind filling it up?"

Example 32.

> hn
> Anthony: 5HPU(6) PSHAW #OK++ PRO-1
> "Of course, I'll do it."

Example 33.

> hn
> Lon: 5HPU(6)
> "All right then."

With data such as examples 31–33 it seems that natural interaction is often characterized by competing social needs between the participants; the use of politeness markers is important in the negotiation and fulfillment of these needs.

To review, the politeness markers in the data serve important functions. They provide some ambiguity, indirectness, or mitigation in the strategy they accompany (requesting or refusing) and also indicate that the speaker is aware of the threat to the independence or community needs of either the speaker or the hearer. Although in some social and speech acts, a more direct style may be used (in support of solidarity, signaled by integrity and sincerity), in the preceding data the strategies used were indirect or at least mitigated. However, if one were to ignore the politeness cues, one might arrive at a more direct interpretation. Deficiencies in understanding these cues may contribute to the Deaf-as-direct stereotype that this study argues against.

REQUESTS

Requests are considered face-threatening acts. This speech activity can be taken by the hearer as a threat to negative face—a desire for power or independence. Hearers can also consider it a threat to their positive face wants—a desire for solidarity or community. In the data I analyzed, all of the requestive actions were performed on record with redressive action (i.e., using mitigating and indirectness strategies), although one could also interpret the on-record preparator strategy (discussed later) as an off-record approach. The mitigating face-threatening strategies varied in their use of positive and negative politeness. Using the CCSARP coding manual (Blum-Kulka et al., 1989) as a general guide to analyzing the requestive action, I begin by dividing the requestive actions found in each of the four situations into supportive moves and the head move.

Supportive Moves

A supportive move is an utterance that is external to the request and that modifies the impact of the head move and its threat to face by providing either aggravating or mitigating strategies. All of the supportive moves in the data used mitigating strategies. These supportive moves are divided into preposed (positioned before the head act) and postposed (positioned after the head act).

PREPOSED MITIGATING SUPPORTIVE MOVES
Preparator.
In using the strategy of preparator, the speaker prepares the hearer for the forthcoming request by asking the hearer about the potential ability to carry out the request. This is done without actually expressing the content of the request. Anthony uses this strategy by asking Joe about his possession of a truck (example 34):

Example 34.

<u>y/n-q</u>   <u>hn</u>
PRO-1 STILL HAVE #TRUCK PRO-1
"Do you still have a truck?"

This preparator allows Anthony to learn whether Joe has the potential to fulfill his request. Alternately, this approach could also be an off-record move since one could interpret it as an indirect request. Given its position in the sequence of the interaction, it seems more likely to be a preparator.

Grounder.

Using a grounder mitigating strategy allows the speaker to give reasons, explanations, or justifications for a request. Anthony uses grounders in each requestive action. In all of these moves, he explains that he has just bought a dresser. The grounder in example 35 makes explicit that the store will not deliver the dresser:

Example 35.
tm_____   tm_____

PRO-1 BUY. PRO-1 BRING. STORE, ORDER-ME SELF BRING. POSS-1 CAR, SMALL. STUCK
"I bought it, but the store told me that I had to haul it myself. My car is too small. I'm out of luck."

The rest of the grounders in the transcript state that he needs to transport it himself (examples 36–38) and therefore needs a truck. Examples 36 and 37 include the explanation that his car is too small:

Example 36.
> CL:"dresser," PRO-1 BUY. PRO-1 MUST BRING HOME.
> PRO-1 CAR, 5HPU(4), TOO-SMALL
> "I brought a dresser, and now I must haul it home. My car is too small."

Example 37.
> PRO-1 BUY CL:"dresser." PRO-1 NEED #TRUCK BRING HOME
> "I bought a dresser, but I need a truck to bring it home."

Example 38.
5HPU(4), PRO-1 BUY NEW CL:"dresser," BEAUTIFUL, 5HPU(4), PRO-1 NEED PICK-UP
BRING HOME, 5HPU(4), PRO-1 LOOK++ #TRUCK, 5HPU(4)
"I bought a beautiful new dresser and need to haul it home. I've been looking for a truck."

Example 39, which is from the fourth and final situation, adds the information that he has already asked around without luck and was told to ask Lon:

Example 39.

> PRO-1 LOOK #TRUCK. YESTERDAY PRO-1 BUY CL:"dresser"
> PRO-1 ASK-AROUND #TRUCK NONE++ 5HPU(4).
> PRO-1 TOLD-ME WHY NOT PRO-1 ASK-TO-Lon
> "I've been looking for a truck because I bought a dresser
> yesterday. I've been asking around and haven't had any
> luck. She told me to ask you."

All of these examples are grounders because they provide explanations (in varying degrees) of the reason for the upcoming request.

Postposed Mitigating Supportive Move

IMPOSITION MINIMIZERS AND PROMISES OF REWARD
Imposition minimizer strategies reduce the burden that the request places on the hearer. In example 40 Anthony minimizes his request by promising to bringing the truck back the next day:

Example 40.

> head forward   y/n-q _____   hn _____
> DON'T-MIND PRO-1 LOAN-TO-ME POSS-3 #TRUCK.
> PRO-1 #BACK TOMORROW, 5HPU(4)
> "Do you mind if I borrow your truck? I'll bring it back
> tomorrow."

In example 41 Anthony minimizes the number of miles he will be putting on Pat's truck. When she disagrees that he lives close by (suggesting that he lives thirty miles away), he responds that it is more like twenty miles. This minimization may be a strategy not only to reduce the imposition placed on Pat but also to shore up his negative face needs by explaining that his estimation of "close" is reasonable:

Example 41.

	y/n-q _____
Anthony:	5HPU(4) ALL RIGHT PRO-1 USE PRO-3 #TRUCK 5HPU
	"Is it all right if I use your truck?"
Pat:	PRO-3 LIVE WHERE
	"Where do you live?"
Anthony:	REALLY SHORT-DISTANCE IX"LEFT" BERKELEY 5HPU(5)
	"It's really close, in Berkeley."

bt/neg _____

> Pat: "shakes head" NOT SHORT-DISTANCE. NOSE-FAR! 30 M-I-L-E-S WOW
> "I don't think it's close. It's very far. About thirty miles."

Anthony: NAW, 20 NOT BAD 5HPU
"Nah, it's twenty, not too bad."

In example 42 Anthony's acceptance of Lon's conditional agreement results in Anthony's commitment to fill the gas tank—in effect a promise of reward. He further reduces the imposition by committing to a particular time for picking up the truck:

Example 42.

 <u>y/n-q</u> _____

Anthony: DON'T-MIND PRO-1 LOAN-TO-ME POSS-3 #TRUCK
"Do you mind if I borrow your truck?"

Lon: 5HPU(6) FINE 5HPU(4) UNDERSTAND #GAS ALMOST RUN-OUT
ON-"E". DON'T-MIND GAS FULL
"That's fine. The only thing is that it's almost out of gas
it's on 'e'. Would you mind filling it up?"

 <u>hn</u>

Anthony: 5HPU(6) PSHAW #OK++ PRO-1
"Of course, I'll do it."

 <u>hn</u>

Lon: 5HPU(6)
"All right then."

Anthony: AFTERNOON TIME THREE-O'CLOCK
"How about today at three?"

Lon: DOESN'T-MATTER NOT PLAN USE ALL-DAY NOT. THINK^SELF
ANY TIME 5HPU(5)
"It doesn't matter. I'm not planning to use it all day. It's up
to you. Any time will be fine."

Anthony: 5HPU(6) POW 5HPU(6) FINE 5HPU(6) PRO-1 TIME THREE-
O'CLOCK, #OK (Anthony gets up)
"Great! Fine, I'll come at three. Okay."

In all three of these examples of imposition minimizers, Anthony attempts to reduce the burden that his request may have on his hearers. This mitigation strategy appears to be conventionalized within Deaf talk.

HEAD ACT

The head act is the minimal unit that can realize a request; it is the core of the request sequence. In the following sections I list the various strategies used in performing the requestive act. These include preparatory conditions and downgraders.

Preparatory Condition: Yes/No Question

This strategy is related to the Searlian felicity conditions outlined previously. An utterance is seen as fulfilling this condition if it makes reference to the feasibility of the request, typically of ability, willingness, or possibility, as conventionalized in the given language. Frequently the speaker will question rather than state the presence of the chosen preparatory condition. This is true in example 43, which occurred in situation two of the transcript. Here Anthony uses the yes/no question construction to conventionally make the request:

Example 43. CAN PRO-1 USE POSS-3 #TRUCK
"Can I use your truck?"

This is considered an indirect speech act because the locutionary structure of this utterance is a yes/no question regarding the hearer's ability. However, the illocutionary force is one of request. This appears to be a conventionalized form of indirect request in ASL.

Phrasal and Lexical Downgraders: Yes/No Questions and Appealers

Phrasal and lexical downgraders serve as optional additions to soften the potential threat to the interlocutors' face needs. They modify the head act internally through specific lexical and phrasal choices. The following examples use a combination of the yes/no question construction and specific lexical appealers. Appealers are elements that speakers use to appeal to the hearer's benevolent understanding. They function to elicit a signal from the hearer. The appealers DON'T-MIND, ALL RIGHT, and #OK (highlighted in boldface type) are common in ASL requests:

Example 44.

bt pg   head forward y/n-q   hn
5HPU(4) **DON'T-MIND** PRO-1 BORROW POSS-3 #TRUCK
"Would you mind if I borrowed your truck?"

Example 45.

y/n-q
5HPU(4) **ALL RIGHT** PRO-1 USE PRO-3 #TRUCK 5HPU(4)
"Would it be all right if I use your truck? It's up to you."

Example 46.

> y/n-q
> 5HPU(4) #OK PRO-1 USE POSS-3 #TRUCK
> "Is it okay if I use your truck?"

The downgraders that Anthony uses in these examples appear to be conventional mitigating strategies that reduce the threat to his hearers. At the same time, he preserves his own needs for independence and community.

REFUSALS

Refusals can also be considered face-threatening acts. In refusing, speakers assert their own negative face (independence) wants over those of the hearer, who has just made a request. In turn, the positive face wants of the hearer and the speaker are also at odds (i.e., they constitute a threat to their sense of community). In light of this double threat, one can commit the act either baldly or redressively. None of the speakers' refusal acts in the data took a direct or bald approach (adhering to the Grician maxims). No one actually said "no." Everyone used some form of redressive action to mitigate the threat to both participants' face wants. The strategies in the data were identified using Beebe's and Cummings's (1996) categories. These strategies are shown in the following examples, with supporting lines from the transcripts.

Statements of Regret

All of the speakers who refused Anthony's request provided a statement of regret rather than stating "no" explicitly (examples 47–50). In addition to the lexical SORRY, all of the refusing speakers use the nonmanual polite grimace (*pg*):

Example 47.

> neg/pg
> Joe: 5HPU(5) SORRY

Example 48.

> pg
> Pat: SORRY

Example 49.

> neg/pg
> Shane: SORRY++

Example 50.

Shane: PRO-1 MUST GO. SORRY NONE# TRUCK, 5HPU(3/5)

Based on these data, to perform a refusal act directly may be a considerable threat to the speaker's and hearer's face wants. Use of the *pg* nonmanual marker seems to have important politeness value in mitigating the force of the refusal.

Excuses, Reasons, Explanations, and Statements of Alternative

Another possible redressive action is to express an excuse or provide an alternative. This strategy was used by Shane, who explains that his brother will have the truck for a week. After pausing to think, he suggests that Anthony go see Pat about borrowing her truck:

Example 51.

```
                            y/n-q_____
  Shane:  . . . PRO-1 THINK. PRO-3 KNOW NS-PAT
          ". . . Let me think, do you know Pat?"
          hn___
Anthony:  P-A-T
          "You mean Pat?"
                       hn_____
  Shane:  THAT! PRO-3 HAVE #TRUCK PRO-3
          "Yes, that's her. She has a truck."
Anthony:  5HPU(2)
          "Oh yeah?"
                   hn___
  Shane:  5HPU(5) OLD 5HPU(5)
          "It's old, though."
          pg____pp_____
Anthony:  OLD! SO-SO
          "No, it's old? Well, that might not be too bad."
  Shane:  REALLY NOT-YET ENGINE-DROP. STILL GOOD++
          PRO-3 GO SEE++ 5HPU(5)
          "It isn't dead yet. It's still pretty good. Why don't you give it
          a try?"
```

Shane's excuse is that his truck is not available because his brother is borrowing it for a week. He then attempts to shore up his positive face wants by offering Anthony an alternate plan.

Statements of Principle

As a mitigating strategy, Joe expresses a statement of principle in situation one. His company simply does not allow him to lend the truck to anyone. By shifting the burden onto the company's policy, he reduces the threat that the refusal poses to Anthony's needs of independence while maintaining the sense of community between Joe and Anthony:

Example 52.

<pre>
                tm_____
Joe: IX"points behind to garage" #TRUCK, IX"points to truck"
       REALLY POSS-3 #CO "nods head"
                             neg_____
       IX"points to company" NOT PERMIT LOAN-TO-OTHERS
</pre>
"My truck really belongs to the company. They don't allow outside people to borrow it."

The strategy of stating a principle is used in ASL conversations to reduce the threat to face.

Attempts to Dissuade Interlocutor: Statements of Negative Consequences

Pat uses the strategy of dissuasion by making clear the possible negative consequences. She asks how far Anthony needs to drive, then explains that the engine might give out because of its age and history of breaking down. Anthony senses her indirect refusal tactic and declines to use the truck:

Example 53.

<pre>
     Pat: PRO-3 LIVE WHERE
           "Where do you live?"
Anthony: REALLY SHORT-DISTANCE IX"left" BERKELEY 5HPU(5)
           "It's really close. In Berkeley."
           neg_____
     Pat: NOT SHORT-DISTANCE. NOSE-FAR! 30 M-I-L-E-S WOW
           "I don't think it's close. It's very far. About 30 miles."
Anthony: NAW, 20 NOT BAD 5HPU(5)
           "Nah, it's 20, not too bad."
           pg/ht_____
     Pat: REALLY PRO-1 DON'T-MIND LOAN-OUT POSS-1 CAR BUT REALLY
           hn___ th_____ pg____
           POSS-1 #TRUCK, OLD, TROUBLE+, AND ENGINE SO-SO.
</pre>

<pre><u>neg/pg</u></pre>

PRO-1 NOT TRUST 5HPU

"I don't mind lending you my car, but my truck is old and often gives us trouble, and the engine is not running great. I don't trust it."

<pre><u>pg</u></pre>

Anthony: REALLY++ PSHAW. PRO-1 BETTER NOT LOAN-TO-ME.

<pre><u>hn/pp</u></pre>

PRO-1 GO LOOK OTHER.

"It's really that bad? Forget it, I'd better not borrow it. I'll look somewhere else."

Because Anthony withdraws his request, equilibrium is restored with respect to both participants' need for independence and community. The use of dissuasion as a mitigating strategy is useful in formulating refusals in ASL conversations.

Setting Conditions for Future Acceptance

The strategy of setting a condition for future acceptance occurred in one of the ASL conversations in the data. In example 54 Cinnie's refusal is more of a put-off. She appears to be willing to lend her truck but adds that it is dirty and may not be in an acceptable condition to be used. Anthony seems to interpret this as a refusal and states that he will look elsewhere. Cinnie then suggests that he wait until Lon comes back with the truck. Anthony accepts this condition and waits for Lon:

Example 54.

Cinnie: FINE++ #BUT IX (thumb) "points right" DIRTY.

IX (thumb) "points right" BACK OIL CL:"spot."

BEFORE MOTOR PRO-1 CL:"put engine in bed, then take out".

<pre>   <u>pp</u></pre>

PRO-1 NOT-YET CLEAN 5HPU(5)

"That's fine, but the truck is dirty. There's an oil spill in the back from when we hauled an engine. It's not clean yet. What do you think?"

<pre><u>pg</u></pre>

Anthony: 5HPU(3) SEE TRY ASK OTHER PRO-3++.

<pre><u>cond</u>   <u>hn</u></pre>

SUPPOSE 5HPU(4) FAIL PRO-1 USE POSS-3 #TRUCK 5HPU(4)

"Well, I'll see if I can borrow someone else's truck. If I can't find one, I'll be back to use your truck."

Cinnie: FINE PSHAW WHY NOT SETTLE-DOWN WAIT L-O-N COME ANY TIME. PRO-3 HAVE #TRUCK PRO-3 5HPU(5)
"Come on, why don't you stick around? Lon will be back at any minute. He will have the truck."

Anthony: 5HPU(6) FINE (sits down)
"All right."

This negotiation appears to satisfy the needs of both people. Anthony's request is not immediately fulfilled, but he is willing to wait in order to have his needs for both independence and community satisfied. Cinnie's face wants are also satisfied. The strategy of setting a condition for future acceptance is an option for ASL signers in performing refusals.

Adjuncts to Refusal

Adjuncts to refusals are attempts to reestablish a sense of positive face despite the standoff produced by the participants' negative face wants. This can take the form of a statement of empathy, such as Joe's use of GOOD #LUCK from the data:

Example 55.   brow raise/hn
                 GOOD #LUCK!
                 "Good luck!"

Joe seeks a recommitment to community and solidarity through his statement in example 55.

Anthony downplays the impact that the refusals have on his need for independence. Lexical items such as PSHAW (example 57) mitigate the threats to positive face or community that the refusal has posed. Another confirmation of the need to reestablish community is the use of leave-taking items that also serve as in-group identity markers, such as the use of THUMB-UP (examples 57 and 58). These have no straightforward equivalent in English but roughly mean "take care." Pat and Anthony use the sign ILY, which also does not have a straightforward equivalent in English (although it has been translated "I love you") and can be considered another in-group identity sign used to show solidarity and community among Deaf people:

Example 56.
Shane: PRO-1 MUST GO. SORRY NONE #TRUCK 5HPU(5)
         "I must go. Sorry I didn't have the truck. You know how it is."

Example 57.
  Anthony: PSHAW, NO PROBLEM (backs up) PSHAW, THUMB-UP (walks away)
             "That's all right, no problem. Take care."
Example 58.
  Shane: THUMB-UP (walks away)
             "Take care."

The use of refusal adjuncts such as these is an important mitigating strategy in restoring the sense of community between participants in an ASL interaction that involves face-threatening acts.

CONCLUSIONS

My analysis and supporting data demonstrate that certain speech activities (e.g., requests and refusals) in ASL conversation lend themselves to the use of conventional indirectness and mitigating strategies. In requests, these include strategies for prepositioned and postpositioned mitigating supportive moves including preparators, grounders, imposition minimizers, and promises of rewards. Within the head requestive act, ASL signers can use indirect yes/no questions and lexical appealers such as DON'T-MIND, ALL RIGHT, and #OK. In requests, ASL signers use statements of regret, excuses, reasons, explanations, alternatives, principles, and negative consequences, as well as conditions for future acceptance. Adjuncts to refusals include the lexical signs PSHAW, THUMBS-UP, and ILY.

Additionally, this study discusses the identification of mitigating gestural and facial expression politeness markers or cues that are essential to framing and interpreting politeness in ASL conversation. In the data the manual 5HPU marker is clustered around phrases and signs that are face threatening. The data also revealed several nonmanual cues that serve as mitigating strategies in face-threatening acts. These include the polite grimace (*pg*), polite pucker (*pp*), and body teeter (*bt*).

Based on this evidence, the style of talk used by the Deaf participants is decidedly indirect rather than direct. The motivations behind the use of indirectness strategies in ASL follow metacommunication dynamics in human interaction such as the notions of face and the double bind paradox. Indirectness in ASL serves the purposes of both defensiveness and rapport.

To repeat the findings from the ethnographic interview data, although a direct style of conversation occurs in ASL, it reflects the politeness of solidarity through the signaling of sincerity. When used in the correct frame of interaction (e.g., greetings, certain Deaf gatherings), directness is not taken as rudeness or a lack of consideration. The direct style also varies according to the participants in the conversation and the context at hand. The source of much of the stereotyping regarding the bluntness or directness of Deaf people may stem from cultural contact with hearing people. An indirect style of conversation is also prevalent and appropriate in certain frames of interaction.

This preliminary work corroborates my original hypothesis: The Deaf-as-blunt stereotype is too broad and reductive given the complexities of the data. A possible source of this stereotype is cross-cultural contact. As Hoza (1999) suggests, professional interpreters, who constantly deal with cross-cultural contact, must broaden their role to include politeness mediation. Part of this role involves dealing with Becker's deficiencies and exuberances of meaning when working between the source and target languages. This includes increasing our microlevel understanding of easily overlooked, yet important cues such as the ones this study identifies. It also includes developing a macrolevel understanding of the politeness dynamics within each language community and also preparing oneself for typical conflicts of politeness needs that may arise in cross-cultural and cross-linguistic contact.

Much work remains to be done to remedy these deficiencies not only on an individual level but also in interpreting research and pedagogy. Some headway is being made in increasing our understanding of the interpretation of narrative and monologic discourse. However, more research and curricula need to be developed in the area of interpreting conversational, dialogic interaction in various speech act and social settings (including face-threatening acts), taking into consideration sociolinguistic variables including economic status, gender, sexual orientation, race, age, and regional dialect, as well as Brown and Levinson's (1987) factors of power, social distance, and relative imposition. This takes on added importance as more interpreters enter the field who are not native ASL signers and lack adequate exposure to the way in which ASL is used in these various settings and acts.[5] Given the length of time it takes to learn ASL at an adequate level for interpreting, as well as the limited opportunities for contact with native signers outside of the classroom (Jacobs, 1996), this is truly a tremendous challenge. Nevertheless, it is crucial in view of the fact that we are seeing an increase in conversational interpreting with the recent advent and tremendous growth of video relay services, which require that interpreter practitioners have high-level skills in interpreting throughout a full range of speech acts and a firm grasp of the styles and strategies in English and ASL conversation.

NOTES

1. This chapter is a revision of an unpublished master's degree capstone research paper originally submitted to the faculty of the Linguistics Department of Gallaudet University in May 1999.

2. I would like to acknowledge and thank Ceil Lucas for advising me and supporting my research efforts, as well as Carolyn Woosley, M. J. Bienvenu, Ben Bahan, and Susan Mather for their valuable insights. I am grateful to Deborah Tannen, Jack Hoza, Melanie Metzger, and Lisa Bordone Roush for their helpful comments. Any errors are attributable to me alone.

3. The reverse stereotype—that hearing people are unduly vague—also exists.

4. Indirect or off-record utterances can be strictly defined as cases in which the syntactic form does not match the illocutionary force and the speaker's intent is ambiguous (see discussion under Indirect Speech Acts). On-record, positive politeness utterances that are mitigated, on the other hand, have a clearer intent but are mitigated via certain markers and strategies. Since both indirectness and mitigation are a move away from doing an FTA directly or baldly, I use the phrase "indirectness/indirectness strategies" as a superset wherein mitigation strategies are subsumed.

5. Furthermore, native signers of ASL who are interpreters-in-training may also need exposure and explicit instruction in English conversation in various speech acts and social settings.

REFERENCES

ASL Shakespeare Project. 2006. http://www.aslshakespeare.com.

Austin, J. L. (1962). *How to do things with words.* Oxford, UK: Clarendon.

Bach, K., & Harnish, R. M. (1979). *Linguistic communication and speech acts.* Cambridge, MA: MIT Press.

Baker, C., & Padden, C. (1978). Focusing on the nonmanual components of American Sign Language. In P. Siple (Ed.), *Understanding language through sign language research* (pp. 27–57). New York: Academic Press.

Becker, A. L. (1995). *Beyond translation: Essays in modern philology.* Ann Arbor: University of Michigan Press.

Beebe, L. M., & Cummings, M. (1996). Natural speech act data versus written questionnaire data: How data collection method affects speech act performance. In S. M. Gass & J. Neu (Eds.), *Speech acts across cultures:*

Challenges to communication in a second language (pp. 65–88). Berlin: Mouton de Gruyter.

Blum-Kulka, S. (1989). Playing it safe: The role of conventionality in indirectness. In S. Blum-Kulka, J. House, & G. Kasper (Eds.,), *Cross-cultural pragmatics: Requests and apologies* (pp. 37–70). Norwood, NJ: Ablex.

Blum-Kulka, S., House, J., & Kasper, G. (1989). Investigating cross-cultural pragmatics: An introductory overview. In S. Blum-Kulka, J. House, & G. Kasper (Eds.), *Cross-cultural pragmatics: Requests and apologies* (pp. 1–34). Norwood, NJ: Ablex.

Bridges, B., & Metzger, M. (1996). *Deaf tend your: Non-manual signals in American Sign Language*. Silver Spring, MD: Calliope.

Brown, P., & Levinson, S. C. (1978). Universals in language usage: Politeness phenomena. In E. Goody (Ed.), *Questions and politeness: Strategies in social interaction* (pp. 56–289). New York: Cambridge University Press.

Brown, P., & Levinson, S. C. (1987). *Politeness: Some universals in language usage*. New York: Cambridge University Press.

Celo, P. (1996). Linguistic and pragmatic aspects of the interrogative form in Italian Sign Language. In C. Lucas (Ed.), *Multicultural aspects of sociolinguistics in Deaf communities* (pp. 132–52). Washington, DC: Gallaudet University Press.

Conlin, F., Hagstrom, P., & Neidle, C. (2003). A particle of indefiniteness in American Sign Language. *Linguistic Discovery* 2(1). http://journals.dartmouth.edu/cgi-bin/WebObjects/Journals.woa/2/xmlpage/1/article/142?htmlOnce=yes.

Durkheim, E. (1915). *The elementary forms of the religious life*. New York: Free Press.

Eelen, G. (2001). *A critique of politeness theories*. Manchester, UK: St. Jerome Publishing.

Emmorey, K. (1999). Do signers gesture? In L. Messing & R. Campbell (Eds.), *Gesture, speech, and sign* (pp. 133–59). New York: Oxford University Press.

Ervin-Tripp, S. (1972). On sociolinguistic rules: Alternation and co-occurrence. In J. Gumperz & D. Hymes (Eds.), *Directions in Sociolinguistics* (pp. 213–50). New York: Holt.

Geis, M. L. (1995). *Speech acts and conversational interaction*. New York: Cambridge University Press.

Goffman, E. (1967). *Interaction ritual*. Garden City, NY: Doubleday.

Goody, E. N. (Ed). (1978). *Questions and politeness: Strategies in social interaction*. Vol. 8 of *Cambridge Papers in Social Anthropology*. New York: Cambridge University Press.

Grice, H. P. (1975). Logic and conversation. In *Syntax and Semantics*. P. Cole & J. L. Morgan (Eds.), Vol. 3: *Speech Acts* (pp. 41–58). New York: Academic Press.

Gumperz, J. (1982). Socio-cultural knowledge in conversational inference. In *Discourse strategies*. New York: Cambridge University Press.

Gumperz, J. (1992). Contextualization revisited. In P. Aver & A. Di Luzio (Eds.), *The contextualization of language* (pp. 39–54). Amsterdam: John Benjamins.

Hall, S. (1989). Train-gone-sorry: The etiquette of social conversations in American Sign Language. In S. Wilcox (Ed.), *American Deaf culture: An anthology* (pp. 89–102). Silver Spring, MD: Linstok.

Hickey, L., & Stewart, M. (Eds). (2005). *Politeness in Europe*. Buffalo, NY: Multilingual Matters.

Hoza, J. (1999). Saving face: The interpreter and politeness. *Journal of Interpretation 12*, 39–68.

Hymes, D. (1974). Ways of speaking. In R. Bauman & J. Sherzer (Eds.), *Explorations in the ethnography of speaking* (pp. 433–51). New York: Cambridge University Press.

Jacobs, R. (1996). Just how hard is it to learn ASL? The case for ASL as a truly foreign language. In C. Lucas (Ed.), *Multicultural aspects of sociolinguistics in Deaf communities* (pp. 183–226). Washington, DC: Gallaudet University Press.

Katriel, T. (1986). *Talking straight: Dugri speech in Israeli Sabra culture*. New York: Cambridge University Press.

Keenan, E. (1974). Norm-makers, norm-breakers: Uses of speech by men and women in a Malagasy community. In R. Bauman & J. Sherzer (Eds.), *Explorations in the ethnography of speaking* (pp. 125–43). New York: Cambridge University Press.

Keenan, S. K. (1993). Investigating Deaf students' apologies: An exploratory study. *Applied Linguistics 14*, 364–84.

Kochman, T. (1981). *Black and white: Styles in conflict*. Chicago: University of Chicago Press.

Koike, D. A. (1992). *Language and social relationship in Brazilian Portuguese*. Austin: University of Texas Press.

Labov, W. (1972). *Language in the inner city*. Philadelphia: University of Pennsylvania.

Lakoff, R. T. (1973). The logic of politeness, or minding your *p*'s and *q*'s. In C. Corum, T. Cedric Smith-Stark, & A. Weiser (Eds.), *Papers from the ninth regional meeting, Chicago Linguistics Society* (pp. 292–305). Chicago: Chicago Linguistic Society.

Lakoff, R. T. (1979). Stylistic strategies within a grammar of style. *Annals of the New York Academy of Sciences 327*, 53–78.

Lakoff, R. T., & Ide, S. (2005). *Broadening the horizon of linguistic politeness*. Amsterdam: John Benjamins.

Lane, H. (1992). *The mask of benevolence: Disabling the Deaf community*. New York: Vintage.

Leech, G. (1983). *Principles of pragmatics.* New York: Longman.

Lentz, E., Mikos, K., & Smith, C. (1992). *Signing naturally: Student workbook, level 2, student videotext.* San Diego: DawnSignPress.

Levinson, S. C. (1983). *Pragmatics.* New York: Cambridge University Press.

Lucas, C., & Valli, C. (1992). *Language contact in the American Deaf community.* San Diego: Academic Press.

Mather, S. M. (1996). Initiation in visually constructed dialogue: Reading books with three-to-eight-year-old students who are Deaf and hard of hearing. In C. Lucas (Ed.), *Multicultural aspects of sociolinguistics in Deaf communities* (pp. 109–31). Washington, DC: Gallaudet University Press.

McLaughlin, M. L. (1984). *Conversation: How talk is organized.* Beverly Hills: Sage.

Mindess, A. (1999). *Reading between the signs: Intercultural communication for sign language interpreters.* Yarmouth, ME: Intercultural Press.

Pietrosemoli, L. (2001). Politeness and Venezuelan Sign Language. In V. Dively, M. Metzger, S. Taub, & A. M. Baer (Eds.), *Signed languages: Discoveries from international research* (pp. 163–79). Washington, DC: Gallaudet University Press.

Registry of Interpreters for the Deaf. (2005). *Professional code of conduct.* http://www.rid.org/coe.html.

Reiss, N. (1985). *Speech act taxonomy as a tool for ethnographic description: An analysis based on videotapes of continuous behavior in two New York households.* Amsterdam: John Benjamins.

Rintell, E. M., & Mitchell, C. J. (1989). Studying requests and apologies: An inquiry into method. In S. Blum-Kulka, J. House, & G. Kasper (Eds.), *Cross-cultural pragmatics: Requests and apologies* (pp. 248–72). Norwood, NJ: Ablex.

Sapir, E. (1958). Speech as a personality trait. In D. Mandelbaum (Ed.), *Selected writings of Edward Sapir in language, culture, and personality* (pp. 533–43). Berkeley: University of California Press.

Scollon, R. (1982). The rhythmic integration of ordinary talk. In D. Tannen (Ed.), *Analyzing discourse: Text and talk* (pp. 335–49). Washington, DC: Georgetown University Press.

Scollon, R., & Scollon, S. B. K. (1981). *Narrative, literacy, and face in interethnic communication.* Norwood, NJ: Ablex.

Searle, J. R. (1969). *Speech acts.* New York: Cambridge University Press.

Searle, J. R. (1975). Indirect speech acts. In P. Cole & J. L. Morgan (Eds.), *Syntax and Semantic,* vol. 3: *Speech Acts* (pp. 59–82). New York: Academic Press.

Searle, J. R. (1976). The classification of illocutionary acts. *Language in Society* 5, 1–24.

Tannen, D. (1984). *Conversational style: Analyzing talk among friends.* Norwood, NJ: Ablex.

Tannen, D. (1994). *Gender and discourse.* New York: Oxford University Press.

Thornburg, L., & Panther, K. (1997). Speech act metonymies. In W. Liebert, G. Redeker, & L. Waugh (Eds.), *Discourse and perspective in cognitive linguistics* (pp. 205–22). Amsterdam: John Benjamins.

Tray, S. (2005). What are you suggesting? Interpreting innuendo between ASL and English. In M. Metzger and E. Fleetwood (Eds.), *Attitudes, innuendo, and regulators: Challenges of interpretation* (pp. 95–135). Studies in Interpretation, vol. 2. Washington, DC: Gallaudet University Press.

Trosborg, A. (1995). *Interlanguage pragmatics: Requests, complaints, and apologies.* Berlin: Mouton de Gruyter.

Van der Auwera, J. (1980). *Indirect speech acts revisited.* Bloomington: Indiana University Linguistics Club.

Van der Kooij, E., Crasborn, O., & Ros, J. (2006). Manual prosodic cues: Palm-up and pointing signs. Poster from the *Proceedings of the Theoretical Issues in Sign Language Research Ninth Conference*, Florianópolis, Brazil, December 6–9, http://www.tislr9.ufsc.br/poster/ els_van_der_kooji_onno_crasborn_johan_ros.pdf.

Watts, R. J. (1992). Linguistic politeness and polite verbal behavior: Reconsidering claims for universality. In R. J. Watts, S. Ide, & K. Ehlich (Eds.), *Politeness in language: Studies in its history, theory, and practice* (pp. 43–69). Berlin: Mouton de Gruyter.

Watts, R. J. (2003). *Politeness.* New York: Cambridge University Press.

Watts, R. J., Ide, S., & Ehlich, E. (Eds.). (1992). *Politeness in language: Studies in its history, theory, and practice.* Berlin: Mouton de Gruyter.

Wierzbicka, A. (1991). *Cross-cultural pragmatics: The semantics of human interaction.* Berlin: Mouton de Gruyter.

Winston, E., & Monikowski, C. (2003). Marking topic boundaries in signed interpretation and transliteration. In M. Metzger, S. Collins, V. Dively, & R. Shaw (Eds.), *From topic boundaries to omission: New research on interpretation* (pp. 187–227). Studies in Interpretation Series, vol. 1. Washington, DC: Gallaudet University Press.

Wolfson, N., Marmor, T., & Jones, S. (1989). Problems in the comparison of speech acts across cultures. In S. Blum-Kulka, J. House, & G. Kasper (Eds.), *Cross-cultural pragmatics: Requests and apologies* (pp. 174–96). Norwood, NJ: Ablex.

Wood, M. M. (1986). *A definition of idiom.* Bloomington, IN: University Linguistics Club.

Informal Ethnographic Survey

1. It has been said by those outside and inside the Deaf community that deaf people tend to be blunt or direct and that hearing people tend to be indirect or vague. What is your opinion about this statement?

   What is your definition of directness?

   What is your definition of indirectness?

2. When citing an example of how deaf people are blunt, the greeting "You've gained weight!" is often mentioned. Would such a statement be considered direct or blunt within the Deaf community?

   If no, why and what social factors would need to be present for this to remain appropriate?

   What factors would make this inappropriate?

   What are other areas of life (for example, physical appearance, HIV status, or age) where directness may be an issue?

3. Is it appropriate to be indirect at times within the ASL signing community? Why?

   What factors would preclude indirectness?

   What are some examples of appropriate indirectness?

APPENDIX B

Transcription Conventions

SMALL CAPS	English glosses
#FINGERSPELLING	lexicalized fingerspelling
L-E-T-T-E-R-S	fingerspelled word
HYPHENATED-WORDS	hyphenation indicates a single sign
++	repetition of a sign
CL:	classifier predicate (quotation marks following this indicate visual/spatial information)
Bob-ASK-TO-Cindy	indicates that verbs include the subject and object referents
(actions)	indicates contextual information

y/n-q_____   yes/no question

DON'T-MIND   line above gloss indicates relevant nonmanual
                         features

/??/   uncertain transcription

APPENDIX C

Situation I

Context: Joe is washing his car in the driveway in front of his closed
garage. Anthony comes up to him.

<pre>
              wh-q_____
Joe: WHY WHAT'S-UP COME HERE
              y/n-q_____ hn__
Anthony: PRO-1 STILL HAVE #TRUCK PRO-1
              hn   wh-q__
Joe: YES IX"points behind to garage" GARAGE IX"point to garage," WHY
Anthony: PRO-1 GO(2h) STORE YESTERDAY, PRO-1 SEE CLOTHES CL:"top and
              sides of dresser"
              CL:"dresser" THAT
              y/n-q____
Joe: OLD
              neg_____   mouth gape_____
Anthony: NEW++, REAL NICE! BEAUTIFUL! WOOD #OAK. PRO-1 LOOK "right"
              FALL-IN-LOVE!
                                  tm___   tm____
              PRO-1 BUY. PRO-1 BRING. STORE, ORDER-ME SELF BRING. POSS-1 CAR,
              SMALL. STUCK.
              "shakes head, grimaces, hands open, head dips"
              head forward y/n-q_____ hn_____
              DON'T-MIND PRO-1 LOAN-TO-ME POSS-3 #TRUCK.
              PRO-1 #BACK TOMORROW. 5HPU
              tm_____
Joe: IX"points behind to garage" #TRUCK, IX"points to truck"
              REALLY POSS-3 #CO. "nods head"
                                  neg_____   head shake/grimace
              IX"points to company" NOT PERMIT LOAN-TO-OTHERS. 5HPU SORRY
Anthony: 5HPU #OK PRO-1 TRY ASK OTHER 5HPU/shrug shoulder
</pre>

152 : DANIEL ROUSH

	<u>brow raise/hn</u>
Joe:	GOOD #LUCK!
Anthony:	THUMB-UP (walks away)
Joe:	THUMB-UP

Situation 2

Context: Shane is sitting on the sideline at a baseball diamond watching a game. Anthony walks up behind and softly touches him on the shoulder. Shane quickly glances over his shoulder, then back at the game. He then turns back to Anthony, who is gazing at the game, and waves HI, then says ONE-MOMENT. Shane turns back to the baseball game to see a strike by the batter. He turns to Anthony and thrusts his head back, then forward as if to say "What's up?"

Anthony:	CAN PRO-1 USE POSS-3 #TRUCK
	<u>grimace</u>
Shane:	SORRY+
Anthony:	5HPU
	<u>hn _____</u> <u>hn _____</u>
Shane:	PRO-1 LOAN-OUT BROTHER. PRO-3 USE ONE ONE-WEEK PRO-3. 5HPU
	(gazes at the baseball game, then back at Anthony)
	WHAT, WHY 5HPU
Anthony:	CL: "dresser," PRO-1 BUY. PRO-1 MUST BRING HOME.
	PRO-1 CAR 5HPU "head nod" TOO-SMALL
Shane:	(gazes at the baseball game, then back at Anthony)
	<u>y/n-q _____</u>
	5HPU "points at Anthony twice" PRO-1 THINK. PRO-3 KNOW NS-PAT
	<u>hn _____</u>
Anthony:	P-A-T
	<u>nod _____</u>
Shane:	THAT! PRO-3 HAVE #TRUCK PRO-3
Anthony:	5HPU
	<u>hn __</u>
Shane:	5HPU OLD 5HPU
	<u>grimace pucker</u>
Anthony:	OLD! SO-SO
Shane:	REALLY NOT-YET ENGINE-DROP. STILL GOOD++ PRO-3 GO SEE++ 5HPU
	<u>pucker</u>
Anthony:	SEE++ (gazes at baseball game)
Shane:	(gazes at baseball game)
Anthony:	(taps Shane lightly on the shoulder)

Shane: (Shane looks at Anthony)

y/n-q

Anthony: PAT STILL LIVE NEAR P-A-R-K

Shane: SAME++

pucker

Anthony: FINE PRO-1 GO

Shane: 5HPU "head nod" (Player hands bat to Shane. He stands,
then turns to Anthony)

PRO-1 MUST GO. SORRY NONE #TRUCK 5HPU

Anthony: PSHAW, NO PROBLEM (backs up) PSHAW, THUMB-UP (walks away)

Shane: THUMB-UP (walks away)

Situation 3

Context: Pat is mowing her lawn. Anthony comes up in front of her,
lowers his head, waves, and holds his arms out. Pat stops mowing.

Pat: GOOD SEE PRO-3. WOW (Pat and Anthony hug)

Anthony: (looks around the yard)

brr   wh-q

NICE MOW AROUND. WHAT HUSBAND MOW

Pat: PRO-3 IN HOUSE WATCH #T-V+ FOOTBALL. REALLY PRO-1 BORED
CRAZY PRO-1

Anthony: PSHAW "shakes head"

Pat: WHAT'S-UP PRO-3 HERE WHAT'S-UP 5HPU

Anthony: PRO-1 BUY CL:"dresser." PRO-1 NEED #TRUCK BRING HOME

y/n-q

5HPU ALL RIGHT PRO-1 USE PRO-3 #TRUCK 5HPU

Pat: PRO-3 LIVE WHERE

Anthony: REALLY SHORT-DISTANCE IX"left" BERKELEY 5HPU

neg   shakes head

Pat: "shakes head" NOT SHORT-DISTANCE. NOSE-FAR! 30 M-I-L-E-S WOW

Anthony: NAW, 20 NOT BAD 5HPU

grimace/head teeter

Pat: REALLY PRO-1 DON'T-MIND LOAN-OUT POSS-1 CAR BUT REALLY

hn th   grimace   neg/grimace

POSS-1 #TRUCK, OLD, TROUBLE+, AND ENGINE SO-SO. PRO-1 NOT TRUST
5HPU

hn/pucker

Anthony: REALLY++ PSHAW. PRO-1 BETTER NOT LOAN-TO-ME. PRO-1 GO LOOK OTHER

<pre>
                  grimace
Pat: SORRY
                              y/n-q/hn
Anthony: ALL RIGHT+, SEE AROUND #OK
           hn
Pat: SURE
Anthony: BYE
Pat: ILY, BYE (goes back to lawn mower)
Anthony: ILY (walks away)
</pre>

Situation 4

Context: Cinnie is sitting on her front porch reading with the newspaper in front of her face. Anthony sneaks up and taps lightly on the front of her newspaper to startle her. She puts down the paper and slaps him playfully.

<pre>
Anthony: HI
Cinnie: SCARE PRO-1 PRO-3 (smiles)
Anthony: (stands back and smiles)
Cinnie: HOW PRO-3
           hn
Anthony: FINE++ 5HPU PRO-1 BUY NEW CL:"dresser" BEAUTIFUL 5HPU PRO-1
           NEED PICK-UP BRING
                                       y/n-q
           HOME 5HPU PRO-1 LOOK++ #TRUCK 5HPU. OK PRO-1 USE POSS-3 #TRUCK
Cinnie: FINE++ #BUT IX(thumb) "points right" DIRTY
           IX(thumb) "points right" BACK OIL CL:"spot"
           BEFORE MOTOR PRO-1 CL:"put engine in bed, then take out"
                            pucker
           PRO-1 NOT-YET CLEAN 5HPU
           grimace
Anthony: 5HPU SEE TRY ASK OTHER PRO-3++
           cond   hn
           SUPPOSE 5HPU FAIL PRO-1 USE POSS-3 #TRUCK 5HPU
Cinnie: FINE PSHAW WHY NOT SETTLE-DOWN WAIT L-O-N COME ANY TIME
           PRO-3 HAVE #TRUCK PRO-3 5HPU
Anthony: 5HPU FINE (sits down)
           y/n-q
Cinnie: READ NEWSPAPER 5HPU
Anthony: 5HPU #SPORTS YES
Cinnie: 5HPU #SPORTS OF-COURSE PRO-3 (hands Anthony the sports section)
Anthony: WHO KISS-FIST BASEBALL TEAM PRO-3. PRO-1 CHICAGO
</pre>

Cinnie:	PRO-1 #SF G-I-A-N-T-S PRO-1
	<u>grimace</u>
Anthony:	LOUSY PRO-3
	<u>pucker</u>
Cinnie:	5HPU POSS-1+ #SF
Cinnie:	(looks down at her newspaper)
	(Lon pulls up in the truck and walks toward Cinnie and Anthony on the front porch)
Cinnie:	(waves hand to get Anthony's attention)
Anthony:	(gazes at Cinnie)
Cinnie:	L-O-N HERE IX (points toward Lon)
Anthony:	(to Lon) HELLO
Lon:	GOOD SEE PRO-3???/ COME-HERE VISIT, WHAT'S-UP
Anthony:	PRO-1 LOOK #TRUCK. YESTERDAY PRO-1 BUY cl:"dresser"
	PRO-1 ASK-AROUND #TRUCK NONE++ 5HPU
	PRO-1 TOLD-ME WHY NOT PRO-1 ASK-TO-LON
	<u>y/n-q</u>
	DON'T-MIND PRO-1 LOAN-TO-ME POSS-3 #TRUCK
Lon:	5HPU FINE 5HPU UNDERSTAND #GAS ALMOST RUN-OUT ON-"E."
	DON'T-MIND GAS FULL
	<u>h n</u>
Anthony:	5HPU PSHAW #OK++ PRO-1
	<u>h n</u>
Lon:	5HPU
Anthony:	AFTERNOON TIME THREE-O'CLOCK
Lon:	DOESN'T-MATTER NOT PLAN USE ALL-DAY NOT.
	THINK^SELF ANY TIME. 5HPU
Anthony:	5HPU POW 5HPU FINE 5HPU PRO-1 TIME THREE-O'CLOCK, #OK
	(Anthony gets up)
Lon:	FINE (shakes hands with Anthony)
Anthony:	THANK-YOU++ (turns to Cinnie) 5HPU PRO-1 LEAVE
	(gives Cinnie a hug) SEE AROUND
Cinnie:	TAKE-CARE
Anthony:	#OK, THUMB-UP (turns to Lon) THUMB-UP (Anthony leaves)

Part III Consumer Considerations

An Invitation to Dance:

Deaf Consumers' Perceptions of Signed

Language Interpreters and Interpreting

Jemina Napier and Meg J. Rohan

Research on signed language interpreting is an emerging subdiscipline of interpreting and translation studies (Pöchhacker, 2004), and the number of research-based publications has been gradually increasing (see Harrington & Turner, 2001; Janzen, 2005; Marschark, Peterson, & Winston, 2005; Metzger, Collins, Dively, & Shaw, 2003; Metzger & Fleetwood, 2005). Typically, these studies have focused on interpreters' production of an interpreted message in one direction, on equivalence and accuracy (Cokely, 1992; Napier, 2002; Russell, 2002), or on the interactive nature of interpreting (Metzger, 1999; Roy, 2000), but very few researchers have examined interpreting from the perspective of the deaf consumer and actually involved deaf people in the analysis of interpreting and interpreters.

Drawing on the work of other linguists (Cameron, Frazer, Harvey, Rampton, & Richardson, 1992), Turner and Harrington (2000) discussed issues of power and method in the research on signed language interpreting and highlighted the following key points: Research should be on, for, and with stakeholders (i.e., those affected by the research or those who have a vested interest in the outcome); people should not be treated as objects (often implied by the term "subjects" rather than "participants"); participants may have their own agendas; and researchers should share their knowledge with the stakeholders.

Various Australian studies have explored the profile of the signed language interpreting profession (Bontempo, 2005; Bontempo & Napier, submitted; Napier & Barker, 2003; Ozolins & Bridge, 1999). For example, studies have examined the output of signed language interpreters from English into Australian Sign Language (Auslan), with investigations of metalinguistic awareness, translation style, and omission production (Napier, 2002), as well as translation processes (Conlon & Napier, 2004; Leneham, 2005), the role of legal interpreters (Banna, 2004), and occupational overuse syndrome (Madden, 2005). Given this background, an investigation of interpreting from the perspective of deaf consumers in Australia is needed not only to include them as stakeholders in the interpreting services and to explore their agenda in terms of quality interpreting services but also to share knowledge about interpreting from a consumer's perspective. This type of research is also needed internationally because no studies to date have explored the experiences of deaf people in working with interpreters over a period of time.

Deaf people have anecdotally discussed their attitudes toward interpreters regarding what they think makes a good interpreter, what they like and need and why (e.g., Baker-Shenk, 1986; Bienvenu, 1987; Corker, 1997). They have also been asked for suggestions for best practice (Stratiy, 2005) and have expressed a need for interpreters to be adaptable to meet the consumer's needs according to the context (Heaton & Fowler, 1997). Interestingly, three deaf university academics (Campbell, Rohan, & Woodcock, in press) state that they consider the universities in which they work—rather than themselves—to be the consumer of the interpreting service. That is, they believe that the interpreter is working to facilitate communication in a specific context that involves not only the deaf person but also those with whom they are communicating. Nevertheless, they describe these deaf academics' clear preferences and expectations from interpreters in this context. They state that they need interpreters to be flexible and well prepared, be able to "interpret on one's feet," adopt a collaborative teamwork approach, demonstrate respect, develop rapport with them and others in the communication context, be trustworthy, provide faithful interpretations, solicit feedback, have a good attitude and comportment, and essentially be an ally. Although valuable, these requirements are based on observations and self-reporting and do not provide an empirical basis that might inform interpreter development and training. The study reported here is therefore pioneering and should provide insight not only for Australian interpreters but also interpreters internationally.

What constitutes a good interpreter or a good interpreting experience? Do different stakeholders have different perspectives? Research of this kind may reveal (or support) what deaf people and interpreters are reluctant to acknowledge. It may also provide evidence for what deaf people and interpreters instinctively know and discuss about the relationship between deaf people and interpreters, whether positive or negative. Nevertheless, by developing an overview that identifies commonalities in what deaf people want from interpreters and what they actually understand from interpretations, all of the stakeholders can work together to ensure consistency and excellence in training and practice.

By collecting information from deaf people themselves, it becomes possible to create a more accurate picture of their perceptions of interpreting and more accurately determine whether the interpreting profession is meeting the needs of community members. In addition, our knowledge and understanding of the interpreting process can be improved by providing greater insight into how we can better work together to ensure quality interpreting services. In order to place the study in context, we provide a brief overview of the Deaf community and the signed language interpreting profession in Australia.

THE AUSTRALIAN CONTEXT

The Deaf Community and Australian Sign Language

Australian Sign Language (Auslan), the natural signed language of deaf Australians, has received de facto recognition by the federal government within the Australian National Language Policy (Dawkins, 1991), and the first Auslan dictionary was published in 1989 (Johnston, 1989). Auslan has its roots in British Sign Language (BSL) and is also closely related to New Zealand Sign Language (NZSL) (Johnston, 2002) but is very different from American Sign Language (ASL). Auslan has a two-handed fingerspelling alphabet and is used throughout Australia but has two distinct dialects: north and south (Johnston, 1989, 1998). Evidence of sociolinguistic variation (Schembri, Goswell, & Johnston, 2004) and language contact (Napier, 2007) also exists.

Estimations of the sign-language-using deaf population in Australia have varied. A commonly cited figure is sixteen thousand. This figure is based on a study conducted by Hyde and Power (1992), in which deaf people were contacted and asked to report how many people they knew who signed and to put the researchers in touch with other deaf people (snowball technique).

According to a scoping study carried out on behalf of the Australian Federal Government (Orima, 2004), many people within the Deaf community believe the deaf Auslan-using population to be much higher than figures reported in the last Australian Bureau of Statistics census of 2001. The census data identified 5,303 Australians who use Auslan to communicate with others at home. Based on an analysis of deaf school enrollments and hearing screening test results, Johnston (2003, 2005) estimates that the number is closer to 6,500.

The Orima deaf Auslan user survey mentioned earlier showed that 82% of deaf people that responded to their survey ($n = 491$) use signed language every day to communicate. Other census information gives us a picture of the demographics of the Deaf community (taken from Orima, 2004):

- Of signing deaf people, 30% completed their high school education (at approximately eighteen years of age), compared with 41% of the general Australian population.
- The signing deaf population is overrepresented in the lower income ranges and underrepresented in the higher income ranges, compared to the general Australian population.
- Of the general Australian population, 42% are unemployed or not in the labor force, compared to 47% of signing deaf people.

According to the Orima (ibid.) survey results, more than 30% of deaf people work in the public sector (for the local, state, or federal government), and almost 30% work in the service industry, with lesser numbers in manufacturing, hospitality, and retail.

Auslan/English Interpreters

An accreditation system (certification system for the qualification of Auslan/English interpreters) has been available in Australia for approximately twenty years, under the auspices of the National Authority for the Accreditation of Translators and Interpreters (NAATI). Spring (2000) provides an overview of the evolution of language services in Australia, including NAATI. Australia is one of the few countries in the world that accredits spoken language and signed language interpreters through the same system (Bridge, 1991; Napier, 2004).

Moreover, NAATI has a panel of Auslan examiners that comprises qualified interpreters, interpreter educators, and deaf consumers. An interpreter receives accreditation by passing a practical examination or completing an approved course. People can apply directly to NAATI and take the examination independently of a training course. Interpreters are required to have achieved NAATI accreditation before accepting paid work in the field. Because of problems with supply and demand, however, many unaccredited interpreters receive paid work in educational institutions and rural areas.

Because completion of a training course is not currently mandatory, many interpreters receive accreditation only by passing the NAATI test, which incorporates assessment of language translation and an examination of ethical behavior. Currently, two levels of accreditation are available for Auslan/English interpreters: paraprofessional interpreter (formerly known as Level 2), which is based on competence in interpreting nonspecialist dialogues, and professional interpreter (formerly known as Level 3), which is based on competence in interpreting specialist consultations that require greater linguistic sophistication.

Interpreter training programs have been available since 1986 (Flynn, 1996) but have not necessarily been offered in every major capital city or held every year. Australia currently has only one university-level training program (Macquarie University in Sydney). However, training courses are available at community colleges for technical and further education (TAFEs) for people who are interested in becoming accredited at the paraprofessional level. After completing the prerequisite introductory, intermediate, and advanced signed language courses, students can then attend a part-time, one-year course and on completion attain a diploma and NAATI paraprofessional-level accreditation. Some TAFEs offer an advanced diploma for students to achieve professional interpreter-level accreditation on completion of the program; alternatively, students can enroll in a postgraduate diploma or master's degree program at Macquarie University.

A demographic survey of 125 NAATI-accredited Auslan/English interpreters (mostly between the ages of 26 and 45) conducted in 1999 (Napier and Barker, 2003) found that 83% of interpreters were female and 70% were accredited at the NAATI paraprofessional level. Napier and Barker found that 77% of the respondents held postsecondary qualifications but only 48% were working toward or had already received a university qualification. Fewer than half of the respondents had undertaken formal interpreter training. Almost half reported working mostly in educational settings.

A more recent but similar demographic picture of Auslan interpreters was drawn by Bontempo (2005) as part of a wider study of interpreters' perceptions of their own competence. Of the 110 NAATI-accredited interpreters surveyed, 67.3% of these were accredited at the paraprofessional level, and 32.7% at the professional level. This demonstrates that the 70:30 ratio found by Napier and Barker (2003) still applies. Of the total number of respondents, 77.3% reported practicing either full time or part time in the profession. The remainder worked in some other capacity, typically as a teacher of deaf students, a booking clerk for an interpreting agency, a community worker, and so on. The majority (74.5%) of the respondents were between thirty and forty-nine years of age (83.5% and 16.5% male). One interesting difference between the Bontempo survey and the Napier and Barker survey is that more than 86% of the respondents held postsecondary qualifications (9% more than cited by Napier and Barker). This may be due to the fact that a university interpreter training program was established soon after the Napier and Barker survey.

Between November 1982 and June 2005, 728 Auslan interpreters were accredited by NAATI (Sherrill Bell, pers. comm., 2005). Of these, 630 were accredited at the paraprofessional level, and 92 at the professional level. This overall figure does not take into account those who are no longer working (because they are deceased or living overseas), nor is it representative of the number of active interpreters, as it is widely known that unaccredited practitioners are working in Australia. The number of practicing qualified interpreters is estimated at 250–300, although this figure is impossible to pinpoint (Napier, Bontempo, & Leneham, 2006). Additionally, unqualified interpreters are working in some states and territories because the increasing demand for interpreters is outstripping the supply, particularly in educational interpreting (Ozolins & Bridge, 1999).

Now that an overview has been given of the Australian Deaf and signed language interpreting context, we review the relevant literature on consumers' perceptions of interpreting.

Research-Based Consumers' Perceptions of Interpreting

As mentioned earlier, few empirical studies have been undertaken of consumers' perceptions of interpreting in both spoken and signed languages. Those that exist have typically sought to answer questions such as these: What do consumers expect from interpreting services? How much do they understand of the interpretations? Are they satisfied with the interpreting services they receive? What types of experiences have they had in working with interpreters? This study addresses these questions as well.

First we describe two key studies in the literature on spoken language interpreting. In order to explore the expectations of users of conference interpretation, Moser (1996) conducted a survey of two hundred delegates attending various conferences. Forty-five percent of the respondents expected that all of the interpretations would be faithful to the original source text, and 34% stated that regular delivery, absence of hesitation, correct grammar, use of complete sentences, and clarity of expression gave the impression of a good interpreter. In addition, more than one-third of the respondents mentioned that interpreters should demonstrate the features of a lively, nonmonotonous voice with clear enunciation in order to convey the feeling of the original message effectively. Moser also reported that approximately one-third of the respondents found it irritating when an interpreter's time lag was too long and felt that it was important for interpreters to retain synchronicity (that is, keep up with the speaker).

Moser (ibid.) examined the relation between respondents' expectations with their degree of experience in attending conferences. Although those with less experience rated good voice, synchronicity, and rhetorical skills on a par with those who were more experienced users of interpreters, significant differences occurred in expectations about the faithfulness of an interpretation. Of the more experienced group, 53% emphasized the importance of a faithful interpretation, compared to only 35% of less experienced respondents. Moser's study essentially found that conference delegates prefer faithful interpretations, that is, those that precisely convey the meaning of the message.

In an alternative environment, Edwards, Temple, and Alexander (2005) explored the experiences of minority ethnic people living in two major cities in the United Kingdom who needed interpreters to gain access to and use of a range of services in the community (e.g., legal, health, and welfare). Bilingual research assistants conducted semi-structured interviews with fifty men and women of Chinese, Kurdish, Bangladeshi, Indian, and Polish descent who varied in age. As with much interpreting research in Australia and elsewhere, Edwards et al. (ibid.) stated that "The majority of evaluations of interpreting provision in the UK has been conducted from a service provider perspective. There has been little work that looks at users' experiences of interpreters, both professional and informal, from their own point of view. Even less research looks at users' preferences regarding who should interpret for them. The few exceptions to this have been single service evaluations, rather than addressing users' views of their broad needs for interpreters" (p. 78).

Thus, the Edwards et al. study sheds light on the perceptions of a different group of consumers, as compared to the professional conference delegates surveyed in Moser's (1996) study. Rather than accuracy and faithfulness, their discussion focuses on the qualities that constitute a good interpreter's and consumers' experiences in using professional interpreters (as compared with family and friends as interpreters). They determined that personal character and trust are important in people's understanding of good interpreting, leading them to prefer interpreters drawn from their own informal networks (i.e., family and friends). Moreover, they concluded that trust may offset consumers' concerns about interpreters' bilingual competence.

Following similar methodologies, research on signed language interpreting has touched on consumers' perceptions by surveying or interviewing deaf people and asking them to comment on their preferences for, or experiences of, interpreting in different contexts. For example, in relation to educational interpreting, Locker (1990) interviewed three deaf American college students about their expectations of interpreters in university lectures. She found that they preferred to receive lecture information through semantically equivalent interpretations of English into ASL rather than through a literal sign-for-word interpretation.

Napier and Barker (2004) reported on a panel discussion with four deaf Australian university students about their perceptions of and preferences for Auslan interpreters' translation style in the university context. All of the panel members stated a preference not only for a meaning-based, "free" approach (i.e., interpretation) overall but also for a more literal approach (i.e., transliteration) when necessary to provide access to academic English or subject-specific terms.

Kurz and Langer (2004) interviewed twenty-nine deaf and hard of hearing students about their mainstream educational experiences and their perspectives on the role and responsibilities of interpreters in that context. They found that students had concerns about clear communication and were conscious of the interpreters' impact on the dynamics of the classroom but were grateful for their presence. They also found that participants reported understanding their interpreters less when they were in high school or college than when in middle school. Although they did not test for statistical significance due to small numbers, they did note a trend: Older participants reported that they did not understand their interpreters well, as compared to younger participants, who said that they did. Furthermore, participants reported that they had to adapt their signing style to make it easier for interpreters to understand them and that this was frustrating and annoying. When they asked the participants to provide a "wish list" for interpreters, Kurz and Langer found that deaf students want interpreters to do the following: (1) interpret everything; (2) not let their personal style interfere with the deaf person's education; (3) let the students make their own decisions; (4) not rely on the deaf consumer; (5) match the deaf person's signing style when providing voice-over; (6) match their signing style to that of the speaker; (7) know their limitations; (8) set boundaries while remaining human; (9) prepare for assignments; (10) ask for repetition when unsure; (11) advocate when appropriate; (12) position themselves appropriately within the deaf person's line of sight; (13) give the deaf person some personal space; and (14) use facial expressions, eye contact, and finger-spelling.

In relation to television interpreting, Steiner (1998) investigated deaf viewers' comprehension of signing style on British television. He interviewed various deaf people and showed them excerpts of different hearing and deaf people signing a news bulletin. He asked them which signer they preferred to watch and also studied their comprehension of the information each signer presented. He found that the expressed preference of deaf viewers' signing style did not always correspond with their actual level of comprehension when watching televised interpreters or deaf presenters.

In defining "entry to practice competencies," Witter-Merithew and Johnson (2005) conducted focus groups with American stakeholders, including interpreters, interpreter educators, interpreting students, deaf people, employers, and policy makers. After interviewing twenty-five deaf people and undertaking focus groups consisting of another fifty-six deaf people, they found that the outcomes listed by interpreter preparation programs do not meet the needs of deaf consumers and that the relationship between deaf consumers and interpreters is complex. Overall, the authors asserted that signed language interpreters must develop competence and expertise in five key areas: theory and knowledge (academic foundation and world knowledge); human relations (interpersonal qualities); language skills (in both signed and spoken languages);

interpreting skills (technical skills in a range of subjects and settings); and professionalism (standards and practices).

In a complementary study Forestal (2005) conducted quantitative research on deaf leaders' attitudes toward interpreters and interpreting. He surveyed 394 deaf professionals in the United States about their experiences with and attitude toward interpreters. Almost 55% confirmed having negative experiences with interpreters. Nearly 84% were satisfied with interpreters they had used within the past two years. The respondents' attitudes correlated significantly with age, frequency of use of interpreters, negative experiences, and satisfaction. In general, the older the respondent and the more frequently they used interpreters, the more positive their attitudes toward interpreters; conversely, the greater the number of negative incidents they experienced, the more negative their attitude.

Although deaf people's perceptions and comprehension of interpreting have been previously discussed, the majority of studies focus on an abstract discussion of hypothetical situations. The purpose of our study was to gain an overview of deaf consumers' perceptions of actual interpreting experiences in a broad range of settings, particularly those settings in which people most commonly work with interpreters. Thus, rather than engage in a hypothetical discussion, we designed a study that would elicit the actual, everyday experiences of deaf people.

RESEARCH QUESTIONS AND HYPOTHESES

In designing this study, we formulated the following research questions:

1. How much choice do deaf people have when selecting an interpreter, and how much control do they have over the ones they work with?
2. Do deaf people generally feel that they understand interpreters?
3. What factors affect their reported levels of comprehension?
4. How satisfied are deaf people with the interpreting services they receive?
5. Does the level of satisfaction change and, if so, according to what variables?
6. What do deaf people perceive as the best and worst things about interpreters?

We hypothesized that deaf people's reported comprehension and satisfaction would be influenced by their prior experience with the interpreter, the interpreter's accreditation level, and the "fit" between the interpreter and the client. We also expected that deaf people would place a higher value on attitude and professionalism than on language proficiency.

In order to test these hypotheses, we designed a study to elicit quantitative and qualitative information from deaf people in their everyday experiences of working with interpreters. Pöchhacker (2004) has discussed three methodological approaches in interpreting studies: fieldwork, surveys, and experiments, and states that the methodology most commonly chosen in interpreting research is experimentation. In order to answer our questions, we decided to begin with a survey and to follow it with a focus group discussion, with a view to an experimental study at a later date.

Method: Survey

PARTICIPANTS

Thirty-one people (23 women and 8 men who lived in Australia and stated that their first or preferred language is Auslan) volunteered to participate in the survey. All of the volunteers rely on interpreters to access information. Five of the participants are native Auslan users. The occupations of all but one participant (who was a student) could be classified as professional: (e.g., accountant, actor, assistant school principal, Auslan teacher, clerk, community officer, community worker, consultant, Deaf awareness trainer, director, events coordinator, film maker, lecturer, liaison officer, manager, postdoctoral researcher, public service officer). The majority (22) of the participants were 30–49 years of age: Of those, 12 were 30–39, and 10 were 40–49; 4 participants were between 20 and 29, and 1 participant was in the 50+ age group.

Procedure

A recruitment advertisement was published in the membership magazine of the Australian Association of the Deaf (AAD), which was sent to more than two hundred members. The researchers also used their own professional and social networks to distribute a call for participants. Those who responded were then sent further information, which included a diary template that was to be completed following each interpreted event during the next four weeks. The template included open and closed questions about each interpreted event. The respondents were asked to rate their responses on a scale and were given opportunities to provide additional extemporaneous comments. They were asked to fill in their diary entry as soon as possible after the event had concluded. Although it was offered to everyone, only one participant requested a videotaped copy of the instructions in Auslan. A deadline of six weeks to complete the diaries was set.

After five weeks, the participants were contacted and asked to send in their completed diary forms. Thirty-one participants returned their forms within ten weeks. This 58.5% return rate is not unexpected from the perspective of previous research. For example, for typical low-response rates, Wray, Trott, and Bloomer (1998) cited an expectation of 20–30%, whereas Babbie (1973) stated that a return rate of 50% is adequate, 60% is good, and 70% is very good (cited in Schiavetti & Metz, 1997, p. 276).

After careful analysis of the diary data, we decided to hold focus groups in order to elicit further qualitative data from deaf people in Auslan rather than English. A focus group is "a carefully planned discussion designed to obtain perceptions on a defined area of interest in a permissive, non-threatening environment" (Krueger, 1994, p. 6; cited in Myers, 1998, p. 85). We felt that collecting further data would help us to better investigate the concepts we were exploring (Cresswell, 1994, p. 177).

Method: Focus Groups

PARTICIPANTS

All of the diary respondents who lived in Sydney (where the researchers are based) were contacted and asked to participate in a focus group in order to discuss their diary responses and general perceptions in more depth. Other deaf people who lived in Sydney but were not involved in keeping a diary were also contacted and asked whether they were interested in participating. This was to provide further validity to the responses of the first group of participants. Two focus groups were held, one with six participants and the other with four (five people were planning to attend, but one person was ill and did not come). Wherever possible, each focus group was balanced for gender, as well as native and nonnative signers, with the participants of the previous diary study. Table 1 provides details of the participants in each focus group.

TABLE I. *Focus Group Participants*

Age group	Gender	Native signer	Occupatiion	Diary respondent
		Focus group 1		
1. 20–29	M	Y	professional	Y
2. 30–39	M	N	professional	Y
3. 40–49	F	N	professional	Y
4. 30–39	M	Y	professional	N
5. 30–39	F	N	paraprofessional	N
6. 40–49	M	Y	professional	N
		Focus group 2		
1. 30–39	M	Y	professional	Y
2. 30–39	F	N	professional	Y
3. 30–39	F	N	professional	Y
4. 50+	F	Y	paraprofessional	N

Procedure

To help them prepare their responses, all of the participants were sent a list of "prompt" questions one week before the focus group met. The questions focused on issues such as what participants like most about interpreters, their notions of an ideal interpreter and interpreter attitude, challenges interpreters face, best and worst interpreting experiences, and preferences for different situations.

For our analysis, the groups were facilitated in Auslan and video-taped for later translation and transcription. The facilitator made minimal input to the discussion, interjecting only to guide participants back to the point or to make connections between different points that were raised.

RESULTS

Not all of the participants completed all of the questions relevant to each interpreting event. Variation in the degrees of freedom reported in the analyses therefore reflects missing data.

Interpreter Selection

The thirty-one participants reported 267 interpreter occasions. The number of events described by each participant ranged from 2 to 18 (M = 8.61, SD = 3.68, Mdn = 9.00).

What happens when the Deaf consumer selects an interpreter? The Deaf consumers chose their own interpreter on only 34% of occasions. For the majority of these (75%), the interpreter they scheduled was their first choice. When Deaf consumers select the interpreters themselves, they know their accreditation; none of the participants recorded "don't know accreditation" on those occasions when they made their own selections.

For 42 of the 90 instances in which the interpreter's accreditation was recorded, an interpreter who held Level 3 certification was chosen; in 42 of these instances, an interpreter who held Level 2 certification was chosen; and in 6 occasions the interpreter held no qualification. For 1 of these 6 occasions, the interpreter was a child of Deaf adults (CODA); for another, the interpreter had been trained but had yet to take the formal certification test (which the interpreter later passed); and for yet another, the interpreter was the consumer's husband. For the remaining 3 instances of choosing nonaccredited interpreters, the reasons given for the choice were the nonavailability of other interpreters, a lack of notice concerning the interpreting occasion (which meant that the choice was based on immediate availability), and a refusal to pay for an interpreter.

What happens when others make the selection? Consultation about interpreter preference was relatively rare when the Deaf consumers did not choose their own interpreter, and consultation reportedly occurred on only 20% of occasions. Nevertheless, on average, the consumers were sanguine about the choice of interpreter: In response to the question "How happy or unhappy were you about this interpreter being booked for you?," the mean response on a 7-point scale (where 7 implies "very happy") was 5.19 (SD = 1.69); the responses ranged from 1 to 7. For 62 of the 170 instances (36%) in which the interpreter's accreditation was recorded, an interpreter who held profession level certification was selected; in 80 of the 170 instances (47%), an interpreter who held paraprofessional level certification was chosen; and in 22 of the 170 instances (13%), the interpreter's accreditation was unknown. For the remaining instances, the interpreter reportedly had no formal accreditation.

The focus group discussions raised this point and highlighted the fact that the selection of interpreters is an important issue that can have a significant impact on deaf consumers (see figure 1).

Focus group 1

P2: I had to decide if I could lip-read the speaker if the interpreter missed something. So I didn't really feel a part of the group. But I thought, "Well, maybe it was just a bad day for her." I knew she had been booked for the next day session in three weeks' time. I turned up on the day, and she was worse than before. I was chairing a group discussion, and I couldn't understand one thing she was saying. I was lost. So I wiped my hands of her.

P3: So did you decide in the first place who you wanted, or did they book for you?

P2: It was booked for me.

P3: Paraprofessional or professional level?

P2: They were both paraprofessional level.

P3: Oh, right.

P2: The interpreter I was talking about had only recently become accredited in the last year. She went through training. I know she went to a training program and got accredited at paraprofessional level. I had to do something positive, so I contacted the person who had booked the interpreters and said, "I can't have her." The booking person said, "She was only a fill-in anyway." But the interpreter herself knew from the previous session that she could not do the job well, but she still said yes to coming again. I don't understand why.

Focus group 2

P2: I have my own professional standards, which I admit are high, the same as all of you do. If I meet an interpreter who doesn't match that, it can feel embarrassing sometimes.

P1: Sometimes you have to take what you can get because there's no one available. It's disappointing, but I understand.

P6: I feel it's okay if we can have control over who we want to interpret. For example, if I'm organizing a meeting, I always supply a list of my preferred interpreters to match the situation. For example, I do a lot of work with telecommunications, so I prefer to use interpreters who have worked in that area a lot already, so they know about the technology [and] the devices and can then interpret well without asking for repeats. There are a lot of abbreviations and acronyms, so I can work with them better. So in that way, I have control.

Let's say I arrive in a situation where someone else has booked the interpreter, I feel that I can't complain. It's between that person and the interpreter, they booked the interpreter, not me. I will accept that; I'm more accepting in that circumstance. However, if I've booked the interpreter, I will complain if I'm not happy because I've made the booking. You see what I mean?

P2: Yes, and you can complain to the agency that you booked with. You have that right.

P6: Yes. In that situation I talked about before involving that embarrassing interpreter, I complained to the agency who booked the interpreter. But it was like talking to a brick wall. I couldn't change their mindset.

Key: P = Participant

FIGURE 1. *Selecting interpreters.*

Prior Experience with Interpreters

When deaf consumers select an interpreter themselves, they almost always (92% of occasions) choose those they have worked with in the past. Even when they do not do the choosing, they have often (80% of occasions) previously worked with the interpreter.

The number of times deaf consumers had worked with the selected interpreter was coded using a 6-point scale. The codes were assigned as follows: Code 1 indicated a prior working relationship on 1–5 occasions (rarely); code 2, 6–10 occasions (infrequently); code 3, 11–20 occasions (sometimes); code 4, 21–30 occasions (relatively often); code 5, 31–50 occasions (often); and code 6 indicated a long-term relationship (more than 50 occasions). Prior experience was reported in 201 interpreting events, and the code ratings ranged from 1 to 6 (M = 2.21, SD = 1.51, Mdn = 2.00).

As expected, a significant difference appeared in the number of previous experiences with the interpreter when the deaf consumers made their own selections (M = 2.77), compared with occasions on which others made the choice for them (M = 1.90), $t(134.66_{adj} = 3.85)$, $p < .001$; mean difference .87; 95% CI: .42–1.31). There was also significantly more variability in deaf consumers' prior experience when interpreters were chosen by the deaf consumers (SD = 1.67) than when others made the selection (SD = 1.31, $F = 8.55$, $p = .004$).

These results also take into account the interpreters' availability. For deaf consumers who chose their own interpreter, their first choice was available only 76% of the time.

The fact that deaf consumers like to work with interpreters with whom they have worked before was clearly evident in the focus group discussions (see figure 2).

Future Selection of Interpreters

On only 21% of occasions did the deaf consumers report that they would not use the same interpreter again. On almost all of these (94%), the interpreter had been selected by someone else. Of the rejected interpreters, 24% were professionals, 54% were paraprofessionals, and 6% had no accreditation (accreditation was unknown for the remaining 16% of the rejected interpreters). None of the professional interpreters whom the deaf consumers had chosen themselves were in the rejected group.

P2: The issue of trust for me depends on my previous experience with the interpreter. I will always give them the opportunity to work with me. If there is voicing work involved, I will willingly sign what I want to say, but at the same time I monitor the interpreter by watching what they do. . . . So I use those methods to decide if I can trust the interpreter to do a good job or not. . . . If I work with a new interpreter, I seem to have a good gut feeling about whether I can trust the person or not. . . . Meeting the interpreter and talking to him/her first makes me tend to think that the interpreter is a good one. In those conversations, if I have not met the interpreter before, I always ask about their previous experience and where they have worked before, how they became involved in interpreting, etc. I always ask those types of questions, so that I can make up my mind about whether the interpreter is a good one.

P3: It's a difficult situation. On many occasions, I've met the interpreter before the job, and I've thought, "Oh no! How am I going to deal with *that* interpreter?" But I have to accept the situation; I have to. I might be thinking, "I know this person can't deal with the type of information that will come up in this lecture, but oh well."

FIGURE 2. *Prior experience.*

Comprehension of Interpreter

The deaf consumers were asked to respond to the question "How well or badly did you understand the interpreter today?" using a scale that ranged from 0 (did not understand anything) to 10 (understood everything). The responses ranged from 0 to 10 (M = 8.48, SD = 1.90, Mdn = 9.00). However, a planned contrast comparing the comprehension level of deaf consumers who had and had not chosen their interpreter showed that the level of comprehension reported by the former was significantly higher (M = 8.95) than that reported by the latter (M = 8.22, $t(221.88_{adj}$ = 3.20), p = .002; mean difference .72; 95% CI: .28–1.17). In addition, significantly more variability appeared in the comprehension reports of those who did not select their interpreter (SD = 2.04) than when the deaf consumers made their own choice (SD = 1.52, F = 6.83, p = .01).

When deaf consumers selected the interpreter and their first choice was available, their comprehension was significantly greater (M = 9.35) than when the interpreter was not available (M = 7.71, $t(22.53_{adj}$ = 3.32), p = .003; mean difference = .49; 95% CI: .6–2.66). Very little variability appeared in the comprehension ratings of interpreters who were a consumer's first choice (SD = .95) and significantly less variability than when the interpreter was not the first choice (SD = 2.19, F = 41.26, p < .001).

Accreditation and Comprehension

Not unexpectedly, the reported levels of comprehension were highest when professional interpreters (M = 9.19, SD = 1.38; i.e., Level 3) were working and lowest when the interpreter had no accreditation (M = 7.60, SD = 2.32). This difference is statistically significant: t(15.47_{adj} = 2.59), p = .02; mean difference 1.59; 95% CI: .29–2.90. The difference in variability of the comprehension ratings is also significant (F = 12.49, p = .001), with greater variability when the interpreter had no accreditation.

There was also a significantly greater comprehension of professional interpreters (M = 9.19, SD = 1.39) than of paraprofessionals (M = 8.08, SD = 1.98, t(219.84_{adj} = 4.91), p < .001; mean difference = 1.11; 95% CI: .66–1.56). Again, greater variability of comprehension ratings was evident when the interpreters held paraprofessional accreditation than when they held professional interpreter accreditation (F = 16.50).

On 8% of interpreting occasions, the deaf consumers did not know the interpreters' accreditation level, but they were unlikely to be professionally accredited. Australia has relatively few interpreters, and they are generally well known. It can be assumed, then, that these interpreters either were paraprofessionals or did not have any accreditation. The comprehension ratings of these interpreters was relatively low and similar to the comprehension ratings of nonaccredited interpreters (M = 7.86, SD = 2.34).

Use of Fingerspelling, Accreditation, and Comprehension

Participants rated the extent of fingerspelling used by the interpreters. The ratings ranged from 0 (did not use fingerspelling at all) to 10 (used a lot of fingerspelling; M = 5.33, SD = 2.34, Mdn = 5.00). There is no significant difference in the extent of fingerspelling used by interpreters (M = 5.66, SD = 2.40) and paraprofessionals (M = 5.18, SD = 2.27, t(219 = 1.53)). The relation between degree of fingerspelling and comprehension was not significant (r = −.10, n = 113). However, when the relation between comprehension and fingerspelling is examined for consumers who did and who did not select their own interpreter, a different picture emerges.

When deaf consumers choose their own interpreters, there is no relation between the extent of fingerspelling and comprehension (r = .03, n = 86).

However, when they do not select the interpreter, greater comprehension is significantly associated with less fingerspelling ($r = -.19$, $n = 164$).

Sign Use and Comprehension

For each interpreting event, the participants rated the approximate number of unfamiliar signs the interpreter used by choosing one of five categories that corresponded to 1 (few) and 5 (many). Ratings ranged from 1 to 5 ($M = 1.39$, $SD = .89$, $Mdn = 1$). Not unsurprisingly, a significant negative correlation occurred between comprehension and the number of unfamiliar signs: the more unfamiliar the signs, the lower the comprehension ($r = -.65$, $p < .001$, $n = 258$).

Interpreters with no accreditation used the greatest number of unfamiliar signs ($M = 1.80$, $SD = 1.27$), whereas accredited interpreters used the fewest ($M = 1.25$, $SD = .72$), although this difference is not significant, $t(15.36_{adj} = 1.64)$). However, significantly more variability appeared in reports of unfamiliar signs used by nonaccredited interpreters.

There was also no significant difference between professional interpreters and paraprofessionals ($M = 1.42$, $SD = .92$, $t(216.83_{adj} = 1.47)$), although significantly more variability occurred in reports of unfamiliar signs used by paraprofessionals ($F = 6.48$, $p = .01$).

Comfort Level, Smoothness of Communication, and Comprehension

The participants were asked to rate how comfortable or uncomfortable they felt while watching the interpreter. To do so, they used a 7-point scale that was labeled at −3 (very uncomfortable), 0 (neither comfortable nor uncomfortable), and +3 (very comfortable). After recoding so that the lowest rating was 1 and the highest 7, the ratings ranged from 1 to 7 ($M = 5.71$, $SD = 1.68$, $Mdn = 6.00$). The participants also rated the smoothness of communication on a 7-point scale that ranged from −3 to +3. This was also recoded, and the ratings then ranged from 1 to 7 ($M = 5.64$, $SD = 1.60$, $Mdn = 6.00$). A significant positive correlation was evident between the two ratings ($r = .87$, $n = 255$, $p < .001$).

As figure 3 shows, the highest comfort ratings ($M = 6.20$, $SD = 1.47$) and the highest communication smoothness ratings ($M = 6.14$, $SD = 1.41$) were reported for professional interpreters. In general, the highest comfort and communication smoothness were associated with those occasions on which the deaf consumers selected the interpreter. Both comfort ratings and communication smoothness ratings were

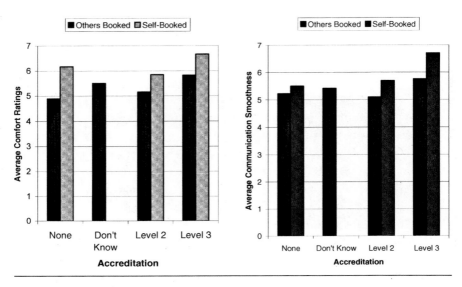

FIGURE 3. *Comfort rating.*

significantly associated with comprehension ratings (r = .71, n = 258 and r = .74, n = 256, respectively).

The focus group participants also stated that comfort was often influenced by how "good" the interpreter was (figure 4).

Overall Satisfaction

Participants were also asked to rate their satisfaction with the interpreter on each occasion, using a 7-point scale that ranged from –3 to +3. This was recoded, and the ratings ranged from 1 to 7 (M = 5.61, SD = 1.66, Mdn = 6.00). As figure 5 shows, the highest satisfaction ratings were associated with self-selected interpreters (M = 6.23, SD = .58), and the lowest overall satisfaction ratings were associated with paraprofessionals who were chosen by other people (M = 4.94, SD = 1.85) and with nonaccredited interpreters, who were also selected by others (M = 5.00, SD = 2.00).

Qualitative Responses: What Do Consumers Like and Dislike?

For each interpreting event recorded in their diary, the participants described the interpreters' two best and two worst features. The responses were coded according to the categories discussed in Campbell, Rohan, and Woodcock (in press) and to categories related to linguistic style. These categories, with a brief explanation, are given in table 2.

What I feel is important is that I can participate in what's going on regardless of if there are hearing and Deaf people in the meeting. When the interpreter is working well and conveying what everyone says, that's excellent. I can feel comfortable. When [hearing people] laugh, I laugh, too. I like when that happens. I think the interpreter has then done a good job.

It's a balancing act. But related to that points to . . . I had one interpreter who was great, and the other was new, and I, to be honest, it was really painful when the good interpreter finished and swapped with the other one; it was signed English. I felt like pushing that person aside. When the first interpreter swapped back, it was so comfortable. It really made a huge difference.

You feel like you only get about half the information; you get only half. Like you watch [the good interpreter], and it's comfortable, it's interesting, you pay attention and understand, and then with the other interpreter your mind wanders, and you can't wait for the other to come back, so you only get half the information.

There were two interpreters working side by side, and I couldn't wait for it to be the other person's turn because he/she is a very good interpreter. I was hoping for the 20 minutes to pass quickly so the good interpreter could start and I could relax and feel comfortable. Then for the next 20 minutes I'd have to struggle to work out what was going on.

FIGURE 4. *Comfort with interpreters.*

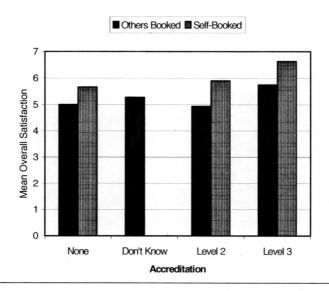

FIGURE 5. *Levels of satisfaction.*

TABLE 2. *Categories of Description*

Coding category	Description	Number of times used: best features (in rounded percentages)	Number of times used: worst features (in rounded percentage)
Expressive signing skills	interpreter produces signs clearly and correctly	82; 18.3%	49; 19.8%
Nonmanual features	interpreter uses facial expressions appropriately and accurately	20; 4.5%	11; 4.5%
Consumer's comprehension	deaf consumer understands the interpreter	9; 2%	4; 1.6%
Receptive signing skills	interpreter understands the deaf consumer's signing	8; 1.8%	12; 4.9%
Voice-over skills	interpreter voices over accurately and smoothly	3; .07%	10; 4.0%
Message translation	message is translated accurately in both directions	55; 12.3%	47; 19.0%
Professionalism		182; 40.7%	83; 33.6%

General, including attitude, commitment, ethics	interpreter has a good attitude and is ethical	80; 17.9%	56; 22.7%
Attire	interpreter dresses appropriately	18; 4.0%	9; 3.6%
Punctuality	interpreter arrives on time for assignments	17; 3.8%	6; 2.4%
Focus on consumer needs	interpreter is flexible and adapts to the consumer's needs according to context	22; 4.9%	3; 1.2%
Teamwork	interpreter works professionally and smoothly with other interpreters	45; 10.1%	9; 3.6%
Situational knowledge	interpreter is familiar with content and/or context	7; 1.6%	9; 3.6%
Personal characteristics	interpreter has good sense of humor, is pleasant and friendly	81; 18.1%	22; 8.9%
Total reports		447	247

POSITIVE ASPECTS

Professionalism was most often (40.7%) cited as the participants' first reported positive feature. Included in the professionalism category were comments that related to very basic aspects of professionalism, such as appropriate dress (17% of the professionalism coded responses) and punctuality (16% of the professionalism coded responses). Expressive signing skills (e.g., "clarity of signs," "fluent and expressive") and personal characteristics (e.g., "flexible," "patient," "friendly," "good sense of humor") each accounted for 18% of the responses concerning the interpreters' positive aspects. Positive comments about the efficacy of the translation accounted for 12.3% of responses (e.g., "appropriate register for English to Auslan," "She gave me very comprehensive interpretation of info being presented," "able to sign at same pace as teacher's instructions").

The second feature (see table 3) cited by deaf consumers as being one of the best features of the interpreters shows a similar pattern, with the greatest number of responses concerning professionalism (29.1%). The next most-used category concerned personal characteristics (20.7%). The message translation category was used for 15.7% of responses. Deaf consumers also made comments that concerned the interpreters' knowledge of the situation (12.3% of responses; e.g., "familiar with content"; "understanding of subjects discussed"; "clearly has university experience and can handle the jargon and technical info").

In summary, it appears that deaf consumers' preferences for interpreters focus heavily on issues relevant to professionalism, expressive signing skills, personal characteristics, and message translation adequacy. Situational knowledge was also a category that was used to code responses.

NEGATIVE ASPECTS

Deaf consumers' negative comments about their interpreters also centered around professionalism, the adequacy of the message translation, personal characteristics, and expressive signing skills. More specifically, mirroring the reports of positive aspects, the most commonly mentioned first feature related to professionalism (e.g., "breached role again," "would often included her personal opinions in her interpreting," "a bit casual in approach—lackadaisical"). In addition, almost 20% of the comments also related to expressive signing skills (e.g., "particular habits, especially bent/

TABLE 3. *Features of Interpreters*

Coding category	Number of times used: best features (in rounded percentages)	Number of times used: worst features (in rounded percentage)
Expressive signing skills	27; 13.3%	14; 17.3%
Nonmanual features	9; 4.4%	5; 6.2%
Consumer's comprehension	3; 1.4%	2; 2.5%
Receptive signing skills	5; 2.5%	4; 4.9%
Voicing	1; .05%	3; 3.7%
Message translation	32; 15.7%	22; 27.2%
Professionalism	59; 29.1%	23; 28.4%
General, including attitude, commitment, ethics	28; 13.8%	15; 18.5%
Appropriate attire	5; 2.5%	1; 1.2%
Punctuality	5; 2.5%	1; 1.2%
Focus on consumer's needs	15; 4.9%	2; 2.5%
Teamwork with other interpreters	6; 3%	4; 4.9%
Situational knowledge	25; 12.3%	4; 4.9%
Personal characteristics	42; 20.7%	4; 4.9%
Total reports	203	81

hooked little fingers all the time—an eyesore!" "poor signing, nervousness," "finger spelling—he/she couldn't spell!"). Inability to provide an adequate translation of the message also accounted for 19% of the comments (e.g., "not getting 'all' the message," "She/he wasn't giving me the info I needed," "unable to keep up and appeared unwilling to ask presenter to slow down"). For the second comment made about the negative aspects of interpreters, 28.4% were coded as relating to professionalism; 27.2%, the quality of the message translation; and 17.3%, expressive signing skills.

REPORTS OF NEGATIVE FEATURES AND ACCREDITATION LEVELS

Focusing on the most frequently used coding categories (professionalism, adequacy of message translation, personal characteristics, and expressive signing skills), the number of times (and the percentage of the number of interpreters) the coding category was used for interpreters with each type of accreditation is shown in table 4.

Table 4 indicates some dissatisfaction with the professionalism of professional-level interpreters because negative comments about the professionalism of 30.4% of professionally accredited interpreters were recorded. However, professional interpreter-level status is supposedly an indicator of professionalism. As we discussed earlier, there are two main

TABLE 4. *Negative Features According to Accreditation Level*

	Unknown accreditation $n = 22$	No accreditation $n = 12$	Para-professional $n = 122$	Professional 105
Professionalism	1; 45%	7; 58%	30; 24.6%	32; 30.4%
General	6	7	18	24
Appropriate attire	3	0	5	1
Punctuality	1	0	2	3
Focus on consumer's needs	0	0	2	1
Teamwork	0	0	3	3
Message translation	3; 13.6%	3; 25%	26; 21.3%	15; 14.3%
Personal characteristics	1; 4.5%	3; 25%	15; 12.3%	3; 2.8%
Expressive signing skills	1	5	29; 23.7%	14; 13.3%

paths to achieving interpreter-level status. Further research is needed to determine whether consumer satisfaction is related to these different paths.

Not surprisingly, more negative comments were made about the adequacy of message translation by paraprofessional interpreters (21.3%) than by professional interpreters (14.3%). However, given that professional interpreters should be displaying high levels of efficacy, negative comments about 14.3% of professional interpreters is disturbing. Again, we discuss this later in the context of training issues.

Fewer complaints about personal characteristics were made about professional interpreters (2.8%) than about paraprofessional interpreters (12.3%). Not surprisingly, fewer complaints were also made about professional interpreters' expressive signing skills (13.3%) than about those of paraprofessionals (23.7%), although again it is a concern that there are any complaints at all about professional interpreters' expressive signing skills. The focus group discussions provided further evidence that deaf consumers' positive or negative comments about interpreters tend to concentrate in the key areas as identified by the diary responses. Examples from each focus group are given in table 5.

In sum, with reference to these categories, the likes and dislikes of the deaf consumers in the focus groups are shown in table 6.

Limitations of the Study

Two features of the current research may limit the generalizability of the results. The first concerns the nature of the participants, and the second involves the mode of delivery. In both the diary study and the focus groups, the majority of participants were university-educated deaf professionals. It is possible to speculate why this was the case, but there is no certain explanation. We feel that a likely reason is that deaf professionals may have a better understanding of the value of research. It may also be due to the fact that the call for participants was sent out in the form of a flyer. Although it was written in plain English, many deaf people may have considered it irrelevant. Moreover, the majority of respondents were in the 30–39 age bracket and therefore of the generation of deaf people who have accessed their university education through interpreters and also use them in their workplace (as compared to most other deaf people, who use an interpreter only for medical appointments perhaps once a year).

This has a bearing on the results as it means that the participants in our study will likely have had different experiences of working with

TABLE 5. *Examples of Focus Group Categories*

Coding category	Focus Group 1	Focus Group 2
Expressive signing skills	What makes an interpreter lovely to watch is that they are easy on the eye. Watching graceful, elegant movement is enjoyable. It's good when someone knows how to play with expression. Sometimes an interpreter may know how to interact comfortably socially and when they start to work, they change "code" and adopt a more formal stance. They might use a smaller or larger signing space because they know there are different levels of expression. That's also what makes a good interpreter, someone who signs the same way at home or socializing as they do when they are working. Recognizing different levels of expression.	"Give me the information! Give me the language, give me everything!" I said at the start, "Please, if you don't know the sign for a word, just finger spell it. I can work it out for myself because I know the language they will use. Just give it to me if you don't know a sign."
Nonmanual features	I think it's unnatural for a person to sign without using facial expression.	Maybe that's the interpreter's role: They have to think through and work out what the possibilities are. Maybe they could be tired, and they think, "I'm not passing on the right information" or "Maybe my facial expression is boring" [laughs]. I think they need to work through some of those things.
Consumer's comprehension	In some of the meetings I go to regularly, I know the interpreters well, so generally I understand everything—no problem. I also use other interstate interpreters because I travel a lot, or I may work with brand new interpreters that I've not met before. I'd say that for most of them, say 80%, I understand just fine, but for 20% of them I don't understand at all.	Or they know you well enough [so that] you can show in your facial expression that you're puzzled or not happy. That's why my favorite interpreter is my favorite. She knows me, so she knows if I don't understand. She can see my facial expression is showing that, so she knows not to summarize but to actually add more information to make sure I understand everything.

Receptive signing skills	There are still a few interpreters who are mindful of that, so I have to make an effort to modify my signing and remember to slow down. It's better for me really because, if I go too fast, they don't understand what I'm saying. So if I slow the pace down, then they understand me.	I know this person is involved socially with the Deaf community, but it looks like he/she is stuck in a rut with their signing; it doesn't improve. I know that person doesn't understand me. Even a few weeks ago that person was booked for a job that I was at. That person will never make it in my opinion.
Voicing skills	A while ago we had the Cluedo evening. The interpreter picked exactly the right voice and accent to match my character. The hearing people commented on how good it was. The Deaf people missed out on that part, but they still got the message through my acting and use of gesture. The hearing people didn't miss out though.	The training required me to be fully involved in discussions and be able to share my experience and to talk about my issues and so on. So that meant the interpreter had to voice for me when I signed. The first time this interpreter had interpreted for me in the course was two months ago. I could see that she found it difficult to voice for me. The interpreter struggled and stumbled, and on some occasions I gave up and spoke for myself.
Message translation	Often Deaf people miss out on things, so I think that interpreters should be able to look at the Deaf client, and, if it seems that the person did not get the message, the interpreter should be able to realize they have done something wrong and modify the way they interpret. They should be able to say, "This is what is meant," then I can laugh as well, which is a big relief for me. That's what I mean: A good interpreter can do that.	I wonder do all interpreters understand Deaf people's finger spelling and Auslan? Are they good at getting the message? I know if someone interrupts me and asks me what I said, it throws me; communication is not smooth. I lose track. I wonder what interpreters out there are like. They ask me sometimes to spell something again, and I do, but sometimes I sign. I wonder about that.
Professionalism	I want the interpreter to be professional, impartial, and dispassionate in some circumstances, but in others it's okay to joke and chat like a group of friends would.	For me it means professional standards. Having a good attitude in my professional job means having professional standards. It means doing what is appropriate.

TABLE 5. *Continued*

Coding category	Focus Group 1	Focus Group 2
General, including attitude, commitment, ethics	It's about attitude, professionalism, timing	There are just some people who have a great attitude automatically—they are just that type of person.
Attire		I had a bad experience at my graduation. I was very embarrassed. The interpreter turned up. . . . Her clothing was really terrible, and I was mortified. Everyone else was dressed formally. . . . [She] looked very unkempt. . . . She should have worn clothes appropriate for the situation.
Punctuality	When an interpreter has the wrong attitude or arrives late, that has a negative impact on the quality of the service.	An example of a bad attitude is an interpreter who turns up late. [all nod] That's my *pet* hate—interpreters who turn up late. I hate it.
Focus on consumer needs	The ideal interpreter is someone who is willing to be flexible, to do their best to understand me, to keep their ears and eyes open, and is willing to be my "ears" and my "eyes" and facilitate the conversation.	I think working with the same interpreter several times helps. Also what you [points to LJ] said earlier about the interpreter approaching the Deaf person before the job starts [JA nods] to talk and work things out and try to match the Deaf person's needs and to work out what is happening.

Teamwork	I totally agree with having two interpreters, but I've had an interesting experience using two interpreters. They had a spat about something when they changed over, and I didn't know what to do. I tried to encourage them to work together, but . . .
Situational knowledge	General knowledge of the content used in that situation, so that I can talk freely and naturally. What I sign might not look sophisticated, but the interpreter knows what I mean and can interpret that into the right form of the language in spoken form. I decided for myself that if I have a choice at all, if I can't have my favorite, I will ask for a Level 3 because most of the things I need an interpreter for are very formal things. Level 2 interpreters can't always cope with that. [JA nods.] They don't know how to manage situations like that.
Personal characteristics	There are Level 3 interpreters out there who have a lot of experience, but they don't have the other characteristics that make them professional. They need to go through a course, get through it, and graduate to be professional. That the person is able to meet others and talk with them. So not only language, because there may be some interpreters who have fantastic signing and voicing skills but are terrified to talk to people on a personal level.

TABLE 6. *Summary of Likes and Dislikes*

Coding category	What focus group participants like in interpreters	What focus group participants do not like in interpreters
expressive signing skills		use incorrect signs; are unable to work into both Auslan and English confidently and accurately
Nonmanual features consumer comprehension receptive signing skills		are unable to work in both Auslan and English confidently and accurately
Voicing		are unable to work in both Auslan and English confidently and accurately
message translation	convey everything that goes on	are unclear, so have to reinterpret meaning do not ask for a repeat when message is not understood
professionalism	work with the client to establish common and preferred signs, protocols, and procedures ask for feedback appropriately ask for repetition/clarification are tactful are prepared for assignments are discreet and do not draw attention to themselves	do not prepare apologize too much for making an error are not receptive to feedback do not stay in role want attention

general, including attitude, commitment, ethics	
Appropriate attire	
Punctuality	are punctual
focus on consumer needs	relate to the client are not controlling communicate the way deaf people do — require change of signing style to meet their needs
teamwork	do not get along with each other (creates tension) do not change over smoothly and quickly with team interpreter
situational knowledge personal characteristics	

interpreters as compared to members of the wider Deaf community. As Hauser, Finch, and Hauser (in press) state, the typical interpreting model may not apply when working with deaf professionals because they have different needs (see also Woodcock, Rohan, & Campbell, in press; Campbell, Rohan, & Woodcock, in press). This limitation will be taken into account in our future research, which will include attending various deaf gatherings (such as sporting, senior, and youth events) and making announcements in Auslan to a range of "grassroots" and professional deaf people in order to capture a range of ages and experiences in working with interpreters.

The second limitation is that the diary study was conducted in English. We attempted to account for this by conducting the focus groups in Auslan. However, we are aware that some deaf people may have been put off by the English structure of the diary template. We initially received fifty-three expressions of interest in participating, but after sending out the information we received only thirty-one sets of diaries. Thus any future diary studies will attempt to circumvent this problem by providing participants with an opportunity to keep a video diary and upload their entries to a website. Nonetheless, we feel that the data collected in this study have presented significant results and provided further insight into the perceptions and preferences of deaf consumers in relation to interpreting.

DISCUSSION AND CONCLUSIONS

Quantitative and qualitative data have been presented with regard to deaf people's perceptions of the quality and standards of signed language interpreting in Australia. The data were collected from deaf people's actual experiences of working with interpreters over a period of time and from discussions about generic experiences and preferences. The goal was to investigate the factors that lead to satisfaction when using interpreters; to investigate consumers' perceptions of what makes some interpreters more understandable than others; to identify the factors that make Auslan interpreters comfortable to watch; and to define the qualities of an ideal interpreter.

We have found that general satisfaction levels are relatively high, although deaf people seem to have little choice in the interpreters they access. Comprehension seems to be significantly higher when deaf people do have the opportunity to choose their own interpreters. However, deaf consumers in Australia have clear ideas on what constitutes an ideal interpreter; for them, the key factors leading to comfort in working with interpreters are understanding of the consumer and context, professionalism, and attitude.

This study highlights the need for interpreters and deaf people to work closely together and demonstrates the importance of conducting research on interpreting with deaf people. Thus, our hypotheses that deaf people's reported comprehension and satisfaction are influenced by their prior experience with the interpreter, the interpreter's accreditation level, and whether they had chosen the interpreter have been supported, although the tests we used to examine these hypotheses did not always reach significance when the focus was on the interpreter's accreditation level.

The generally high satisfaction levels are pleasing to see, especially when compared to the fact that a 1987–1988 study by the National Association of the Deaf in the United States found that 70% of the deaf individuals who participated were dissatisfied with interpreting quality (cited in Marschark et al., 2005, p. 346). This demonstrates that either interpreters have come a long way in improving their skills and attitudes or deaf people have a better understanding and appreciation of how to work with interpreters, or both.

This study highlights the importance of consulting with deaf people in order to investigate their notions of interpreting and their attitudes toward interpreters. As Edwards et al. (2005) have stated in their study of ethic minority interpreters in the UK, it is important to look at the common issues in consumers' experiences of working with interpreters. Adhering to the recommendations of Turner and Harrington (2000), this research has been "on, for and with" stakeholders, and the participants have been given an opportunity to discuss their own agendas. The next stage is to share this knowledge with the relevant stakeholders.

The study also demonstrates that interpreters and deaf people need to work together in order to achieve success in every interpreted event and also to improve standards generally in the interpreting profession. Various authors have discussed the co-construction of meaning between interpreters and interlocutors (Turner & Brown, 2001; Wadensjö, 2002; Wilcox & Shaffer, 2005) and the need for deaf people and interpreters to cooperate with one another to achieve successful communication (Napier, Carmichael, & Wiltshire, in press). To put it in the words of the focus group participants (see figure 6), the relationship between interpreters and deaf people can be considered as "an invitation to dance." We hope interpreters will take note of the likes and dislikes expressed by the deaf participants in this research and will seek to dance in a way that is beneficial to everyone.

The Australian Association of the Deaf has a policy on interpreting that states that "interpreting between Auslan and English is an essen-

Focus group 1

P3: If I picture the ideal interpreter, I think of an imaginary line like a boundary that is always moving, moving, moving, depending on the situation. Sometimes the boundary moves away [from the interpreter] to more of a cultural bridge, and passing on information is a lesser role, and other times the balance is different with the Deaf client. I think the interpreter should know and be aware of how to move the boundary in different situations.

P1: Like a dynamic interpreting situation. Excellent. That's interesting.

P2: What P3 said is excellent. It's called an "invitation to dance." The communication is based on, "I'll meet you and invite you to dance," and once our communication is established, then we can go forward. It's like you're inviting the interpreter to dance with you.

P3: I think my criteria are: one, knowing the Deaf person, knowing what they are capable of and where they stand in the circumstances with the hearing people. Knowing how to behave if it's a social situation, an informal situation, or something very formal. Recognizing the Deaf person's status amongst the hearing people and recognizing the hierarchy that exists. An interpreter who can do that is my ideal.

P1: I was thinking about that boundary idea. [points to P3] Do you mean that you would you rather lead or control the situation, or the interpreter do that, or somewhere in between?

P5: I'd never allow the interpreter to control it.

P2: It's a dance. It's like a dance.

P1: Who is in control of the situation?

P2: Ginger Rogers and Fred Astaire. Who's leading?

P1: I know. I understand that, but is it you [points to P2] dancing with the hearing person, or you [points to P2] dancing with the interpreter?

P2: Both. It's a triangle [draws a vertical triangle in front of body] in a way.

P1: Is it possible to work out that way? Can you dance with three people?

P6: Of course, yes.

FIGURE 6. *An invitation to dance.*

P4: She's [points to P3] talking about an ideal. That's her dream, a wish list.

P1: I know. That's what I mean: Do you ideally want to control the interpreter or have the interpreter control the situation?

P3: I mean that flexibility is there, but the interpreter knows that they should never control the situation. I don't know how to express it.

P6: I feel that the interpreter is a communication facilitator. That person knows when to become silent or when to become assertive or passive.

P1: You mean a communication facilitator, in not the same way as a telephone? Not completely impartial?

P6: No, not like a telephone.

P1: So the person has a relationship with both parties.

P6: Yes. Because I don't have access to the radio, I don't have access to information in the same way hearing people do. It's different because I use my eyes. I see captions, I see everything I need to see. I don't hear anything. In some situations, I can see a lot of discussion going on, and the interpreter might say that they are talking about . . . a "hearing joke," which I miss out on. I don't laugh because I don't understand it. The interpreter might explain, "This is what it means." I might just shrug or I might laugh, too. I control the circumstances, not them [the interpreter]. That's where I need to be able to laugh along with everyone else. Often Deaf people miss out on things, so I think that interpreters should be able to look at the Deaf client, and if it seems that the person did not get the message, the interpreter should be able to realize they have done something wrong and then modify the way they interpret. They should be able to say, "This is what is meant," then I can laugh as well, which is a big relief for me. That's what I mean: A *good* interpreter can do that.

P1: Back to what you [points to P3] were saying before about the boundary, I'd love for interpreters to have prior awareness, so that if communication goes off track, they realize where it happened and with who and make moves to repair it. It's awareness of the dynamics that the interpreter has innately through education. It includes being aware of the Deaf person's language level and being able to adapt and convey the spoken message to match. Is it wrong that they improve it a bit?

FIGURE 6. *Continued*

tial aspect in the life of the Deaf Community and enables equal participation by Deaf persons in the wider community. Often it is the principal means by which a Deaf person accesses the wider community in which they live" (AAD, 2006). We suggested the following key points are essential for the promotion of effective working practices by signed-support AAD language interpreters in Australia:

1. Signed language interpreting is a highly skilled profession that requires funds for appropriate professional training programs.
2. Signed language interpreting is an area of signed language linguistics that has not been sufficiently researched, and research in this area is a matter of priority.
3. A strong relationship with the Australian Sign Language Interpreters Association (ASLIA) is necessary, and communication and consultation between the leaders of the AAD and the ASLIA must occur regularly.
4. Interpreters must be appropriately trained and accredited by the National Accreditation Authority for Translators and Interpreters (NAATI) at the paraprofessional, professional, and conference interpreter levels.
5. Employers of interpreters must employ only those individuals who possess Auslan/English interpreting accreditation from NAATI.
6. Interpreters should not be engaged as paid interpreters for appointments with their own deaf family members (parents, children, siblings, and partners).
7. All interpreting practitioners should be members of the ASLIA.

Given these recommendations from the AAD, we would like to present an invitation to dance to the Deaf community, ASLIA, AAD, interpreting service agencies, interpreter education institutions, and other stakeholders worldwide—to work together to disseminate the findings of this study and to share knowledge and information about interpreters and interpreting, with the hope that we will continue to see further improvement. We conclude with suggestions for training, service delivery, and research.

Training

- We suggest that ASLIA, AAD, and other training institutions collaborate on a series of face-to-face information workshops, bringing interpreters and deaf people together to discuss interpreting issues, the interpreter's role, and effective strategies for working together.
- We suggest that Macquarie University and other TAFE institutions establish advisory groups with members of the Deaf community, AAD, and ASLIA to ensure that training programs are delivering the kinds of interpreters that deaf people want.

- We suggest that an interpreter training network be established to enable interpreter educators to share information, resources, and exercises and to ensure that interpreting students are receiving similar instruction.
- We suggest that NAATI introduce mandatory training requirements in Australia, with a move toward university qualification as the foundation for interpreter training and education (following the current efforts of the Registry of Interpreters for the Deaf in the United States).

Service Delivery

Given that a significant element of the study centered on deaf people's opportunities to choose their interpreters, we recommend that, wherever possible, interpreting service agencies provide options to deaf consumers to select their preferred interpreters. The results from this study show that this makes a significant difference in the outcome of the interpreted event. Many interpreting agencies in Australia and elsewhere already adhere to such a policy, but the fact that only 34% of deaf participants in this study were able to choose their interpreters shows that this practice is obviously not consistent.

Research

Although this was the first study of its kind to investigate deaf consumers' experiences in working with interpreters in their everyday lives, the data still rely on self-reporting and personal perception. Thus, further empirical quantitative and qualitative research is needed to develop a more comprehensive picture of signed language interpreting practices in Australia, and we plan to extend this research with four further studies (pending funding):

- a Web-based, signed language diary study with larger numbers from the wider Deaf community in Australia and with replications of the study in other countries in order to obtain a worldwide picture of consumers' perceptions of interpreting
- an in-depth qualitative discourse analysis of perceptions of interpreting as reported by deaf and hearing people, as well as interpreters. A further four focus groups have already been conducted with hearing consumers and interpreters, so we have planned to carry out an analysis of attitudes toward interpreting by drawing on the appraisal theory of systemic

functional linguistics (Halliday, 1994; Martin & Rose, 2002), which analyzes the language that people actually use to give further insight into their attitudes about a topic.

- a cross-linguistic study of deaf consumers' comprehension of an interpreted text as compared to the comprehension of hearing consumers who rely on interpretation into other spoken languages
- a cross-linguistic study of deaf consumers' comprehension of interpreted texts in English-speaking countries but into different signed languages (e.g., Auslan, ASL, New Zealand Sign Language, Irish Sign Language, South African Sign Language)

ACKNOWLEDGMENTS

The funding for this study was provided through Jemina Napier's Macquarie University postdoctoral research fellowship. Earlier discussions of preliminary data from this study were presented at the Supporting Deaf People Online Conferences in 2005 and 2006 (see http://www.directlearn.co.uk/). We would like to thank all of the deaf people who participated in the study; the Australian Association of the Deaf for distributing the call for participants; Andrew Myles and Maree Madden for their assistance with data entry, transcription, and analysis; and Louise Reynolds and Chris Candlin for their support.

REFERENCES

Australian Association of the Deaf. (2006). Interpreting policy. www.aad.org.au (accessed December 12, 2006).

Babbie, E. R. (1973). *Survey research methods*. Belmont, CA: Wadsworth.

Baker-Shenk, C. (1986). Characteristics of oppressed and oppressor peoples. In Marina L. McIntire (Ed.), *Interpreting: The art of cross-cultural mediation* (pp. 59–71). Silver Spring, MD: RID Publications.

Banna, K. (2004). The role of interpreters in the courtroom. Research report, Macquarie University, Sydney, Australia.

Bienvenu, MJ. (1987). Third culture: Working together. *Journal of Interpretation 4*, 1–12.

Bontempo, K. (2005). A survey of Auslan interpreters' perceptions of competence. Postgraduate certificate in linguistics research, Macquarie University, Sydney, Australia.

Bontempo, K., & Napier, J. In press. A skills gap analysis of sign language interpreters. *Sign Language Translator and Interpreter 1*(2).

Bridge, M. (1991). The relevance of the NAATI testing system for sign language interpreters. Paper presented at the National Conference of the Interpreter and Translator Educators Association of Australia, RMIT University, Melbourne.

Cameron, D., Frazer, E., Harvey, P., Rampton, M. B. H., & Richardson, K. (Eds). (1992). *Researching language: Issues of power and method.* New York: Routledge.

Campbell, L., Rohan, M., & Woodcock, K. (in press). Educational and academic interpreting from the other side of the classroom: Working with Deaf professors as opposed to Deaf students. In P. C. Hauser, K. Finch, & A. Hauser (Eds.), *Deaf professionals and designated interpreters: A new paradigm.* Washington, DC: Gallaudet University Press.

Cokely, D. (1992). *Interpretation: A sociolinguistic model.* Burtonsville, MD: Linstok.

Conlon, C., & Napier, J. (2004). Developing Auslan educational resources: A process of effective translation of children's books. *Deaf Worlds 20*(2), 141–61.

Corker, M. (1997). Deaf people and interpreting: The struggle in language. *Deaf Worlds 13*(3), 13–20.

Cresswell, J. (1994). *Research design: Qualitative and quantitative approaches.* London: Sage.

Dawkins, J. (1991). *Australia's language: The Australian language and literacy policy.* Canberra: Australian Government.

Edwards, R., Temple, B., & Alexander, C. (2005). Users' experiences of interpreters: The critical role of trust. *Interpreting 7*(1), 77–96.

Flynn, J. (1996). Reflections on sign language interpreting. Paper presented at the National Deafness Conference, Hobart, Australia, May 25.

Forestal, L. (2005). Attitudes of Deaf leaders toward signed language interpreters and interpreting. In M. Metzger & E. Fleetwood (Eds.), *Attitudes, innuendo, and regulators: Challenges in interpretation* (pp. 71–91). Washington, DC: Gallaudet University Press.

Halliday, M. A. K. (1994). *An introduction to functional grammar.* London: Edward Arnold.

Harrington, F. J., & Turner, G. H. (Eds.). (2001). *Interpreting interpreting: Studies and reflections on sign language interpreting.* Coleford, UK: Douglas McLean.

Hauser, P., Finch, K., & Hauser, A. (In press). One size does not fit all: The need for a new interpreting paradigm. In P. Hauser, K. Finch, & A. Hauser (Eds.), *Deaf professionals and designated interpreters: A new paradigm.* Washington, DC: Gallaudet University Press.

Heaton, M., & Fowler, D. (1997). Aches, aspirins, and aspirations: A Deaf perspective on interpreting service delivery. *Deaf Worlds 13*(3), 3–8.

Hyde, M., & Power, D. (1992). The use of Australian sign language by Deaf people. *Sign Language Studies 75*, 167–82.

Janzen, T. (Ed). (2005). *Topics in signed language interpreting: Theory and practice*. Philadelphia: John Benjamins.

Johnston, T. (1989). *Auslan dictionary: A dictionary of the sign language of the Australian Deaf community*. Maryborough, Victoria: Deafness Resources Australia.

Johnston, T. (1998). *Signs of Australia: A new dictionary of Auslan*. Sydney: North Rocks Press.

Johnston, T. (2002). BSL, Auslan, and NZSL: Three signed languages or one? In A. Baker, B. V. D. Bogaerde, & O. Crasborn (Eds.), *Proceedings of the Seventh International Conference on Theoretical Issues in Sign Language Research* (pp. 47–69). Hamburg, Germany: Signum.

Johnston, T. (2003). W(h)ither the Deaf community? Population, genetics, and the future of Auslan (Australian Sign Language). *American Annals of the Deaf 148*(5), 358–75.

Johnston, T. (2005). W(h)ither the Deaf community? Population, genetics, and the future of Auslan (Australian Sign Language). *Sign Language Studies 6*(2), 225–43.

Krueger, R. A. (1994). *Focus groups: A practical guide for applied research*, 2d ed. Newbury Park, Calif.: Sage.

Kurz, K. B., & Langer, E. C. (2004). Student perspectives on educational interpreting: Twenty Deaf and hard of hearing students offer insights and suggestions. In E. A. Winston (Ed.), *Educational interpreting: How it can succeed* (pp. 9–47). Washington, DC: Gallaudet University Press.

Leneham, M. (2005). The sign language interpreter as translator: Challenging traditional definitions of translation and interpreting. *Deaf Worlds 21*(1), 79–101.

Locker, R. (1990). Lexical equivalence in transliterating for Deaf students in the university classroom: Two perspectives. *Issues in Applied Linguistics 1*(2), 167–95.

Madden, M. (2005). The prevalence of occupational overuse syndrome in signed language interpreters in Australia: What a pain! In M. Metzger & E. Fleetwood (Eds.), *Attitudes, innuendo, and regulators: Challenges of interpretation* (pp. 3–70). Studies in Interpretation Series, vol. 2. Washington, DC: Gallaudet University Press.

Marschark, M., Peterson, R., & Winston, E. A. (Eds). (2005). *Sign language interpreting and interpreter education: Directions for research and practice*. New York: Oxford University Press.

Martin, J. R., & Rose, D. (2002). *Working with discourse: Meaning beyond the clause.* New York: Continuum.

Metzger, M. (1999). *Sign language interpreting: Deconstructing the myth of neutrality.* Washington, DC: Gallaudet University Press.

Metzger, M., Collins, S., Dively, V., & Shaw, R. (Eds.). (2003). *From topic boundaries to omission: Research on interpretation.* Studies in Interpretation Series, vol. 1. Washington, DC: Gallaudet University Press.

Metzger, M., & Fleetwood, E. (Eds.). (2005). *Attitudes, innuendo, and regulators: Challenges of interpretation.* Studies in Interpretation Series, vol. 2. Washington, DC: Gallaudet University Press.

Moser, P. (1996). Expectations of users of conference interpretation. *Interpreting 1*(2), 145–78.

Myers, G. (1998). Displaying opinions: Topic and disagreement in focus groups. *Language in Society 27*, 85–111.

Napier, J. (2002). *Sign language interpreting: Linguistic coping strategies.* Coleford, UK: Douglas McLean.

Napier, J. (2004). Sign language interpreter training, testing, and accreditation: An international comparison. *American Annals of the Deaf 149*(4), 350–59.

Napier, J. (2007). Comparing language contact phenomena between Auslan/English interpreters and Deaf Australians: A preliminary study. In C. Lucas (Ed.), *Multilingualism and sign languages: From the Great Plains to Australia* (pp. 39–78). Sociolinguistics of Deaf Communities, vol. 12. Washington, DC: Gallaudet University Press.

Napier, J. (In press). Cooperation in interpreter-mediated monologic talk. *Discourse and Communication.*

Napier, J., & Barker, R. (2003). A demographic survey of Australian sign language interpreters. *Australian Journal of Education of the Deaf 9*, 19–32.

Napier, J. (2004). Accessing university education: Perceptions, preferences, and expectations for interpreting by Deaf students. *Journal of Deaf Studies and Deaf Education 9*(2), 228–38.

Napier, J., Bontempo, K., & Leneham, M. (2006). Sign language interpreting in Australia: An overview [Cover story]. *VIEWS* (April).

Napier, J., Carmichael, A., & Wiltshire, A. (In press). Look-pause-nod: A linguistic case study of a Deaf professional and interpreters working together. In P. C. Hauser, K. L. Finch, & A. B. Hauser (Eds.), *Deaf professionals and designated interpreters: A new paradigm.* Washington, DC: Gallaudet University Press.

Orima. (2004). *Supply and demand for Auslan interpreters across Australia.* Canberra: Australian Government Department of Family and Community Services.

Ozolins, U., & Bridge, M. (1999). *Sign language interpreting in Australia.* Melbourne: Language Australia.

Pöchhacker, F. (2004). *Introducing interpreting studies.* New York: Routledge.

Roy, C. (2000). *Interpreting as a discourse process.* New York: Oxford University Press.

Russell, D. (2002). *Interpreting in legal contexts: Consecutive and simultaneous interpretation.* Burtonsville, MD: Sign Media.

Schembri, A., Goswell, D., & Johnston, T. (2007). NAME Dropping: Evidence of Sociolinguistic Variation in Australian Sign Language. In C. Lucas (Ed.), *Multilingualism and sign languages: From the Great Plains to Australia* (pp. 121–58). Washington, DC: Gallaudet University Press.

Schembri, A., & Johnston, T. (2004). Sociolinguistic variation in Auslan Australian Sign Language: A research project in progress. *Deaf Worlds: International Journal of Deaf Studies* 20(1), 78–90.

Schembri, A., & Johnston, T. (2007). Variation in fingerspelling in Australian Sign Language. *Sign Language Studies.*

Schiavetti, N., & Metz, D. E. (1997). *Evaluating research in communicative disorders,* 3d ed. Boston: Allyn and Bacon.

Spring, M. (2000). Evolution of language services in Australia: From infant to teenager. In R. Roberts, S. A. Carr, D. Abraham, & A. Dufour (Eds.), *The critical link 2: Interpreters in the community: Selected papers from the second international conference on interpreting in legal, health, and social service settings.* Philadelphia: John Benjamins.

Steiner, B. (1998). Signs from the void: The comprehension and production of sign language on television. *Interpreting* 3(2), 99–146.

Stratiy, A. (2005). Best practices in interpreting: A Deaf community perspective. In T. Janzen (Ed.), *Topics in signed language interpreting* (pp. 231–50). Amsterdam: John Benjamins.

Turner, G. H., & Brown, R. (2001). Interaction and the role of the interpreter in court. In F. J. Harrington & G. H. Turner (Eds.), *Interpreting interpreting: Studies and reflections on sign language interpreting* (pp. 152–67). Coleford, UK: Douglas McLean.

Turner, G. H., & Harrington, F. (2000). Issues of power and method in interpreting research. In M. Olohan (Ed.), *Intercultural fault lines: Research models in translation studies.* Vol. 1: *Textual and Cognitive Aspects* (pp. 253–66). Manchester, UK: St. Jerome.

Wadensjö, C. (2002). The double role of a dialogue interpreter. In F. Pöchhacker & M. Shlesinger (Eds.), *The interpreting studies reader.* New York: Routledge.

Wilcox, S., & Shaffer, B. (2005). Toward a Cognitive Model of Interpretation. In T. Janzen (Ed.), *Topics in signed language interpreting* (pp. 27–50). Amsterdam: John Benjamins.

Witter-Merithew, A., & Johnson, L. (2005). *Toward competent practice: Conversations with stakeholders*. Alexandria, VA: Registry of Interpreters for the Deaf.

Woodcock, K., Rohan, M. J., & Campbell, L. M. (In press). Where are the Deaf professors? *Higher Education*.

Use of Space during an English-to-ASL

Interpretation When a Visual Aid Is Present

Amy Frasu

The goal of this research was to investigate methods of incorporating visual aids into interpretations from spoken English to American Sign Language (ASL). With data obtained from interviews with deaf consumers, three approaches to the use of space were analyzed. The motivating question for this research was, Is it cognitively dissonant for a deaf person to view an interpretation that does not match the spatial orientation of a visual aid?

A visual aid is a specific arrangement of graphics and/or text (e.g., a diagram, map, PowerPoint slide). Audience members who are not deaf can see the visual aid and listen to a spoken presentation simultaneously. However, deaf members of the audience integrate visual information contained in the visual aid with that in the ASL interpretation. This creates a challenge for ASL-English interpreters, as they must convey overlapping verbal and visual information to deaf individuals.

LITERATURE REVIEW

Use of Space in ASL

Unlike spoken languages, ASL uses physical space in grammatically significant ways. Space serves not only the syntactic function of indicating prosodic features of ASL discourse but also operates topographically to indicate locations of referents. "The space within which signs are articulated can be used to describe the layout of objects in space" (Poizner, Klima, & Bellugi, 1987, p. 193). According to studies of ASL structure (Klima & Bellugi, 1979; Liddell, 2003; Valli & Lucas, 1992), signers can manipulate space to refer to the locations of objects in the real world (e.g., provide directions from one place to another), tokens (i.e., ideas represented in neutral space), and temporal relationships (i.e., use of an imaginary timeline).

The location and production of signs in space is known as *spatial mapping*, a strategy for referring to areas of space that represent concepts. "Signers use spatial mapping to reflect their mental representation of discourse structure to the audience, expecting that the audience will use the spatial maps to build their own mental representations of the discourse and arrive at an understanding of the text that is similar to that of the signer" (Mather & Winston, 1998, p. 185). Spatial mapping is a critical component of ASL discourse because it enables the addressee to create coherence and cohesion.

Perspective in ASL

In typical ASL discourse, the participants face one another directly. They manipulate spatial mapping to indicate their various frames of reference and usually describe a scene from their own perspective (Valli & Lucas, 1992). The physical location of the items the interlocutors are discussing determines whether they use the speaker's perspective.

When two ASL speakers describe the locations of objects not present in the immediate surroundings, the canonical spatial representation of this scene is created according to the speaker's mental map of his or her physical location relative to the objects. In order to comprehend the intended message, the viewer must subsequently perform a 180-degree mental rotation of perspective (lexical items produced on the right are visualized on the left, and vice versa). For example, an ASL speaker may depict an imaginary map in space, indicating western regions to the left and eastern regions to the right. An addressee facing the speaker would see the east to the left and the west to the right but cognitively visualizes the images from the opposite perspective. Emmorey, Klima, and Hickok (1998) concluded that this mental rotation is not difficult and is in fact preferred by deaf people if the interlocutors are not looking at the same real-world scene.

Emmorey and Tversky (2002) compared the ways in which ASL speakers and English speakers manipulate perspective when describing the location of objects. If two English speakers are viewing the same scene, they each choose a spatial perspective to describe the position of items in their shared environment (e.g., "Grab the one closest to you" or "It's the one to my left"). Emmorey and Tversky's findings show that, when English speakers provide spatial descriptions, they typically promote cohesiveness by adopting the addressee's perspective rather than their own.

When two ASL speakers discuss objects in their immediate environment, they often use what Emmorey (2002) has referred to as *shared space*. A direct relationship exists between the real-world environment and the shared space of ASL speakers. In this type of situation, the use of space is based on neither the speaker's nor the addressee's direct perspective; rather, these perspectives are combined into one shared space based on the actual location of the objects. "The speaker's signing space is simply 'mapped' onto the jointly observed space" (Emmorey & Tversky, 2002, p. 6).

Use of Space and Perspective during ASL-English Interpretation Tasks

Johnson (1992) analyzed problems faced by ASL-English interpreters when a lecturer describes a diagram and by deaf students who simultaneously attempt to see an interpreted message and a visual aid. Her study concluded that the interpreter's visualizations, use of space, and classifiers must remain consistent with the speaker's intended message. As a result of competing visual images, deaf consumers may develop a distorted view of the diagram description.

There is currently no standard practice for the incorporation of visual aids into English-to-ASL interpretations. Roy's (2002) commentary in *VIEWS*, the professional newsletter of the Registry of Interpreters for the Deaf (RID), proposes that it may be cognitively dissonant for a deaf student to see a written equation that is read from left to right, while the direction of the interpretation moves from right to left. Interpreters may follow their own personal theories on this topic, but it has not been explored or documented by researchers.

Previous research has not been conducted on the way in which ASL-English interpreters integrate visual aids with the visual mode of ASL. This study focuses on the use of space, the mental mapping of realized objects, and shared space in ASL-English interpretations. This research may serve as a foundation for future investigation.

METHODOLOGY

The Study

This study was a qualitative analysis of thirty interviews with deaf individuals. Each participant in the study watched a recording of an

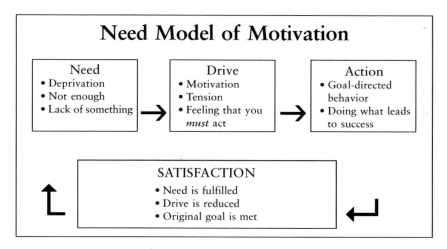

FIGURE 1. *Visual aid.*

English-to-ASL interpretation. The interpretation was repeated three times, with each segment utilizing a different spatial representation of the presenter's diagram. The participants provided feedback about each version of the interpretation and expressed their reactions to the different ways the interpreter used space and perspective in order to convey concepts.

The Interpreted Lecture

The lecture was a three-minute monologue about a psychological model, titled the "Need Model of Motivation." The speaker gave an explanatory lecture in consultative register about the manner in which psychological needs result from emotional needs. She referred to a cyclical process in which a person's feelings of deprivation cause an internal drive to change and take action; when a goal-directed behavior eventually leads to success, the goal is satisfied, and the person can move on to face a new need. The cycle is represented by figure 1.

The Perspectives

Three versions of the interpretation were shown to each participant. One version was rendered from the interpreter's perspective, one from the audience's perspective, and one from the perspective of shared space:

1. The interpreter's perspective uses space according to the interpreter's visualization of the diagram (figure 2).

FIGURE 2. *Interpreter's perspective of* NEED.

2. The audience perspective's uses space to parallel the audience's view of the diagram (figure 3)
3. The perspective of shared space integrates signs with the diagram in the jointly observed space of the interpreter and the audience (i.e., the interpreter turns her eye gaze and points to the diagram) (figure 4).

The recency principle (Miller & Campbell, 1959) states that the last (most recent) item in a series may be preferred over previous items. To diminish this influence, I randomized the order of the interpretations into three sets. Because the order was varied, the probability of the participants' preferring a certain interpretation due to chronology was reduced.

The Interpreter

The interpretations used in this study were performed by an RID-certified ASL-English interpreter with ten years of professional experience. Of the thirty deaf participants, twenty-nine had never before worked with this interpreter. The interpreter's anonymity increased the likelihood that the participants would focus on feedback about the interpretation rather than on previous knowledge of this particular interpreter.

FIGURE 3. *Audience's perspective of* NEED.

FIGURE 4. *Perspective of shared space* NEED.

Structure of the Interviews

The participants in this study were recruited at Gallaudet University through flyers and e-mail announcements. The advertisements requested participation by deaf people who wanted to give feedback about interpreting. Participants were chosen randomly according to their availability to take part in a one-on-one interview for approximately thirty minutes. None of the participants knew the specific topic of the study before watching the interpretations.

The interviews were conducted in ASL by a hearing graduate student at Gallaudet University. Each interview took place in a room with a video camera, TV, and VCR/DVD player. All of the participants were given a copy of the diagram depicted on the video and a clipboard with blank paper in order to take notes if needed. In order for me to objectively examine their responses, the participants were filmed as they watched and discussed the interpretations.

After one uninterrupted viewing of all of the segments, each participant was asked to give feedback about the interpretation, specifically, what that person intuitively recognized as important. The interviewer asked, "FEEL WHAT? FEEDBACK WHAT?" and purposely did not elicit comments about any specific aspect of the interpretations.

If a participant's initial comments did not address mental rotation and the use of space, the interviewer directly inquired about this topic. Following the participant's spontaneous feedback, the interviewer explained the different perspectives in the three versions and disclosed the purpose of the study. Each participant was given the option of watching the interpretations again and stopping at points of interest for further discussion.

The participants' comments and preferences were documented on videotape. Based on this information and the participants' demographics, several patterns within the interview data were analyzed.

The Participant Group

All of the participants provided information about their background, including general facts regarding family, ethnicity, education, gender, and age. The participants were a representative sample of deaf consumers from a variety of backgrounds. As a group, these participants represented members of the Deaf community who routinely receive services from ASL-English interpreters.[1]

The worldview and opinions of any individual are shaped by that person's life experiences; a variety of factors shape these views for all people. These factors include gender, ethnicity, and culture (Scollon & Scollon, 2001; Tannen, 2001). It is common for culturally Deaf people to feel bonded by experiences of oppression, a common language, and the sharing of a visual world (Lane, Hoffmeister, & Bahan, 1996). Identity as Deaf may supersede identity based on other factors, such as gender (Kelly 2001). In addition, age, educational background, and family play an influential role in the development of a deaf person's worldview (Lucas, Bayley, & Valli, 2003).

The experiences deaf people have growing up within the Deaf community (or finding it later in life) shape their cultural identities, as well as their attitudes about language (Padden & Humphries, 1988). Deaf people who are raised by Deaf parents are exposed to language models that differ from those learned by individuals from hearing families. Similarly, deaf students who are educated in schools for deaf children are raised in a linguistic atmosphere that differs from the one experienced by those who were mainstreamed in hearing classes.

In this study 23.3% of the participants stated that they were raised by Deaf parents. Twelve participants were educated in schools for deaf children, five attended mainstream schools, and eleven went to programs in both settings. A separate category was assigned for two participants who attended schools that used no signed language (figure 5).

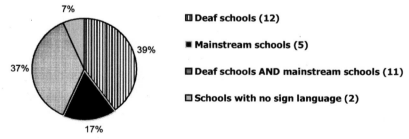

FIGURE 5. *Participants' educational background demographics.*

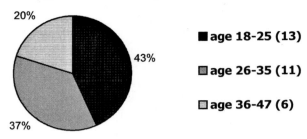

Ages of Participants

20%

43%

37%

■ age 18-25 (13)

▨ age 26-35 (11)

☐ age 36-47 (6)

FIGURE 6. *Participants' age demographics.*

Participants were grouped in the following age categories: 18–25, 26–35, or 36–47 (figure 6). These ranges were based on Lucas, Bayley, and Valli's (2003) age framework in their study of linguistic variation in ASL. The age spans parallel major philosophical changes in the recent history of deaf education in the United States.

People born between 1957 and 1968 (the 36–47 age range) were educated at a time when schools typically encouraged signing and speaking at the same time. In Lucas's study, this age group seemed more authoritarian about the "correct" production of signs, such as whether DEAF should be signed from chin to ear or from ear to chin. Their pattern of rigidity may be attributed to the struggle to accord ASL the status of a rule-governed language. Other age groups seem more willing to accept variation in ASL vocabulary and production. "The prescriptivism seen here in the use of citation forms may be regarded as a tool in maintaining the hard-won recognition of ASL" (Lucas et al., 2003, p. 170).

People born between 1969 and 1978 (ages 26–35) were more likely to be exposed to ASL in their classes due to trends in deaf education, such as the bilingual-bicultural philosophy. The youngest participants in this study, who were born between 1979 and 1986 (ages 18–25), were not old enough to have been involved in the Lucas et al. ASL variation research; the sociolinguistic impacts of their educational background is not yet known.

The participants were equitably represented by age, gender, educational setting, and family background. The majority (76.7%) were Euro-American; therefore, there was not a critical mass of people from different ethnic backgrounds (figure 7).

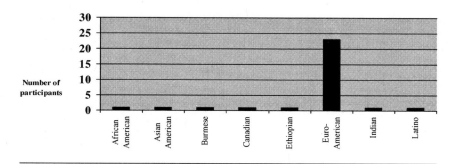

FIGURE 7. *Participants' ethnicity demographics.*

However, the sampling represented diversity within the Deaf community according to other characteristics. Of the 30 total participants, 16 were female, 14 were male, 1 person had Usher syndrome, 2 people did not learn ASL until adulthood, and 3 people were Deaf interpreters.

RESULTS

Participants' General Feedback

The flexible nature of the interview elicited feedback on the use of space and perspective, as well as many other areas. The participants also made comments about cognitive processing, accuracy, linguistic usage, and demeanor. Although this extraneous feedback was beyond the scope of this project, the perceptiveness of their observations is noteworthy.

Related to cognitive processing, the participants' comments included discussions about preparation, visualization, processing time, external processing, and background knowledge. They also mentioned issues of equivalency, matching the speaker's affect and style, and suggestions for alternative interpretations (e.g., ways to express the concepts of "drive" and "need" in ASL). When analyzing the interpreter's demeanor, they discussed issues of confidence, credibility, and professionalism.

A great deal of feedback concentrated on the linguistic features of the interpretation. The participants commented on the cohesion of the message, topicalization, pace, pausing, eye gaze, and facial expression. They discussed examples related to constructed dialogue, syntax, repetition, mouthing, and production of signs and fingerspelling.

Participants' Comments about the Visual Aid

The participants provided a variety of responses about the interpreter's use of space, perspective, and representation of the diagram. Figure 8 outlines the translations of these comments.

Participants' Comments

Version	Comments in favor	Comments in opposition
Interpreter's perspective	I prefer to flip the perspective myself.	This version was difficult to follow.
	It is not distracting if the interpretation does not match the direction of the diagram.	The direction of the cycle goes the wrong way.
Audience's perspective	Less confusing, less mental work	I never see Deaf people rotate perspective; only interpreters do that.
	Watching an interpretation is different than conversations with Deaf people.	
	It is the interpreter's job to make the message easy to watch.	
Perspective of shared space	Clear connection between visual aid and interpreted message	Touching the visual aid is not a realistic option.
	The presenter's words cause the hearing audience to look; pointing accomplishes the same goal.	This seems like it is meant for children. The interpreter's pointing is distracting.
	Referring directly to the visual aid is better than recreating the object in space.	
	This version got my attention.	
	It is natural to interact with the visual aid.	

FIGURE 8. *Participants' comments*

TABLE 1. *Participants' Preferences*

Category	Total #	Interpreter's opinion	Audience's opinion	Shared space opinion
All participants	30	13.3%	20.0%	66.7%
Deaf parents	7	14.3%	14.3%	71.4%
Hearing parents	23	13.0%	21.7%	65.2%
Deaf school	12	16.7%	8.3%	75.0%
Mainstream school	5	20.0%	40.0%	40.0%
Deaf school and mainstream experiences	11	9.1%	9.1%	81.8%
Learned ASL as an adult	2	0.0%	100.0%	0.0%
Deaf interpreters	3	0.0%	0.0%	100.0%
Females	16	6.3%	18.8%	75.0%
Males	14	21.4%	21.4%	57.1%
Age 36–47	6	0.0%	16.7%	83.3%
Age 26–35	11	27.3%	18.2%	54.5%
Age 18–25	13	7.7%	23.1%	69.2%

Participants' Preferences

The main analysis of the interviews concentrated on which interpreted version the participants chose as their dominant preference. In order to correlate the participants' choices with their demographics, the subtotal of people in each category who preferred a specific perspective was divided by the total number of people in that category. For example, twelve of the sixteen females in the study (75%) preferred the shared space perspective. Table 1 shows the data categorized by the participants' characteristics.

FINDINGS

Although patterns emerged in the interviews, it is evident that the Deaf community has multiple perspectives on this topic. Even if they did not have a strong preference prior to the interview, the participants expressed an interest in directly discussing this issue with other interpreters in the future. Those who had adamant opinions said that interpreters should *ask them* how to handle the incorporation of visual aids in order to meet their specific needs.

Interestingly, 83.3% of the interviewees did not notice the difference between the interpreter's perspective and audience's perspective versions until it was described to them directly. Only five of the thirty of the participants independently recognized the intentional rotation of perspective.

The preferences of the five participants who noticed the perspective shift (without the interviewer's guidance) showed no patterns according to age, ethnicity, or education; however, 80% were raised by hearing parents. No participants in this category chose the interpreter's perspective as their first choice, and four out of five chose the shared space perspective as their first-choice preference.

The Shared Space Perspective

Of the thirty participants, twenty (66.7%) preferred the interpretation based on the shared space perspective. In all but one category, the majority of participants chose the shared space version as their main preference: females (75%), males (57.1%), participants with hearing parents (65.2%), participants with Deaf parents (71.4%), students from mainstream programs (40%), students from schools for deaf children (75%), students from a combination of mainstream and deaf school programs (81.8%), ages 36–47 (83.3%), ages 26–35 (54.5%), and ages 18–25 (69.2%). The only participants that did not choose the shared space perspective were those who learned ASL as adults.

The Deaf interpreters in this study all chose the shared space interpretation and had no compelling preferences regarding the other two perspectives. They commented that pointing, eye gaze, and other linguistic features were paramount to issues of mental rotation.

Of the total number of participants, 46.7% specifically stated a preference for pointing and interaction with the visual aid because it was more visual, showed spatial relationships, linked ideas, and promoted attention and involvement. The participants also mentioned that the shared space technique was more similar to the method used by a deaf presenter and was easier to process. Another 13.3% approved of the pointing with some reservations; they suggested pointing only to establish a new concept or to help simplify an extremely complicated diagram; in any event, these participants should always avoid disrupting the speaker's presentation.

An additional 23.3% completely disliked seeing the interpreter point. They described it as unrealistic, said that it distracted from the source message, and was more suitable for children. One participant commented that the interpreter looked like a meteorologist.

The Audience's Perspective

The second most favored version was the audience's perspective, which was chosen by 20% of the participants. In their comments, 53.3% of the participants stated that the interpreter's use of space should match the audience's perspective of the visual aid, but most of that 53.3% ultimately preferred the shared space version as their main choice.

The participants who grew up in mainstream schools likely had the most frequent exposure to interpreted discourse throughout their lives, but in this study they did not provide a consensus about the incorporation of visual aids in interpretations. Their responses showed no definitive patterns: Two chose shared space, two chose the audience's perspective, and one chose the interpreter's perspective.

Both of the participants who learned ASL as adults preferred the audience's perspective. They mentioned that occasional pointing was an effective technique but felt it would be more appropriate for the interpreter to use neutral space rather than repeatedly refer to the diagram.

The Interpreter's Perspective

The interpreter's perspective was the least favored version and was chosen by 13.3% of the sample group. Participants who chose this version commented that mental rotation was not taxing or distracting. Three-fourths of the participants who favored the interpreter's perspective were males in the 26–35 age group who were raised by hearing parents. All of the participants in this category expressed misgivings about the shared space version due to the interpreter's direct interaction with the visual aid. These were the individuals noted previously who commented that in the real world, an interpreter would not interact directly with visual aid; that this approach was more suitable for children than adults; and that, for a simple example like this model, the pointing was unnecessary.

CONCLUSIONS

The interview findings lead to the following conclusions:

1. Many deaf consumers prefer viewing the shared space approach to interpretation, which incorporates pointing and looking at the visual aid.

2. Preliminary evidence supports interpretation strategies that match the visual aid by using the shared space perspective and/or the audience's perspective.

These conclusions are based solely on this small representative sample of deaf consumers. Interpreters and interpreter educators should not use the results of this research to support a universal method of incorporating visual aids into interpretations. Rather, this research provides evidence that interpreting is not a one-size-fits-all process. The Deaf community has varied opinions on this subject, and interpreters should continue to meet the needs of each consumer on an individual basis.

LIMITATIONS OF THIS STUDY

The majority of the limitations of this study were related to the complex logistics of producing the stimulus tape. Creating a set of brief, interesting, and undistorted interpretations that were varied solely by use of space was extremely challenging. For the sake of consistency among the versions, the interpretation favored English word order, which is a concern that was raised by several deaf participants, as well as the interpreter. In six of the interviews the video playback machine rendered a slightly distorted video image, which distracted the participants. This was remedied for the other participants.

Because the interpreter and the visual aid were the primary focus of the study, the speaker's image was not shown in the recording. Many of the participants wanted to see the speaker in order to analyze the context of the interpretation. In retrospect, it would have been preferable to include the speaker's image on the screen, possibly by using picture-in-picture format.

CONSIDERATIONS FOR FUTURE RESEARCH

Over the course of the interviews and the data analysis, several new questions arose regarding visual aids and perspective, as well as the importance of investigating deaf consumers' ideas about the interpreting process. It is hoped that this project will serve as a basis for further investigation. Future research about interpretation with visual aids should explore the following issues:

- analysis of deaf presenters' and Deaf interpreters' incorporation of visual aids into their use of space
- comparison of reactions to different types of visual aids (e.g., maps, grids, graphs, equations, 3-D objects, and so on)
- investigation into the Deaf community's opinions of interpreter behavior (such as touching a visual aid) in a variety registers and genres
- analysis of combined approaches of shared space/audience perspectives and shared space/interpreter perspectives
- analysis of possible correlations between consumers' preferences and specific geographic regions
- replication of this project with a larger and more diverse sample group
- replication of this project with children and/or young adults

Summary

This study has examined ways in which interpreters may effectively incorporate visual aids into English-to-ASL interpretations. When interviewed, the majority of the deaf participants stated that the shared space perspective was highly effective because it included clear use of eye gaze and pointing. This preference may be based on the topic-comment structure of ASL. In contrast, some of the participants favored the interpreter's or the audience's perspective rather than the shared space approach. A significant number stated that the interpreter's use of space should match the diagram.

The visual mode of ASL creates a unique challenge for ASL-English interpreters to convey the contextual information of visual aids in their work. Further research is needed in order to address this issue for the benefit of interpreters and consumers.

NOTES

1. In this study, the word "Deaf" with a capitalized "D" specifically denotes a community of deaf people who are users of American Sign Language and are members of a distinctive culture (Padden & Humphries, 1988). The term "deaf" in lowercase letters is an adjective that describes an audiological condition and may also refer collectively to Deaf, hard of hearing, and late-deafened individuals as a group.

REFERENCES

Emmorey, K. (2002). *Language, cognition, and the brain: Insights from sign language research*. Mahwah, NJ: Erlbaum.

Emmorey, K., Klima, E., & Hickok, G. (1998). Mental rotation within linguistic and nonlinguistic domains in users of American Sign Language. *Cognition 68*, 221–46.

Emmorey, K., & Tversky, B. (2002). Spatial perspective choice in ASL. *Sign Language and Linguistics 5*(1), 3–25.

Johnson, K. (1992). Miscommunication in interpreted classroom interaction. In D. Cokely (Ed.), *Sign language interpreters and interpreting* (pp. 120–61). Burtonsville, MD: Linstok.

Kelly, A. B. (2001). How Deaf women construct teaching, language, culture, and gender: An ethnographic study of ASL teachers. PhD diss., American Studies, University of Maryland, College Park.

Klima, E. S., & Bellugi, U. (1979). *The signs of language*. Cambridge, MA: Harvard University Press.

Lane, H. L., Hoffmeister, R., & Bahan, B. J. (1996). *A journey into the Deafworld*. San Diego: DawnSignPress.

Liddell, S. K. (2003). *Grammar, gesture, and meaning in American Sign Language*. New York: Cambridge University Press.

Lucas, C., Bayley, R., & Valli, C. (2003). *What's your sign for PIZZA?: An introduction to variation in American Sign Language*. Washington, DC: Gallaudet University Press.

Mather, S., & Winston, E. (1998). Spatial mapping in an American Sign Language narrative. In C. Lucas (Ed.), *Pinky extension and eye gaze: Language use in Deaf communities* (pp. 183–210). Sociolinguistics of the Deaf Community series, vol. 4. Washington, DC: Gallaudet University Press.

Miller, N., & Campbell, D. T. (1959). Recency and primacy in persuasion as a function of the timing of speeches and measurements. *Journal of Abnormal and Social Psychology 59*(1), 1–9.

Padden, C., & Humphries, T. (1988). *Deaf in America: Voices from a culture*. Cambridge, MA: Harvard University Press.

Poizner, H., Klima, E., & Bellugi, U. (1987). *What the hands reveal about the brain*. Cambridge, MA: MIT Press.

Roy, C. (2002). An interpreting puzzle: Math equations. *VIEWS* (June).

Scollon, R., & Scollon, S. B. K. (2001). *Intercultural communication: A discourse approach*, 2d ed. Malden, MA: Blackwell.

Tannen, D. (2001). *You just don't understand: Women and men in conversation*. New York: Morrow.

Valli, C., & Lucas, C. (1992). *Linguistics of American Sign Language: A resource text for ASL users*. Washington, DC: Gallaudet University Press.

Contributors

Lisa Frey Barrick
Interpreter
Birmingham, Alabama

Susan Foley-Cave
Interpreter
Centre for Deaf Studies
The University of Dublin/Trinity College
Dublin, Ireland

Amy Frasu
Interpreter
San Antonio, Texas

Lorraine Leeson
Director
Centre for Deaf Studies
The University of Dublin/Trinity College
Dublin, Ireland

Liza B. Martinez
Director
Philippine Deaf Resource Center
Quezon City, Philippines

Jemina Napier
Senior Lecturer, Coordinator,
    Translation, and Interpreting
    Programs
Department of Linguistics
Macquarie University
New South Wales, Australia

Meg J. Rohan
Lecturer
School of Psychology
University of New South Wales
New South Wales, Australia

Daniel Roush
ASL Specialist
Interpreter Training Program
Eastern Kentucky University
Richmond, Kentucky

Roberto R. Santiago
Interpreter
Los Angeles, California

Index

Page numbers in italics indicate tables or illustrations.

Shaffer, B., 63
shared space perspective, 208, 209, 214–19
spatial mapping
    consumer preferences, 214–19
    literature review, 204–6
    research design, 206–13, 218
Spring, M., 162
Steiner, B., 167
stereotypes, 103–5, 112, 119, 144, 145n3
Stokoe, W., 105, 117
supportive moves, 134–37

Tannen, D., 110–11, 115, 115, 119–20
television interpreting, 167
Temple, B., 165–66, 193
Titone, D., 5
training, 196–97
translation theory, 6–8
Tray, S., 4, 10–12, 27, 119
triadic interactions, 46–47
Turner, G., 159, 193
Tversky, B., 205

Tytler, A., 7–8, 10

Valli, C., 9, 212
Van der Kooij, E., 126
Vásquez, V., 27
Venezuelan culture, 118–19
Vilar-Sánchez, K., 8
Virginie, L., 5–6
visual aids, 204, 214–19
voice interpreting
    code-switching
        research study, 79–85
        types/examples, 75–79, 86–91
        variables impacting, 92–98
    consumer perceptions, 180, 183, 187

Wadensjö, C., 54, 64
Wierzbicka, A., 110
Wilcox, S., 63
Winston, E., 18, 126
Witter-Merithew, A., 167
Wood, M., 5
Woodcock, K., 178
Woodward, J., 73–74